ADST-DACOR Diplomats and Diplomacy Series

SERIES EDITOR
Margery Boichel Thompson

Since 1776, extraordinary men and women have represented the United States abroad under widely varying circumstances. What they did and how and why they did it remain little known to their compatriots. In 1995, the Association for Diplomatic Studies and Training (ADST) and DACOR, an organization of foreign affairs professionals, created the Diplomats and Diplomacy book series to increase public knowledge and appreciation of the professionalism of American diplomats and their involvement in world history. In *Eye on the World*, Anthony Quainton offers a clear and engaging account of the competing visions, dilemmas, and messiness of the foreign policy process, along with the candid, often self-critical story of his remarkably diverse life in international service.

EYE ON THE WORLD

A Life in International Service

ANTHONY C. E. QUAINTON

An ADST-DACOR Diplomats and Diplomacy Book

Potomac Books

An imprint of the University of Nebraska Press

Library of Congress Cataloging-in-Publication Data
Names: Quainton, Anthony C. E., author.
Title: Eye on the world : a life in international service / Anthony C.E. Quainton.
Description: [Lincoln, Nebraska] : Potomac Books, an imprint of the University of Nebraska Press, [2022] | Series: ADST-DACOR Diplomats and diplomacy series | "An ADST-DACOR diplomats and diplomacy book."
Identifiers: LCCN 2021047032
ISBN 9781640124035 (hardback)
ISBN 9781640125322 (epub)
ISBN 9781640125339 (pdf)
Subjects: LCSH: Quainton, Anthony C. E. | United States. Foreign Service—Biography. | United States. Department of State—Biography. | Diplomats—United States—Biography. | Ambassadors—United States—Biography. | Diplomatic and consular service—United States. | United States—Foreign relations—1945–1989. | United States—Foreign relations—1989– | BISAC: BIOGRAPHY & AUTOBIOGRAPHY / Historical | HISTORY / World
Classification: LCC E840.8.Q27 A3 2022 | DDC 327.2092 [B]—dc23/eng/20211122
LC record available at https://lccn.loc.gov/2021047032

Set in Adobe Text Pro.

For Susan, my constant partner on this long journey

Think only of the past as its remembrance gives you pleasure.

—JANE AUSTEN, *Pride and Prejudice*

Contents

Illustrations

Preface

This is a story of a long and complex life lived in eleven different countries across all the inhabited continents. In my professional career I served nine presidents and twelve secretaries of state. It is both a personal story that begins on one side of the North American continent and ends on the other and a political history of my interaction with some of the major crises of our time. Between my upbringing in Seattle and Victoria and my retirement in Washington DC lie over forty years in Europe, Africa, Asia, and Latin America. In reflecting on these many years, I came to realize the extent to which I had been influenced by empires: British, French, and Spanish. Everywhere I lived or served had at one time been a part of the great colonial enterprise, which began in the sixteenth century with the discovery of the New World by the Spaniards and which lives on today in the independent postcolonial countries of the third world.

My life was thus shaped by the history of the many places where I lived as either a student or a diplomat. I carried much of the political and emotional baggage of the British colonial system, of which the United States was once a part. I lived in a white man's world, a European world, with all the assumptions of cultural superiority that went with that heritage. I was educated in and accepting of an array of values deeply rooted in European and Judeo-Christian history. While I served in countries whose fundamental values were drawn from Islam, Hinduism, and Buddhism, my lens was always that of an outsider, of a white European / North American. Indeed, my education, for all the many virtues and values it instilled, whether in Canada, the United States, or England, carried with it some sense of the white man's burden and of the missionary instinct, both religious and political, that went with it. I was never a colonialist trying to directly control the destiny of far-flung peoples, but I did believe in the American effort to make the world safe for democracy and in the values of a liberal world order. In my time in Nicaragua and Peru, many expected or feared that I would be a proconsular figure directly influencing the outcome of local elections or political movements. It was not a role that I accepted or ever desired to carry out.

I do not pretend to be entirely impartial in my judgments. They are the result of the particular education and value system that formed me. I do not apologize for this perspective but confess that it had a powerful hold on me. There were times when I profoundly disagreed with the consequences of that vision and the essential rightness of our Western cause. Those moments I attributed to a distorted interpretation of that vision, which during the Cold War often led us to slight our own democratic values in the cause of defeating a rival atheistic and totalitarian system.

This story is told largely through the prism of my own memory. While I had some documentary sources in the form of letters and diaries from my youth and some declassified telegrams from my time in Nicaragua and Peru, this account does not claim to be a fully documented recounting of events. It is largely based on memory. As a result, the story is necessarily limited and incomplete. The generosity and encouragement of my American University colleagues sustained me throughout the long writing process.

Much of my past is missing for a variety of reasons, including simple failure of memory or a desire not to reveal every ambiguous detail of my life. Family members have reviewed chapters, correcting and amplifying my own memory. In particular, my wife, Susan, with whom I have shared over sixty years of my odyssey, was essential in keeping me on the straight and narrow when it came to descriptions of events and of my own interaction with them. This work would not have been possible without her, as indeed my life story would be incomplete without her essential role in it.

This book would also not have been possible without the patient, expert, and professional editing of Margery Thompson. She saved me from innumerable errors of fact and expression.

EYE
ON THE
WORLD

PART 1
Child of Empire

1

Seattle Beginnings

A long and event-filled life must begin somewhere. In my case it was under the care of the Sisters of Providence. I entered the world at Providence Hospital, one of Seattle's best, on April 4, 1934. My grandfather, the dean of Christ Church Cathedral in Victoria, British Columbia, Cecil Samuel Quainton, sent a brief congratulatory telegram from his deanery expressing the hope, not entirely fulfilled in later years, that I would grow up to be a "Christian gentleman and cricketer." I was the first and, for seven years, my parents' only child. My father, Cecil Eden Quainton, was a junior assistant professor on the faculty of the University of Washington, where he taught European history. He arrived in Seattle in September 1924 after completing his undergraduate degree at Cambridge University's Queens' College. My mother, Marjorie Oates, had been born in California but moved to Canada as a young girl and grew up in Victoria, on Vancouver Island. She had moved to Seattle with my father some four years before my birth. My mother, of Irish stock, was Roman Catholic, and my father, son of a distinguished clergyman in Victoria, was Anglican. As was expected in those days, I was baptized and raised a Catholic.

My grandparents were all very British. Dean Quainton had come to Canada in 1913 to preach a mission on the Canadian prairies. A powerful preacher, he was rector of a small parish in Yorkshire, England, when he was asked to take over the Anglican church in Brandon, Manitoba. He stayed there until 1917, when he and his wife, Minnie Collins, and their two sons moved to Victoria, where he had been called to be dean of a yet-to-be-built cathedral. My maternal grandfather, Arthur Faulkner Oates, was educated at the modest local grammar school in Bradford, also in West Yorkshire, and trained as a solicitor in London. In 1898 he sold his assets, joined a syndicate of some twenty other young men, and sailed for the Klondike to make his

3

fortune in the goldfields of the Yukon, efforts that ended in catastrophe and bankruptcy. He then drifted first to northern California, where he married his longtime Irish sweetheart, Hannah Josephine Roche, the eldest of twelve siblings from County Cork. She was a successful and talented dressmaker who became a buyer at the White City, San Francisco's fabled department store. Arthur, however, could never make ends meet, and his failure in California led the family, including my mother and my aunt Florence, to move to Victoria, where they settled into that very special Anglo-Canadian world.

My parents were liberal, leftist one would say today, as was the university faculty in general. In fact, the state legislature investigated the university for un-American activities during the witch-hunting days of the late 1940s and early 1950s. My parents faithfully read *The Nation* and the *New Republic* and voted, I think, for the Socialist Party's candidate Norman Thomas. My father considered joining the Abraham Lincoln Brigade to fight the fascists in the Spanish Civil War. For all that, he was an Englishman to the core. He loved cricket, whisky, and the English classics. He even maintained the English mannerism of carrying his handkerchief in his sleeve.

I remember little of my first six years, when we lived in Washington Park, a solidly middle-class neighborhood close to Lake Washington. We had a small, one-story bungalow. At age four I went to the Bush School, a rather snooty school for girls that admitted boys only for prekindergarten and kindergarten. I then had a brief time at a Catholic parochial school on Capitol Hill, in the center of Seattle. My only vivid memory from that period is of a turtle my parents brought back for me from the San Francisco World's Fair in 1939. Like all turtles of that era, it came in a small plastic bowl with an island in the center on which sat a solitary plastic palm tree. The turtle had painted on its back some reminder of its Californian origins.

In 1940 my parents bought a much larger house in the Highlands, an exclusive gated community north of the city. Actually, our house was just outside the gates, adjacent to the Seattle Golf Club, but we were part of the gated community and had full use of the recreation center, pool, and tennis courts that went with membership. Why my parents decided to live in such an exclusive neighborhood is still something of a mystery to me. The Boeings lived in the Highlands, as did the Pigotts, the founders of Pacific Car and Foundry, now Paccar, one of Seattle's leading industries. The other residents were prominent lawyers, doctors, and bankers. It was not a community with many children. I can remember knowing only three other boys my age. There were also five or six girls roughly my age. We all went to different schools but went regularly to dancing class together. Those classes had various levels of cotillions, culminating in the annual Snow Ball at the Olympic Hotel, where Seattle's debutantes were presented to the grandes dames of the community. A series of parties for the would-be debutantes preceded the white tie affair and consumed much of the winter holidays between one semester and the next. Bringing out one's daughter cost the parents of the debutante a small fortune. I was asked to partner debutantes during at least two of these seasons, perhaps reflecting the general paucity of eligible males in the world of Seattle society.

Seattle's leading families, a self-consciously elitist group, were enormously generous to me, the son of a university professor. Although I was a small, asthmatic boy, they often invited me to their houses to play. In the summer they invited me to stay at the Country Club, an equally exclusive summer community on Bainbridge Island. There I learned to play tennis and attempted an occasional round of golf on the sandy course below the houses facing out onto Puget Sound.

Because of the paucity of contemporaries, my life in the Highlands was a relatively lonely one. I would have occasional weekend overnights with one or two other boys my age, although their parents worried unnecessarily about serving fish on Friday to this Roman Catholic child. The Milwaukee Road, Northern Pacific, and Great Northern railway lines ran along the coast just below the Highlands. We would often picnic on the beach, accessible only through the Highlands. We swam, paddled, counted freight cars, and put out our pennies to be flattened on the tracks as the trains came through.

After we moved to the Highlands, I entered first grade at St. Anthony's Parochial School, now Christ the King School, adjacent to the parish where we attended mass on Sundays. It was a traditional Catholic school run by the starched and wimpled Sisters of Charity of the Blessed Virgin Mary, an order known for its formidable discipline and commitment to absolute orthodoxy. They were led by Father Gerald Fitzgerald, who had founded the school and parish only ten years before as Seattle expanded rapidly to its north. The nuns put the fear of hell into a young boy. We were constantly exhorted to avoid occasions of sin, never to eat meat on Friday, and strictly to observe the fasting and dietary prescriptions of the church. It was a patriotic Catholicism wherein, as in public schools, each day began by our solemnly pledging allegiance to our flag, not then under God.

I made my first Communion there and was raised with all the orthodox prejudices of the time. I remember being strongly exhorted never to pray in a Protestant church. Should I somehow find my way to a Protestant wedding (or funeral), I was not to say the Protestant version of the Lord's Prayer. My father, the nuns reminded me, was certain to go to hell as long as he remained a Protestant. My mother thankfully and repeatedly assured me that on this one theological point, the good sisters were in error.

After Pearl Harbor, the announcement of which I remember hearing on the radio in our living room as I was listening to a Seattle Rainiers baseball game, the family became more patriotic. We endured gasoline and butter rationing. I learned to identify the various planes being used by our air forces, as well as the Nazi and Japanese air forces, by looking up at models of those planes that hung above my bed. In May 1942 I took part in a St. Anthony's School entertainment in which I closed out the program playing Uncle Sam in a short play entitled *Americans All*. Later in 1943 I dressed up as Uncle Sam in a red, white, and blue tailcoat and top hat for a meeting of the local PTA. The organizers persuaded me to sing Irving Berlin's

"Any Bonds Today?" in support of the war effort. The bond program had already become a popular hit in a Bugs Bunny cartoon that urged Americans to "buy a share of freedom today." (Mercifully, I was not to sing in public again for over thirty years, when, in the role of Rodolfo, I sang "Paper Doll" on the embassy stage in New Delhi in a production of Arthur Miller's *View from the Bridge*.) The war effort encouraged children to save, and I had specially designed books in which I affixed small-denomination saving stamps until I had enough to receive a ten-dollar war bond.

I stayed at St. Anthony's through the third grade, when the school proposed that I be skipped to the fifth grade. Skipping grades in those days was generally thought to be a great honor and indication of academic promise. My parents, convinced that skipping was a bad idea both socially and educationally, intervened and sent me away to boarding school in Victoria, British Columbia, where, ironically, I got even further ahead of my peers than if I had stayed in Seattle.

I spent summers in Seattle, with occasional trips to the ballpark to see the AAA Seattle Rainiers play. Mostly, however, I spent long hours at the Highlands community swimming pool or played catch on a field adjacent to the pool. Although we did not talk about racism much at the time, we were a racially conscious community. In the late 1940s United Nations Under-Secretary-General Ralph Bunche came to speak to a foreign affairs group in Seattle hosted by one of the few liberal Highlands families. His hosts proposed that he be taken to swim in the communal pool, only to be advised that he could not swim there because he was Black.

The highlight of the summer was the Fourth of July party. The whole community gathered for a traditional picnic preceded by swimming and diving competitions and a series of races on the open lawn. In the evening, the lone tennis court was gaily decorated with Chinese lanterns. Fels-Naphtha was scattered on the cement court to facilitate dancing to music played by a local disc jockey, and of course there were fireworks. It was still a time when one could buy Roman candles and rockets and launch them from one's own backyard. We reveled in lighting firecrackers, which we threw with great glee at one another's feet.

Our house in the Highlands was quite large. Not all the rooms were furnished, so I had two vast empty sunrooms in which to set up my electric train and build castles with blocks, Lincoln Logs, and Lego, the materials changing with advancing age. The house was set above a rather steep slope without much garden in which to play but with numerous magnolia trees to climb. In July 1941 my brother, Rodney, arrived, and from those days onward my parents' attention was divided.

My family lived what seemed to me a conventional life. My parents had a glass of Scotch whisky before dinner, played bridge with friends regularly, faithfully listened to Jack Benny and Fred Allen on Sunday afternoons, and socialized with other members of the History Department and the more liberal members of the Highlands community. We had a dog for several years, a large spotted Dalmatian, but I never really loved him and seventy years later cannot remember his name. I had my chores taking out the garbage and cleaning my room, among others. I was also able to help in the kitchen. I made ice cubes for my parents' evening tipple by putting hot water into the metal ice cube tray and placing it on the large block of ice in our icebox. We had no electric refrigerator at that time. It was wartime, and butter was rationed, so we carefully took the cream off the top of the unhomogenized milk and vigorously shook it in a Mason jar until the milk could be strained and the butter saved. The alternative was dreadful white margarine, which had to be artificially colored by a bright orange powder.

I was largely left on my own. In 1942 I became a chicken rancher on a small scale. At Easter of that year I attended an Easter egg hunt in the Pigotts' extensive garden. The prize I won for finding a golden egg was two small live chicks, which I brought home in triumph. My parents were not amused. The chicks lived for several weeks under the four-legged kitchen stove in a box they quickly outgrew. My parents helped me create a chicken run at the back of the house in an abandoned and dilapidated summerhouse. We put up chicken wire to enclose the area, and the chickens prospered. I acquired several more and for the remainder of the war sold eggs to my parents at a greatly discounted price.

In the summers my parents expected me to work to supplement my modest pocket money. Living close to a golf club provided an easy opportunity, and from the time I was twelve onward I caddied for Seattle's rich and famous, including its oldest and most distinguished citizen, Joshua Greene. Usually I would carry only one bag, but on occasion I would struggle around the course with two. I got only a dollar a round, although the tips were often quite generous. I learned a fair amount about golf and was able to give players advice about which iron they should use for a particular shot, but I never really learned to play or had any desire to do so.

Our stay in the house in the Highlands was relatively brief. My father died shortly after our return from Mexico, where he had been teaching in 1945–46 at the Colegio de México. After his death, my mother was forced to sell the house. She then worked as a receptionist in the offices of Dr. Sydney Hawley, a prominent Seattle gynecologist. We had little money for luxuries. All of my ties were hand-me-down Countess Mara silk ties from Bill Boeing, the founder of the great aviation company. Summer camp in the San Juan Islands, where many of my friends went each summer, was out of the question. Nonetheless, we did not feel poor, nor was I raised to resent the fact that I could not afford everything my richer contemporaries could.

After the sale of our large house we moved at the suggestion of other Highlands families to the caretaker's cottage adjacent to the recreation area / community center. It was a tiny cottage but sufficient for the three of us. By then I was a freshman at Lincoln High School, one of the six major Seattle high schools. The year and a half I spent at Lincoln High left little impression. I made few friends at school and did not have much of a social life there, being so much younger and smaller than my classmates. My only real friends were those from the Highlands: the boys with whom I played desultory catch and the girls with whom I went to dancing class.

By the time I was in high school I was offered jobs in two of Seattle's banks, the Seattle First National and Seattle Savings and Trust, both of whose major owners or stockholders lived in the Highlands and wanted to help my mother's boy find work. I was quite adept at the backroom work at the banks and learned how to use check-sorting and posting machines and other technologies of the time. I was often entrusted with taking the day's checks each evening to the clearinghouse where checks were manually exchanged among the various banks of the city.

I tried to enhance my pocket money in other ways, one of which was to become a babysitter. I was always terrified that something awful would happen (it never did) and I would not be able to cope. My most notable charge was Michelle Dunn, after whom I was told the Washington State Chateau Ste. Michelle Vineyards were named. For a while I also had a paper route delivering the *Seattle Post-Intelligencer*. The route began about half a mile from our house in the Highlands and took me around the neighborhood at a very early morning hour.

Early on I acquired what was to become a lifelong passion for theater. For my fourteenth birthday I was taken to see Tallulah Bankhead in the touring production of Noël Coward's *Private Lives*. A year later, on my way to boarding school on the East Coast accompanied by my aunt, I was taken to see Henry Fonda in *Mister Roberts* and Judy Garland in a revue at Radio City Music Hall. I tried whenever possible to see shows on and off Broadway throughout the remainder of my high school and college career. As plays were rather expensive, the movies provided second-best entertainment. In Seattle I would regularly go downtown to one of the four major movie theaters on a Saturday to see a double bill, often involving the latest Abbott and Costello movie and/or a roaring western.

My earliest years held few outings of moment. One that I remember clearly took us as a family to the thirty-fifth-floor observation deck of the Smith Tower, which at thirty-eight stories had been the highest building west of the Mississippi at its construction in 1914. From the observation deck one had a glorious view over Puget Sound unobscured by the multistoried forest of massive towers that make up Seattle's business district today. At least twice during my childhood years I went with my parents to see the Ringling Bros. and Barnum & Bailey Circus. The big top was set up adjacent to the principal railroad station. The wild animals, the flying trapeze and high-wire artists, the jugglers and the clowns enthralled me. But more fascinating for a small boy were the sideshows: the fire eater, the sword swallower, the bearded lady, the midget Tom Thumb, and the Giant. After one of these visits my parents bought me a giant's ring, seemingly almost big enough to put over my entire wrist. It was a strange and in some ways a forbidden world that captured a ten-year-old's imagination. It was there that my longing for more exotic worlds began, oblivious as I was to the exploitation of the sideshow artists or the performing animals. That sensibility, I regret to say, was decades away.

I should add a word about that interlude year in Mexico. It was an improbable opportunity for my father. He did not speak Spanish, nor had he any previous experience in Latin America. As a result, teaching was a great strain, since much of what he had to say had to be translated for the benefit of his students. We set out by car in our 1938 Plymouth early in 1946. It took us well over a week to get as far as El Paso, from where we took the train to Mexico City. I remember very little of the trip beyond the heat of the Southwest and the stops for glasses of fresh orange juice at wayside stands in California. My father should never have accepted the post. He had a severely weakened heart resulting from teenage rheumatic fever. The altitude of Mexico City was contraindicated, and it ultimately weakened him to the point that he passed away from congestive heart failure only four months after our return, just short of his forty-seventh birthday.

But the family loved Mexico. We traveled widely, to Cuernavaca, Taxco, and Oaxaca, and made many friends in the expatriate community. They shared the same expatriate colonial tastes as my parents, notably, a love of bridge and gin-and-tonics. We had tea at

Sanborn's near the Zócalo and enjoyed the company of a series of British friends. I attended the American high school in Mexico City for the second half of the eighth grade and the first half of the ninth. I found schoolwork so easy that at the age of twelve I was already in high school when I returned to Seattle at the end of 1946.

We lived in an apartment not far from the Paseo de la Reforma, the city's grand main boulevard, and close to Chapultepec Park. The city was not overcrowded in those days, and it was easy to get to the vast imposing temples at Teotihuacán and the floating gardens of Xochimilco, neither the worse for tourist wear as they are today. Both were sources of fascination for me, and I brought home a series of small Aztec artifacts, which adorn our living room to this day. The floating gardens were romantic places of relaxation. They could be visited on flat-bottomed boats extravagantly decorated with fresh flowers. Floating mariachi bands accompanying them were a special delight. I also became fascinated by bullfighting. I had my own cape and sword and spent many idle hours practicing my passes, always imitating the great Spanish matador Manolete, whom I saw fight in the Mexico City bullring that year.

At the end of the year we made the drive back to Seattle. The trip has left no impact on my memory, but I was aware of my father's rapidly declining health. Shortly after our return his illness confined him to the master bedroom upstairs, and I moved to a ground-floor room to be out of the way. I saw him only a few times, weak and pale, in his bed. Several months after our return I watched from behind my bedroom door as he was carried out to a waiting ambulance, never to return. Although I had just turned thirteen and had spent much time with my parents, I retain only a few unconnected images of my father. I can see him playing cricket on the grounds of the University of Washington. I remember him patiently teaching me to ride a bicycle in our driveway and instructing me on how to tuck my shirttails between my legs to keep my shirt front trim and confined within my trousers. Sunday afternoons were always spent with my parents listening to their favorite comedy shows, hosted by Jack Benny and Fred Allen.

At thirteen I enrolled in Lincoln High School, where I was by far the youngest student in the sophomore class. I was small, insecure, and very immature. My years in Victoria and my studies in Mexico had put me ahead of my American peers. I was a good student and had no problem with my studies. I made very few friends. I joined the Lincoln Rail-Splitters, a service organization that kept the campus clean and picked up trash as its principal service obligation. As the years have gone by, the images of my years in Seattle have faded, while others have taken their place. Yet I continued to think of Seattle as my home and the Pacific Northwest as my region, even though I never returned to live there after my departure for boarding school in 1949. It was where Susan and I always returned on home leave from our various Foreign Service posts.

2
The Victoria Connection

Victoria, British Columbia, was not the largest jewel in the imperial crown, but until the 1950s it was one of its proudest and brightest ornaments—a refuge for retired Englishmen, with all the charms of England but with a mild Pacific climate and none of the hardships of postwar Britain. Named for the queen empress, it was proud of its Englishness. Its principal hotel, the Empress, was one of the great Canadian Pacific Railway hotels, self-consciously traditional and Victorian. It served high tea with clotted cream, scones, and all the accompanying delicacies of its English model. American tourists who came to Victoria in droves, then as now, were attracted not only by the high teas but also by the chance to buy Irish linens, Scottish tartans, Spode and Wedgewood china, Indian teas, and so forth, all advertised as available at extraordinary bargains. This somewhat pseudo-Englishness could be cloying, but Victoria's residents were happy to be part of the empire and to live in one of its most loyal remote outposts.

All that changed dramatically in the twenty-first century. British Columbia in general and Victoria in particular became truly multi-cultural. The Union Jack gave way to the maple leaf, and "O Canada" replaced "God Save the Queen." Ethnic restaurants now abound. English retirees are fewer, foreign, mostly Asian, tourists more numer-ous. The effort to project a British atmosphere persists in the shops along Government Street, in the teas at the Empress, and in the carriage rides around Beacon Hill Park and the small but charm-ing harbor, from which in the late nineteenth century my maternal grandfather set sail for the Yukon.

Although I was born and grew up in Seattle, the focal point of my first decade was not Seattle but to the north, in British Columbia, on Vancouver Island, in Victoria. All of my grandparents lived in

Victoria. My parents met and were married there. My father, who had been born in England, moved there with his parents in 1917 from Brandon in Manitoba, where my grandfather had been called from his Yorkshire parish to be rector after a spectacular preaching tour in 1913. My father taught for several years at St. Michael's School, a small traditionally English-style boarding and day school in Victoria. Before coming to Victoria, he had already completed a degree at the University of Manitoba at the age of seventeen, winning a medal from Canada's governor general. In Victoria he waited to go up to Cambridge University's Queens' College, his father's college, where he ultimately earned an upper-second-class degree in history and thereafter went on to a teaching post in the History Department at the University of Washington.

What this meant for me was that part of my summer holidays and most, perhaps all, of my Christmases were spent in Victoria, usually celebrated with my maternal grandparents, Arthur and Josephine Oates, Grandpa and Granny to me. My paternal grandparents, Dean Cecil Samuel Quainton and his wife, Minnie Collins, do not figure in my story, since they died in 1938, shortly after their retirement and return to England, when I was only four. However, they had a strong impact on the Victoria community. Since coming to Victoria from Brandon in 1917, the dean had become a pillar of Victoria society. He was a handsome, charming, learned, and dedicated churchman and a brilliant preacher—the very model of a Victorian dean.

When my parents met and married in Victoria, their marriage was something of a scandal. The Anglican dean's son marrying a Catholic family's daughter was thought to be socially and religiously inappropriate. Reportedly, the dean had to preach to his flock about the matter. Though he was the soul of toleration, Victorians were not. My parents were married in 1930 in the sacristy of the Church of Our Lady of Lourdes in Oak Bay, on Vancouver Island's south coast. My mother was described in the *Daily Times* as "one of the popular members of the younger social set in Victoria." In those days "mixed" marriages could not be solemnized in the church proper.

Both parents remained true to their respective faiths but were totally respectful of each other's convictions. As the Roman Church required, my brother and I were raised Catholic, but I was allowed to accompany my father for Christmas services at Christ Church Cathedral, a building constructed during my grandfather's tenure as dean. Not an exclusionary Anglican, my father maintained a lifelong friendship with a Catholic nun, a former student with whom he corresponded on a regular basis.

For much of their lives my maternal grandparents, the Oateses, lived in Oak Bay, a small suburb close to the center of Victoria. They were not a happy couple. My grandfather failed at many jobs, beginning with his effort to make his fortune in the Klondike in 1898. As part of a syndicate of young Englishmen he had sailed from Liverpool around Cape Horn with the dream of riches easily made. He was quickly disillusioned once he arrived in the Yukon. The syndicate broke up in acrimony, my grandfather found no gold, and he emerged from the experience bankrupt. Settling then in northern California, where my mother was born, he tried his hand as a postmaster and as a supervisor of Chinese coolies building the Union Pacific Railroad. This must have been a humbling experience for a man who had qualified in England as a solicitor. After a series of failures, the family moved north to Victoria, where Arthur Oates had begun his Canadian adventures over a decade earlier.

Little is known about the family's early time in British Columbia. Suffice it to say, when the war broke out in 1914, Arthur enlisted in the Canadian forces and went to Europe to fight. Whether he saw combat is unknown, but shortly after returning he moved out of the family home and went north to Port Hardy, where he became a struggling day laborer and part-time solicitor. He sent money back regularly to support his family. His wife, my grandmother, against all odds raised two girls to the standards of middle-class gentility expected of families in Victoria. Both girls received a "finishing school" education at the Poplars, a school long on deportment and French and light on subjects of serious intellectual content. Neither went to university, and both my mother and her younger sister, Florence, bitterly regretted their lack of formal education.

The Oateses bought a house at 2347 Windsor Road early in the Second World War with money lent to them by their son-in-law, my father, as part of the small legacy he received on the death of the dean. There they remained until their deaths several decades later. Arthur Oates had returned from up island to work briefly in the wartime shipyards of Victoria. He retired in the early 1940s to spend his remaining years ensconced in a large, heavily upholstered chair in the living room. I remember him there, quietly smoking cigarettes, which I was allowed to roll for him. He talked little but was always companionable and immensely interested in my education. Family lore has it that when he first returned from Port Hardy, he was made to sit in the adjacent dining room as a kind of punishment for past sins. His wife, harboring some long-held grudge, would not allow him to stay in the same room with her. Whether the cause of her anger was some real or imagined infidelity during the time he served in England during the Great War or his abandonment of the family to move away from Victoria will never be known. Suffice it to say, relations between them were not warm, although as a small boy I did not discern the tension. By the time I knew him, he had returned to the living room, which he and his wife shared in what seemed a largely companionable silence.

I think of those childhood Christmases in Oak Bay with special affection. We dined on traditional English fare, including turkey and plum pudding. We put on party hats and pulled Christmas crackers, laughed over the jokes they contained and the small gifts inside. We listened solemnly to the king's broadcast to his people in the empire, of which we were a far-flung part. We played cards or roulette in the afternoon and sometimes visited my uncle Eric and his family to play family charades. The house on Windsor Road was small but comfortable, faux Tudor in style, with stucco white walls and black beams. It never seemed small to me. I took for granted the quiet gentility of this very English neighborhood. Tweed was the dress of choice for most of its inhabitants, and canes and dogs were common. Walking to the sea a scant five blocks away or playing in the open Windsor Park, which was even closer, was always an exciting outing.

We went back and forth from Seattle to Victoria by ferry. These were not the broad-decked ferries of Puget Sound or the fast catamarans of today. Rather, they were sleek steamers with royal names: Princess Alice, Princess Charlotte, and the like. They were miniature versions of their oceangoing counterparts. We often had a stateroom in which to rest for what was only a five-hour run up to Victoria. And we breakfasted in the elegantly appointed dining room: white tablecloths and napkins, silver, and traditional English fare. The breakfasts, which I particularly enjoyed, included oatmeal porridge, kippered herrings, soft-boiled eggs in silver-plated eggcups, brown toast, and marmalade. To my young eyes these trips were more than mere ferry rides; they were cruises up one of North America's most beautiful inland waterways.

I have a vague recollection, perhaps imagined, of standing solemnly on the sidewalk on Government Street in downtown Victoria clutching a Union Jack when the king emperor, George VI, came on his last visit to Canada in May 1939 just before the outbreak of the Second World War.

The only prolonged periods of time that I spent in Victoria were the two and a half years that I attended St. Michael's School. My father, English by birth and attitude, believed it would be good to get a young boy out from under maternal apron strings as soon as possible. Although I was happily attending a small Catholic parochial school near our home in the northern suburbs of Seattle, in 1943 I was about to be skipped from the third to the fifth grade. My parents, who were skeptical of this rapid promotion, decided to send me away at age nine to a small boarding school in Victoria where my father had taught twenty years before. Since both my mother's sister and my father's brother lived there, it did not seem quite as radical to them as it did to their friends in Seattle, for whom boarding school was virtually unknown at any age and completely unimaginable for a child of nine.

I was not happy at St. Michael's. I was lonely, sickly, and one of only three American boys at this very English and very alien institution. Dr. Arnold would have felt at home in the discipline-driven environment at St. Michael's. While it was not quite a Dickensian Dotheboys Hall, it had a certain Victorian character to it. Headmaster Kyrle Symons, in flowing Oxonian robes, ruled the school with an iron hand. He had founded the school a quarter-century before, and it remained a miniature version of a nineteenth-century English preparatory school. Spare the rod and spoil the child was at the heart of his system. Education was often enforced through publicly administered sharp whacks on the outstretched hand with a ruler affectionately dubbed by the boys "Flattie." Occasionally, discipline was imparted with a cane across the offending rear end of a recalcitrant boy, administered exclusively by the headmaster. I was beaten only once: for having stolen blackberries from the backyard of a house adjacent to the boarding house. The beating had its desired effect. I never stole blackberries again.

Even in the fourth grade we studied Latin and French, as well as English, penmanship, and mathematics, but not much science. We did read Caesar's *Gallic Wars* in our second year, studying from a thin dense grammar entitled *Elementa latina*. Longman's French grammar performed a similar service for our French classes. We were not expected to love our subjects. They were vehicles for our improvement. I retain a fondness for the one Latin phrase I can still remember from those days, "Caesar adsum jam forte, Pompey aderat," a phrase that gave our juvenile minds great pleasure as we imagined the different dietary propensities of Caesar and his rival Pompey. We sat at what already seemed aged desks with an inkwell in the corner of each. As a result, we were ink-stained most of the time. Many of the desks were carved with the names or initials of former students, who had used their penknives to record their presence at the school.

Our uniform consisted of a gray flannel suit, short trousers with a gray flannel shirt, school tie (blue and black horizontal stripes), and a cap. We also had a sports outfit for drill on the school playground and games after school. Drill was conducted with white poles, and we were instructed in all the ways to slope and present arms, change shoulders, and do precision drill. This precision was put on display once a year for admiring parents and friends at the annual prize day on the lawn of one of Oak Bay's premier mansions.

In an extraordinary way, this little school was an outpost of empire. We were very conscious that on maps of the world almost half of the globe was pink. We collected stamps from remote colonies such as Bechuanaland and British Honduras, distant islands such as St. Helena and St. Kitts, and all the dominions, including Newfoundland, not yet part of Canada. We read Rudyard Kipling and Sir H. Rider Haggard, or, more correctly, the headmaster would read their works to us boarders on Sunday evenings after dinner. We loved the exploits of Allan Quartermain and his loyal Zulu sidekick, Umslopogaas. Our weekly assemblies in the gymnasium were often presentations by war heroes who described daring escapes from Nazi prisoner of war camps. We did not sing "O Canada" but "God Save the King." The Canadian flag still had the Union Jack in one corner. We were part of the empire on which the sun never set. That world and that empire are now long gone and often reviled, so it is hard to imagine the extent to which small boys, even American boys, in one of the empire's far-off corners, could be inspired by the colonial and imperial dream. We were part of it, and to us it seemed good, even noble.

We did not forget, however, that we were in Canada. Although our official sports were cricket and soccer, our passion was ice hockey. Our heroes were Maurice "the Rocket" Richard and Gordie Howe of the Montréal Canadiens and Detroit Redwings, respectively. In our spare time we played the equivalent of ice hockey in a scruffy weed-infested backyard lot behind the boarding house. We pretended to be our favorite National Hockey League teams. We had no puck but used a tennis ball and broken boards as sticks. Our fervor was undiminished by this lack of equipment.

It was wartime. Canada became part of the war effort long before America entered. One of the headmaster's sons, Michael, had enlisted and was killed in the Battle of Britain. Another, Ned, also joined up and was away for almost all my time at the school. He returned in 1945 to spend the remainder of his life teaching at the school alongside his elder brother Kyrle Junior, who did not go to war. We had several boys in the boarding house who had been evacuated from the Blitz. We were expected to contribute a portion of our meager pocket money to support Dr. Barnardo's Homes in Britain, which looked after orphans and other displaced children. Rationing was very much in effect. We had little sugar on anything, including our morning porridge, but we did manage to salvage some granulated sugar from our Sunday corn flakes to add to the unsweetened cocoa that was our standard breakfast drink. We had one orange a week as our only fruit ration. Otherwise we survived on a diet of bread and beef dripping, steam puddings, and lots of cabbage.

In the boarding house the dozen or so boarders slept in traditional dormitories, rooms with six or eight beds side by side. We went to bed at fixed hours whether the sun had set or not, and we rose together early each morning. We hid small treasures, candy mainly, in small holes in the oilskin wallpaper. We were allowed one bath a week in an inch of tepid water, often shared with other boys. It was an austere existence, yet the housemaster, young Kyrle and his wife, Tiny, truly cared for us and were unfailingly kind, notwithstanding the stern discipline they imposed. We did our homework together in a dank common room beside the house, heated by a small pot-bellied stove charged to red heat to keep us warm in the winter. We did not complain much. Complaints were contrary to the stiff upper lip philosophy of the school, although when I got home to Seattle for the vacations, I let my parents know how unhappy I was. They too were not entirely satisfied with what they saw. One Christmas I came home with impetigo and another uncleanliness disease. They tried to express concern to the headmaster, who dismissively told them that if they did not like the way he ran the school, they could take their little boy out and send him elsewhere.

I did get a small respite on the weekends. On Saturdays there were always outings for the boarders: walks to Foul Bay or Oak Bay beaches and hikes on Mount Tolmie and Mount Douglas, among others. On Sundays I invariably walked down Windsor Road in the morning to attend mass with my Aunt Flo, a devout Catholic who never missed a mass. I became an altar boy at Our Lady of Lourdes Church, where my parents had been married, and learned all the intricacies of the Latin mass. After church I would come back to Windsor Road to eat lunch, play in the yard, and roll cigarettes for my grandfather. Aunt Flo acted like a mother to me in those years. She had been a well-known athlete in her youth, a major figure in West Coast badminton tournaments. The house on Windsor Road was full of trophies of her triumphs. She never lost her love of sport and was a regular golfer until aging limbs made golf no longer possible.

She did not, however, have an entirely sunny personality. In her later years she came to resent that her sister succeeded in marrying and escaping the suffocating social climate of Victoria and that she had been left to care for two aging parents on her own. While she had succeeded as an officer in the Canadian Customs Service, starting as a secretary and rising to become an inspector, she never felt fulfilled in what she had achieved and remained jealous of her older, more beautiful, and more socially accomplished sister. My brother, who came to St. Michael's several years after me, became even closer to Aunt Flo. We were both to some degree surrogates for the children she never had, though she felt we never fully recognized or valued what she had done for us.

Occasionally, I would spend weekends on the farm in Colwood, where my uncle Eric and aunt Gladys lived with their two daughters, Dalla and Stephanie. Although I suffered dreadfully from asthma when I went there, it was a refreshing change from the constrained life of the school. The Eric Quaintons had a cow, Juno, which I was allowed to milk, a series of huge Great Danes, and several acres of orchard, scrub, and forest within which to play. I remember their sawdust-fired stove, not so much for the stove itself but for the large barn adjacent to the house where the sawdust was stored. What fascinated me at ten or eleven was not the sawdust but the stag beetles that lived in it. These we caught and preserved. I spent many happy hours exploring the property with my cousins, both tomboys who loved the outdoors. For a brief period, my uncle tried raising turkeys, but turkeys are notoriously difficult to raise, and the endeavor failed miserably when most of the birds died.

Uncle Eric was a remarkable man. Like my father, he had immigrated with his parents in 1913 to Brandon in Manitoba. In the mid-1920s he went on to Queens' College, Cambridge, where he had a career not distinguished by academic success. He took a third-class degree but won a "half blue" in ice hockey, a blue being what Americans would call a varsity letter. Supposedly, one of the highlights of his time in England occurred during the general strike of 1925. According to family lore, he drove streetcars in Birmingham as part of the government's effort to break the strike. He returned to Canada in the late twenties and immediately became a schoolmaster at St. Michael's and a nearby school, Malvern House. He divided his time between the two schools for much of his career, morning at one, afternoon at the other. This way he would not have to lunch with the boys, for whom he had a certain dislike, and could regularly visit his bookie in a seedy back street shop in the center of Victoria.

He loved to play cricket for the Five C's (the Christ Church Cathedral Cricket Club), gamble on the horses, drink beer, play charades, and enjoy the pleasures of the outdoors. Indeed, gambling seems to be in the family genes, as the first newspaper from which I learned to read was the *Daily Racing Form* in preparation for trips with my father to Seattle's great but now long-deceased Longacres track. Both Uncle Eric and Aunt Flo were addicts of local horseracing both on the island and in Vancouver. Uncle Eric was a crusty, acerbic, cantankerous schoolmaster, but for all that he was much beloved by his pupils.

His wife, Gladys, had been born in Shanghai to a wealthy British merchant family that had retired to Victoria in the 1920s. Under American immigration law she was a "Chinese Person" and hence came under an immigration quota of only one hundred per year. This meant that when the University of Oregon offered Eric a chance to teach at about the same time my father went to the University of Washington, she could not get a visa. I never sensed much resentment, as both she and Eric were both proudly British and somewhat scornful of the United States. They were equally scornful of Canadian prime minister Pierre Trudeau and his effort to make Canada bilingual. For them Canada would always be Anglophone. Gladys's China background was an important part of her life and influenced both my cousins, who adapted Chinese motifs in their painting and pottery. She was an articulate, strong-willed woman with a love of birds and dogs. A committed and talented gardener, she surrounded her house with annuals and perennials alike and kept a large aviary filled with small, variegated songbirds. She was not a gambler and did not suffer fools or small boys gladly. Both she and Eric treated me with exceptional kindness.

As the years went by, my life moved to the eastern United States and then into the wider world. My visits to Victoria became less frequent but continued during summer holidays from boarding school and college and on home leaves in the Foreign Service—first with my mother, then with my wife, Susan, and eventually with our children. Always the focus of our visits was the family: the aunts, uncle, and cousins. Our children came to enjoy the same beaches where I had played as a boy and the same family parlor games that had so delighted me at wartime Christmases. As time went by they also shared in more adult social events, enjoying restaurant meals with Aunt Flo (always the same restaurants and always beginning with the same Manhattan cocktail) and spending time with the Eric Quaintons in their second house in the country, where they could share a gin and tonic before lunch or a whiskey before dinner. One drink usually became two, as it was Gladys's firm conviction that "one could not fly on one wing." The cousins were often there: Dalla with Jeremy, her Royal Canadian Navy husband; and Stephanie alone and divorced but by then a famous Canadian watercolorist. Deaths also brought me back—for my parents, both buried in the crypt of Christ Church Cathedral next to the dean's ecclesiastical chair, or for the funerals and memorials for Aunts Gladys and Flo.

The connection with Victoria took an unexpected dimension in 2010, when I was invited to become an advisory governor of St. Michaels University School, successor to the little school on Windsor Road I had attended over sixty years before. As a governor, I returned to the school once or twice a year for board meetings and participated in vigorous discussions about the future of the school, now grown to almost a thousand students from grades kindergarten through twelfth. Unlike its World War II predecessors, it has become quite cosmopolitan, requiring its students to study Japanese rather than Latin. Military-style drill is gone, but the school hymn remains as written by Dean Quainton almost a century ago. A third of the boarders are from China, but dozens of other nationalities are represented as well. It has become one of the great schools of Canada: proud of its successes and its intellectual and athletic leadership in British Columbia and beyond. It retains not only the St. Michael's hymn but also its motto, *Nihil magnum nisi bonum* (Nothing is great unless it is good). The boys and girls who attend are proud to shout its other motto: *Vivat!* (Long may it live!) That one word captures the long-standing place of Victoria in my life.

3
Go East, Young Man

My life in Seattle effectively came to an end with my acceptance at Phillips Academy Andover in Massachusetts in the fall of 1948. For all our English and Canadian connections, we were decidedly a western family. We had no ties—physical, familial, or academic—with the East Coast. So it was something of a shock to find myself traveling across the continent to a world not of Victorian sensibility but of New England Puritan rigor. While I returned to Seattle for holidays and visited Victoria in the summer and on Foreign Service home leave, I never returned physically or emotionally to the Northwest, where I had spent the first fourteen years of my life.

That I went east at all was entirely serendipitous. In the fall of 1947 the *Saturday Evening Post*, which our family, like almost all others in America, read avidly, featured an article with colored pictures of a school on a hill, Phillips Academy Andover. I was enchanted by the beauty of this school and said wistfully to my mother that it would be wonderful to go to a school like that. Since we had no connections to New England and no money for private school education (my mother was then working in a doctor's office as a receptionist), this was clearly an idle thought.

Several weeks later my mother found herself seated at a dinner next to a man who enquired politely of the young widow how her boys were getting on. Well, she assured him, recounting my life and activities at Lincoln High School. For reasons that are not apparent, she then mentioned the *Saturday Evening Post* article. To her astonishment her dinner partner was an Andover graduate, in fact, the only graduate of Andover in Seattle. He immediately expressed an interest in my education and offered to get me a place at his old school. He wrote to the headmaster, John Kemper, praising this bright

Northwest boy and urged the school to admit him. To my mother's and my surprise, the school offered me a place on condition that I pass the school's entrance examination. The school sent me the examination for entry into Mathematics 2 and English 2. In addition to being asked to interpret William Blake's poem "The Clod and the Pebble," I had to write a three-hundred-word essay on the theme "Sunday at Home." To my surprise I passed and was admitted as a Lower Middler (sophomore in Andover's lexicon) with a full room, board, and tuition scholarship of $1,400 annually, a sum far beyond my mother's meager resources.

So it was in the fall of 1948 that I set off for the East in the company of my mother's aunt, my great-aunt Violet Roche. Auntie Vi, a delightful English-born spinster, was the art needlework buyer in Seattle's largest department store, Frederick and Nelson. Every year she traveled to New York to purchase the latest stock for her department. Since she would have had to make the trip at some point that fall, she offered to escort me to Andover. We traveled by train in a sleeping compartment via Chicago to New York, then on to Boston, the only feasible or financially acceptable way of getting back and forth to Seattle. Each year I crossed the continent in the summer and the fall via one of the various rail lines then existing: the Great Northern, the Northern Pacific, the Milwaukee Road, the Union Pacific, and once, when I was at Princeton, across Canada on the Canadian Pacific. For reasons of expense, I made these trips sitting up, an intolerable hardship in retrospect, but as a teenager I hardly thought to complain. Because I could not afford to go home at Christmas or Easter, I spent all my holidays in Philadelphia with Eugenia and Jack Atwood, old family friends. They took me in as if I were one of their own children, and I came to feel a part of their family. Aunt Eugenia, as I came to call her, was the sister of Richard Fuller, who had built the Seattle Art Museum, filled it with Oriental, particularly Chinese, treasures, and then given it to the city of Seattle. His museum, still located in Seattle's Volunteer Park, remains one of the greatest collections of Oriental art in America.

I arrived at Andover in early September 1948 and went straight to Cheever House, the dormitory where I was to spend my first year. The housemaster, Frank "Deke" DiClemente, was a no-nonsense chemistry teacher and wrestling coach. My roommate was a boy from New Jersey, Irv Kelsey. Although we lived together for the entire academic year, we never became friends and parted ways after that first year. My experience in Cheever House was not altogether a happy one. In the spring of that first year I wrote a rather scathing essay in my English class describing my room as a "cell at Alcatraz." I claimed that it was "bleak, cold and sparsely scattered with furniture dating from the antediluvian period."

Andover in the late 1940s was then, and in many ways still is, a university for teenagers. The array of academic options was extraordinary. The faculty was of university caliber, and there was a strong sense from the headmaster on down that this was the finest school in America. Unlike St. Michael's School, it did not pride itself on discipline or a rigid curriculum. It encouraged openness and challenged students to explore ideas to the maximum extent possible. Originally a Congregationalist foundation, Andover continued to retain a role for religion. There were chapel services each week and compulsory churchgoing on Sundays. Catholic boys were allowed to fulfill that requirement at St. Augustine's, the local Andover parish church.

My roommate in my second (Upper Middle) year, Bob Jessup, with whom I lived in Adams House, also left little mark. I remember him as a champion table tennis player whose skills I spent many long hours in the basement of the Commons trying to emulate. I had a much closer relationship with my final roommate, Peter Smith, a gifted musician who spent most of his senior year composing a string quartet. We became good friends, although we lost touch after going our separate ways to Yale and Princeton. I was a rather shy and self-absorbed teenager and made few lifelong friends. The one exception was Richard Ullman, who went on to have a distinguished professorial career at Princeton and who as a Rhodes scholar at Oxford took part in Susan's and my wedding. After the ceremony Richard drove us to Heathrow airport in his sporty but dilapidated convertible.

Almost every afternoon Peter Smith and I had tea with our housemaster, Emory Basford, one of Andover's legendary English teachers. A gentle and learned man with a deep commitment to teaching, he was a convinced Anglophile from the great English tradition. He could be stern and inflexible, certainly did not believe in coddling young minds, and seemed to have come from central casting for the later British TV series *To Serve Them All My Days*. As is the case with so many great teachers, his life was entirely wrapped up in his students. We drank Lapsang Souchong tea and ate pound cake with him. He encouraged us to think broadly about the world and about literature and conveyed to us his love of Wordsworth and the *Lyrical Ballads*. These were not teaching sessions but serious open-ended discussions. To the degree that I had a mentor at Andover, it was he. He certainly played an important part in the next stage in my career. Against my mother's wishes, he encouraged me to apply for an English-Speaking Union Schoolboy Fellowship to study at an English public school for a postgraduate gap year before going to Princeton. Those teas were the highlight of my three years at Andover.

I cannot say I was particularly happy at Andover. I regarded many of my peers with disdain and found them hard to engage. I concentrated on my studies and generally did well, although I just barely failed to be elected to the Cum Laude Society because of a disastrous encounter with calculus, which I could not fathom and for which I received a well-deserved 65. I enjoyed my other studies, particularly the advanced Latin courses, doing Virgil and then Horace and Catullus, with Dr. Gillingham, a strict and rather austere Englishman who loved his subject and conveyed that love to his small coterie of dedicated Latinists. Having read Caesar's *Gallic Wars* as a small boy at St. Michael's, I immediately entered third-year Ciceronian Latin and had no difficulty in going on to the more advanced courses that Dr. Gillingham taught.

The English and history departments were particularly strong. I look back with fondness on those professors: Dudley Fitts, rotund and Buddha-like, explaining Greek tragedies, which he had recently translated; and "Doc" Darling, the renowned and feared American history teacher, who forced us through the uniquely Andover history-learning style, in which we in effect wrote our own American history text. We were given essentially blank pages with one or two topics on each, with appropriate citations, and were then left to our own energy and devices to extract the necessary information and record it.

Andover was a school that valued athletics. I was not particularly good at sports and had no chance of being a varsity athlete. In my Upper Middle Year, that is, the junior year at most high schools, I tried out to become the manager of the track team. I was one of three assistant managers, who spent time moving hurdles, setting up races, and providing water to more skilled classmates on the team. The manager of the team received a varsity letter, entitling him to wear a large white A on the then-fashionable heavy navy blue sweater. Alas, I was not chosen to be the manager and received instead a smaller white A, a junior varsity equivalent that the two of us who were not selected had earned. As for the prestige sports, football, ice hockey, and wrestling, I had no place in them. Overall, I suffered through the many hours of compulsory outdoor activity without achieving any special proficiency. But I did take up fencing, thought in those days to be a rather effete sport, and on reaching England in my gap year I competed successfully in it.

Although not competitive on the athletic field, I entered virtually every academic competition open to me. I won prizes for recitation and declamation, reciting essays of Robert Benchley and Stephen Leacock, as well as the Cratchit dinner scene from Dickens's *Christmas Carol*. I tried out for the school Shakespeare production of *Antony and Cleopatra*, gaining the rather modest role of eunuch and servant to Cleopatra. (The school paper described my portrayal as "engaging.") I played the lead role in the annual Latin play, Plautus's *Curculio*, also called *The Weevil*. I was an active member of the Philomathean

Society, the school's debate club, and in my senior year represented the school in the annual Andover-Exeter debate, speaking in the affirmative on the topic "Resolved: A sense of humor serves mankind more than a sense of propriety." In short, I was active, engaged, and productively expanding my horizons. Like most of my peers I was admitted to a selection of Ivy League schools. (Over sixty classmates alone went to Yale.) I decided on Princeton, which had offered me a generous $1,900 scholarship.

While I left the school with only a handful of lifelong friends, I look back on those three years with considerable affection, despite my overall lack of joy in them. I learned to think, speak, and write clearly. I survived the sexual and social anxieties of the teenage years and emerged, if not a butterfly, at least a somewhat more mature adolescent, reasonably well prepared for the rigors and challenges of university life. Reflecting my parents' views, I was already a confirmed liberal. In my first term at Andover, I wrote a paper my teacher described as "eloquent" entitled "All Americans?" in which I denounced discrimination against "negroes" and Jews and the failure of our country to live up to its constitutional guarantees of life, liberty, and the pursuit of happiness. Those views sustained me across the many decades to come.

Many years later I became a member of the Andover Alumni Council for a five-year term. I also returned at regular five-year intervals for class reunions, where I quickly came to realize that my teenage disdain for my peers, which I too often demonstrated as a student, was in no way justified. The beauty of Andover's campus, its classical buildings, some now two hundred years old, overwhelmed me as a young teenager and remain deeply embedded in my memory of that "school on a hill" that had so captivated my imagination more than half a century before.

4
English Interlude

Before I got to Princeton, a gap year in England intervened. As noted earlier, my housemaster at Andover, Emory Basford, had suggested that I apply for an English-Speaking Union Schoolboy Fellowship to spend a year at an English public school. (Public school in British parlance meant a private school, now referred to as an independent school.) My mother's opposition arose from her suspicion of Basford's intentions. He had taken several of us for a weekend to Deer Island off the coast of Maine, where he had a summerhouse. She feared sexual misbehavior then, as any parent, I suspect, would now. Nothing of the kind occurred. In any event, I went ahead and applied and was thrilled to find myself selected to go to Sherborne School in Dorset. It was a school of which I knew nothing, but research quickly showed that it was a major boarding school in the west of England founded by King Edward VI in 1550 on land that had once been a Benedictine monastery. I felt it a great honor to have been chosen. Today, with so many study abroad options available to graduating high school seniors, this program has fallen on hard times, and neither Andover nor Sherborne still participates. Both are the losers. My mother, who was about to remarry, thought I was making a mistake and that I should go direct to Princeton. She tried unsuccessfully to dissuade me from accepting the fellowship but ultimately acquiesced in something I passionately wanted to do.

England had a strong fascination and sentimental interest for me. My father and paternal grandfather had both gone to Queens' College, Cambridge. In addition, I had had a taste of British-style education as a nine-year-old when I was sent away to that small boarding school in Victoria, British Columbia, where my uncle taught and where, before going up to Cambridge, my father had also taught. I expected Sherborne to be like St. Michael's, a somewhat more benign version of Dickens's Dotheboys Hall. In some ways, it was.

Sherborne sent me information about its academic, religious, and sports programs, as well as a detailed list of clothing that had to be procured in advance. Andover was a school with a very loose dress code. Although we still wore coats and ties, there was nothing that could be called a uniform. Not so at Sherborne, where all the boys wore gray flannel suits, shirts with highly starched detachable collars, and a school tie. A straw boater decorated with house colors had to be worn whenever boys went out into the town. There was also a fair amount of sports clothing for the required gym periods and the rugby and cricket seasons, in which all boys took part. For my mother the challenge was to find the required shirts and collars. Collarless dress shirts were almost completely out of fashion in America at that time, although Brooks Brothers still carried a few, mainly for clergy who needed something to which a Roman collar could be attached. Eventually, the shirts and collars were found.

In September 1951 my mother packed me off across the country to join the other scholars to board the *Queen Elizabeth*, sailing for Southampton. My old family friends, the Atwoods, drove me to New York from Philadelphia and saw me safely aboard after a day of sight-seeing in New York, culminating in a lobster dinner at the Waldorf Astoria Starlight Roof.

The ship was abominably hot, particularly in the claustrophobic cabins of third class. One of my cabin mates, Nicholas Monck, became a good shipboard friend. He was a charming old Etonian who went on to have a distinguished career in the British civil service. I was most unimpressed by my fellow ESU scholars, whom I criticized for their slovenly dress. As I put it in my diary, "They all dress like people from the slums." I enjoyed myself playing bridge and deck tennis, gambling on horse races and bingo, and occasionally dancing in the Winter Garden. I regret to say that I had already adopted English mannerisms and was often mistaken for an English schoolboy rather than an American scholar.

On arrival, John Melvin, my housemaster-to-be, met me at the dock and drove me up to the school. He kindly and gently introduced me to the rules of the school and of Harper House. I arrived full of apprehension about what would be in store for me. Previous scholars had told me before my arrival that Sherborne had not had many American boys. The English-Speaking Union apparently thought that a transatlantic transplant was unlikely to flourish under the harsh discipline for which the school was known. Sherborne assumed that American fellows, all of whom came from eastern U.S. prep schools, had been coddled in an atmosphere of moral and intellectual laxity. These Americans had previously been advised to steer clear of Sherborne in general and at Sherborne of Harper House in particular, which had the reputation of being the most rigorous of all the Sherborne houses in which students lived and ate. Nonetheless, Harper House was my assigned destination.

Although I had completed my secondary education, I was not particularly well prepared for the intellectual demands of the British system. I had studied a variety of standard subjects: French, English literature, American history, Latin, chemistry, and music appreciation. However, I was not ready for the intense specialization of the final years of English secondary education. In most subjects the boys were far more advanced than I, particularly in Greek, Latin, and modern languages. The only options open to me seemed to be history and English, and these were the subjects on which I concentrated as I joined the boys who were preparing for their A-level examinations in the summer of 1952. The teachers were superb, in particular "Buffer" Brown, Lecky Bruce, and Michael Hart. I loved the curriculum and came away from that year with a fascination for Tudor history and a love of the poetry of Gerard Manley Hopkins.

Harper House was a strange rabbit-warren kind of place, with prefects' studies on the ground floor, additional studies to which I was assigned in a prefab building in the back next to a World War II bomb shelter, and a series of dormitories and study rooms upstairs. I shared a study with Denis Bethell, an extremely studious and devout student who went on to win a scholarship to Lincoln College, Oxford, and then to teach at Trinity College Dublin. He had spent the war years in Victoria, where, to my amazement, he had been taught by my uncle at another small boarding school. We were instantly friends, and later at Oxford I stood as his godfather after his conversion to Roman Catholicism.

Sherborne in those days was intensely Anglican. There were only two Catholic boys in the school: myself and a slightly more junior boy, also in Harper House, Peter Saunders, who went on to become a Dominican priest and missionary in Zimbabwe and Lesotho. We would go off to the eight o'clock Sunday morning mass while the few devout Anglican boys in the house would go to early Communion in the school chapel. The rest of the day was heavy-duty Anglicanism. At ten we had an hour-long divinity lecture by Headmaster Robert Powell, followed by morning prayer at 11:00. The lecture was dry, abstruse, and I think above the heads of most boys. While we were free to roam the countryside on Sunday afternoons, we had to be back by 6:15 for evening prayer in the chapel, followed by forty-five minutes "studying dogma." The day ended with prayers beside our beds. For me, that meant a total of four hours of churchgoing. I remember nothing of the dozens of sermons I heard, except one on Peter's call to the apostles, "Let us go fishing," something we all longed to do.

Life in Harper House was highly regulated. I was in a dormitory with nine other boys. We rose at 7:15, had the required cold bath, breakfasted, and headed off to classes attired in our distinctive boater with a pale blue band denoting our house. Meals were a trial for me. My table manners left much to be desired, and I was regarded by the prefects as a slightly savage American who was frequently caught talking with his mouth full, a solecism for which punishment was immediately imposed in the form of a run around either short or long "slopes," that is, the valley in which Sherborne lies. I think one slope was a mile and a half and the other three miles. A prefect followed on a bicycle to make sure that one did not slack or slow to a walk. These punishments were a great trial for me, as was the favorite afternoon sport, Hares and Hounds, in which boys followed an elaborate trail around the countryside set by one of the senior boys. Due to my asthma, I suffered greatly from running in the cold.

With rationing still in effect, my first official duty was to register with the police and apply for a ration card. Because of wartime shortages, meals were heavy on starch, potatoes, and steam pudding, supplemented by small quantities of meat and larger quantities of cabbage and Brussels sprouts. Water was the usual beverage, except in the morning and evening, when tea was provided. To my astonishment, members of the rugby team were allowed, perhaps even required, to drink beer at lunch, an extraordinary offering when seen through the eyes of an American schoolboy at whose school drinking would have led to dismissal.

The rules of the house were firm but unstated. One could not address a prefect directly. One replied to questions with some formula such as "please, thank you, please," even when one was being asked if one wanted to be disciplined. Presence in study hall was recorded by the single Latin word *sum*. As an American, I was spared some of the corporal punishments that were routinely administered by the prefects. I was never caned, although caning was common. I did have to run around the "slopes" and do "lines"—copying out in my best handwriting, never very good, endless passages of English prose on foolscap sheets.

My delinquencies were minor. In addition to faulty table manners, I was often faulted for not having dusted my study carefully enough, a fact determined by a prefect who inspected each study with white gloves to detect any signs of dust. One of the punishments I hated the most was one referred to as "calling," which required one to rise at seven, get fully dressed, undress, have a cold bath, get fully dressed again, undress again, and then have a second cold bath. All of this had to be accomplished in ten minutes. The dormitory prefect, who remained comfortably in bed, monitored one's progress. This punishment was imposed for a fixed number of days, usually a week, and failure to complete the routine on time led to the imposition of an additional day.

While I never became a prefect, something about which I was deeply disappointed, I was given supervisory responsibilities in my last two terms that involved being present while younger boys did their evening homework. Like the young Scrooge, they sat in a cold room on hard wooden benches with no back and solemnly went through their "prep" in absolute silence. My only function was to ensure silence and to rap them across their kidneys with a ruler if they seemed to be slumping from fatigue or were not sitting up straight on their benches. I must confess I rather enjoyed this power.

There were, of course, lighthearted moments. All was not study and punishment. I remember especially the Harper House supper on one of the last days of term. It included a special meal, with roast pork, mince pies, and plum pudding. There were speeches by the youngest boy, a graduate, and the housemaster. The evening ended with house theatricals, including a pantomime, "The Babes in the Woods." I was chosen to play one of the minor roles, that of Fairy Foxglove!! This was hardly a role of which one could boast in the United States, but it occasioned laughs aplenty at the time to see a tutu-clad American cavorting in this rather unconventional role. The term ended in chaos several days later when all the junior students got up early to throw the prefects into a cold bath. All the normal strict rules of behavior were abandoned for that morning before the students boarded the school train for London and dispersed to their homes around Britain.

During this year I had two holidays on the Continent. After celebrating a very traditional English Christmas with the Bethells, my study mate's family in Deal, I went on to Cologne, Germany, to stay with Michael Hart, a teacher at Sherborne, and his family. Michael was a young history teacher who had recently taken a brilliant first-class degree at Keble College, Oxford. German by birth, he had escaped to England before the Second World War. His father was head of German railways in the Rhineland. They were wonderfully hospitable in their apartment, which overlooked the great Cologne cathedral, which had miraculously survived the ravages of war. The city itself was still badly damaged, and for a seventeen-year-old it was an eye-opening experience to see the damage created by the Allied bombing. The Harts decorated their apartment with the traditional Christmas tree, but on its branches were real candles, which when lit in the evening gave the small apartment an almost magical appearance. We also traveled down the Rhine to the Mosel River, where the Harts went each year to buy a supply of wine.

For my second holiday, between the spring and summer terms, Michael Hart and I were together again. We decided to visit Italy and Yugoslavia and set out by train to Rome, Florence, Venice, and then via Trieste to Rijeka, down the coast to Split and Dubrovnik, and finally back across the country via Mostar and Zagreb. The highlight of the trip was our stay in Rome, where I systematically visited all the major basilicas and ancient sites. My family had arranged through the American College that I would get a ticket to a papal audience with Pius XII. On the morning of our second day in Rome I awoke to find a letter from the papal secretary granting me an audience that same day. It was a large audience, including a group of American soldiers and sailors, whom Vatican officials had instructed to give three cheers when the pope arrived and departed. My impression was that most of the Americans in the audience were Protestants, although they had brought rosaries to be blessed and given to friends at home on their return. (I, too, had brought a rosary to give to my grandmother in Victoria.) I was impressed by the pope's modesty. He entered attended by Raphael-costumed chair bearers, as I observed in my diary. He gave a short address in English on Christian unity and then moved among the attendees, enquiring about their families and hometowns. All either kissed his ring or shook his hand (or both).

In Rome and Florence, Michael and I did most of the ancient and ecclesiastical sights together. However, our relations became increasingly strained. We quarreled incessantly over big issues such as religion and trivial things such as the perfect cheese to have after dinner and whether it could be taken with coffee or not. By the time we got to Venice we were barely on speaking terms. Michael announced that we would have to make our way back to England separately. I considered returning directly to England but decided to carry on alone.

Somehow, I managed to complete a trip through Yugoslavia, then an extremely inhospitable country. This was my first introduction to an authoritarian Communist regime. The iron fist of the Tito regime was evident everywhere. On the beaches along the coast there were militia stationed to prevent Yugoslavs from escaping by small boat across the Adriatic to the safety of Italy. Everything seemed gray and uninviting. All tourism was controlled by the state tourism agency, Putnik. On my return, at Slavonski Brod, a small station, I encountered a former German U-boat captain and his dog, Fritz. The captain terrorized the other diners by making Fritz jump up on a table and snarl at the Yugoslavs. It was my first rather unpleasant taste of an encounter with a Nazi.

Harper House left me with one enduring skill: I can still fold my pajamas into two perfect squares. Learning to make my bed to the high standard imposed by the prefects was one thing, but folding one's pajamas was infinitely more difficult and was taken seriously as part of the morning inspection of one's dormitory. The uniform of the day was always a gray suit, a white shirt with a heavily starched detachable collar, a house tie, and, of course, one's boater. My shirt and its detachable collar were a constant trial. Although starched to a bright shine, the collars caused scratchy abrasions on my neck. We were issued two collars a week and only one shirt, so students were well turned out on Wednesdays and Sundays but increasingly scruffy on the intervening days.

School days were full and rewarding. I took history and English, the only two subjects for which an American secondary education had prepared me. With other sixth-form boys I prepared for the Advanced and Scholarship-level papers, which I eventually took in the summer of 1952. One of the essays I chose to write for the so-called general paper was "What qualifications for world leadership are shown by the United States of America?"—a question that could still be asked six decades later.

The history department was particularly strong, led by a venerable Sherborne institution, "Buffer" Brown, who taught history in snuff-encrusted tweeds and with a wonderfully rich sense of humor. He was ably supported by Michael Hart. The year focused heavily on the Tudors and Stuarts. I developed a fascination with that period of English history, which I continued during my studies at Princeton on returning from England. I remember the English staff less well, although the senior master, Lecky Bruce, remains in my memory because of his intimidating stammer. The set books of that year included *The Rape of the Lock*, *The Lyrical Ballads*, and the collected poems of Gerard Manley Hopkins. They remain among my literary favorites.

Sherborne in those days was also a school of muscular Christianity. Sports then, as now, played a large part in school life. I played both rugby and cricket. (I had played a little cricket as a small boy in Victoria and found I could hold my own at a modest level.) I had done fencing at Andover and joined the Sherborne fencing team, traveling with the team to other schools in the region, including Downside, Bryanston, and Wellington. Wednesdays were given over to the Cadet Corps. As an American citizen, I announced that it would be inappropriate for me to put on the king's uniform, and so I was sent to play squash with the thirteen-year-old boys, who were too young to join the corps. A lifelong love of squash resulted, although it was humiliating to be repeatedly defeated by thirteen-year-olds. Although I never became good at sports, I did receive my school colors, the American equivalent of a letter, for fencing, having been only one of two boys from Sherborne who won their bouts at a quadrilateral fencing tournament at Bryanston School.

On several occasions I was asked to write for the Harper House magazine, *The Harpoon*. It was a rather amateur mimeographed affair. At the end of my first term I wrote a short article about democracy in American schools in which I caustically criticized the increasing democratization of Andover and my perception that whatever a majority of students wanted they got. I cited the change in chapel rules the previous year, whereby the Bible was almost completely eliminated, to be replaced by music services and readings from secular authors such as Donne, Shaw, and Eliot. I also poked fun at Andover's decision to provide a refrigerator in every house at the students' request. In the end, however, I concluded that the democratic system of internal elections for clubs and student organization did lead to an emphasis on efficient and effective leadership. In the spring I wrote about the upcoming American presidential elections, trying to explain the primary and convention systems for selecting candidates. I concluded that the Republicans would win and that the victor would be Senator Taft, the leading Republican candidate at the time. In the summer issue I wrote a piece entitled "Yugoslavia: A Police State in the Western World," reflecting my travels over the spring break with Michael Hart. I spared no criticism of the Tito regime while acknowledging some of the egalitarian aspects of Communism.

The summer issue of the much more professionally produced school magazine, *The Shirburnian*, carried my article entitled "American Democracy and English Snobbery," which in many ways summed up my young impressions. I was a rather opinionated and arrogant young man, with a substantial capacity for disdain of British manners and mores. I was particularly struck by the lack of freedom in the British system and the ways in which leadership was imposed on the basis of ability and not popularity. I concluded with the following words, "I can certainly feel thankful to Sherborne for attempting, with doubtful success, to teach me the principles of discipline." Although I may have given up the cold bath and the buttoned coat, I shall always respect "the system" for turning out such high-quality material despite its occasional snobbery and intolerance. The article received "mixed criticism," including some very favorable comments and some very derogatory.

When I left Sherborne at the end of July, a fellow Harper House student, Dennis Pack-Beresford, invited me to join him at Fenagh House, his family's Irish country estate. I was impressed by the large house and its extensive grounds, rock garden, miniature golf course, and one of the finest collections of bamboo in the British Isles. Fenagh House seems in retrospect to have been a modest Irish counterpart of Downton Abbey. The colonel raised prized white sows and cocker spaniels. The house was filled with portraits and busts of the family's two founders, Sir Denis Pack and Viscount Marshal Beresford, both of whom served in the Napoleonic Wars and the British effort to seize Buenos Aires in 1812. Everywhere there were relics of the family's past greatness, which, it occurred to me, would not return unless income and estate taxes were reduced. The servants referred to Mrs. Pack-Beresford as "the Lady," and I was called "Master Tony," a new and unfamiliar title.

The Pack-Beresfords were very much a part of Anglo-Ireland. They kept their distance from the Catholic world around them. I was taken to meet the Anglican vicar for a discussion of an upcoming fair on the grounds of Fenagh House. The fair was to include donkey rides, clay pigeon shooting, and fortune telling. As a somewhat fastidious Roman Catholic, I was scandalized by the fortune telling at what was to be an Anglican fair.

I greatly enjoyed my stay in Ireland. During that short visit I managed to kiss the Blarney Stone, attend the Dublin Horse Show (where I was more impressed by the elegance of the attendees' dress than the skill of the riders), admire the Book of Kells, and marvel at the general cheapness of restaurant meals.

Overall, Sherborne was a wonderful interlude between my American secondary and tertiary education. It gave me both a chance to travel on the European continent and a taste of post-Dickensian England and of what Dr. Arnold sought to achieve in his vision of how young boys could be molded into men. I was to return to England three years later as a Marshall scholar at Christ Church, Oxford, where I reconnected with several old Shirburnians, who had done their national service while I was working on my BA. My affection for England, which had begun in British Columbia, was enhanced at Sherborne and confirmed at Oxford. I look back on my year in Harper House with considerable affection. There were disappointments that I had not been made a prefect, but there was also the great satisfaction at having successfully passed my A-level examinations. The school had a lifelong impact on me. The warmth with which I was received, the friends I made, and the subjects I studied were permanent legacies. While I returned to Princeton with a somewhat fruity English accent and manners that were rather too Anglicized for my family's taste, I had no regrets at having spent my gap year in the heart of the glorious West Country of England, memorialized by Thomas Hardy.

5
A Tiger in My Tank

In the summer of 1952 I returned to Seattle in preparation for starting at Princeton in the fall. Once again, I worked in a Seattle bank to earn money to cover modest incidental expenses at Princeton. I had not visited Princeton and knew little of what to expect. Before going to England, I had received a large scholarship to cover room and board and tuition—worth $1,900 in those far-off days, compared with my full scholarship at Andover of only $1,400. I had a small student loan of some $499. Overall, I thought myself very lucky.

I entered Princeton with sophomore standing, claiming rather disingenuously to the university authorities that my A-levels in history and English in England were really the equivalent of freshman-year work. As a result, I was exempted from the university's general education requirements, including science, and managed to complete my studies in three years. In many respects this was a mistake. It limited my academic flexibility by reducing the number of courses I could take.

It was also a mistake socially. I knew little of the Princeton system on my arrival, but I quickly learned that the sophomore year was the one in which one chose or was chosen to join one of the Prospect Street dining clubs. This choice was important, for in those days the university provided no dining facilities for upperclassmen. The alternative to eating in a dining club was to eat at the Balt, a greasy spoon on Nassau Street.

Bicker, the process by which a sophomore found his way into an eating club, was a nightmare for me. I had few friends by the beginning of my second semester and knew virtually no upperclassmen. Sitting in my room night after night waiting for recruiting teams from one of the clubs to come and interview me was a source of great anxiety. Even worse were the three nights when I went to Prospect Street to open-house receptions at the various clubs. You went to the club that had shown some interest in you during the "bicker period." If they offered you a place, you signed up at once; if not, you were given a quick tour of the club and politely shown the way out. At the end of the first night I had not found a club that would take me. Luckily, on the second night I was offered a place in Key and Seal, where for my final two years I ate all my meals and made many good friends.

Happily, my roommate in those final years, Roger Lloyd, was also a member of Key and Seal. Roger had come to Princeton from Stowe, an English boarding school much like Sherborne, and we shared many interests and cultural tastes. We have remained friends across the decades. He was best man in my wedding, and the reception following was held at the Lloyds' home on Boars Hill near Oxford.

I was academically ambitious, and early on in my Princeton career I was enticed to apply to the Special Program in the Humanities (SPH). A small, elite program, SPH enabled its members to complete their departmental coursework and comprehensive examinations in their junior year, leaving them free to focus on producing a larger and more elaborate senior thesis than that produced by other Princeton undergraduates. SPH required us to take a group seminar on aesthetics, given by the distinguished Princeton philosophy professor Arthur Szathmary; otherwise, we were free to pursue our idiosyncratic intellectual enthusiasms. I started studying Chinese, continued with advanced Russian, and took a course on ancient history. There was little coherence in what I was doing. I was, however, privileged to work with one of Princeton's leading historians, E. Harris Harbison. Having taken his course on the Renaissance and Reformation, I decided to write my senior thesis on Christian humanism and the Protestant Reformation, focusing on Erasmus, Thomas More, and the Spanish cardinal Francisco Jiménez de Cisneros. The thesis was assessed as "mature, comprehensive, and well-balanced" but criticized for occasional factual slips and a complete lack of proofreading. Throughout my senior year I continued to work closely with Professor Harbison. He became my mentor, encouraging me eventually to put my name forward for the Rhodes and Marshall Scholarships.

Overall, I was reasonably successful at Princeton. My grades were good, and I enjoyed the classes I took in my history major, especially one taught by Gordon Craig. We read Craig's monumental work *The Diplomats, 1919–1939*, in which he portrayed a series of American and European diplomats and their roles in the period leading up to the Second World War. It was this course that sparked my interest in what was to become my chosen career. Beyond my academic work, I found the social life of the eating clubs difficult, requiring lots of drinking and the constant strain of finding blind dates for football weekends.

The one place where I was active and found great pleasure was as a member of the Whig-Cliosophic Society, or Whig-Clio, as it was commonly known on campus. It was housed in a small white faux Roman temple building at the center of the campus. While it hosted traditional debates, it also liked to think of itself as modeled on the Oxford and Cambridge Unions, where speeches did not follow the minutely prescribed rules of traditional American debating. As an active member of the debate team I took part in many Whig-Clio meetings and discussions. Among the propositions I defended were some lively and unlikely subjects such as "History in bunk"; "A bird-dog is better than a kennel dog"; "Germany should be rearmed and France embalmed"; "The hydrogen bomb was more of a blessing than a bane to humanity"; and finally, a topic that might still be relevant for debate fifty years later, "This assembly is still ready to support the President's Cabinet of Millionaires." I also achieved a certain notoriety by defending with my roommate, Roger, Whig-Clio's vice president, who was impeached for a lack of seriousness in presiding over debates. Despite our best efforts, he was ousted by a large margin.

I also took part in several productions and poetry readings sponsored by Theatre Intime, the small on-campus theater group in which I appeared in several minor roles. One had to be especially talented to take on major parts. The star of Theatre Intime at the time was Ben Piazza, who went on to a big career in Hollywood. My subsequent love of acting, which was to play a substantial role over my years in the Foreign Service, got strong encouragement at Princeton.

Princeton in the 1950s maintained its compulsory Sunday chapel requirement. It could be fulfilled not only in the university chapel but also in one of the other places of worship in town. In my first year, Father Hugh Halton, a brilliant young Dominican fresh from a doctorate at Oxford, came to Princeton as the new Catholic chaplain. He established the Aquinas Center for the university's Roman Catholic students. I attended mass regularly at the Aquinas Center until my junior and senior years, when the center went through an extraordinary change. Father Halton, on a trip across Ohio, heard on his car radio an address by Walter Stace, a distinguished Princeton professor of religion. Halton, believing that he had heard the Antichrist, on his return to campus began to preach ever-more-strident sermons, denouncing the religion department for its heretical and anti-Christian views. Relentlessly, he went after atheistic radicalism on campus, which he insisted was inconsistent with the academic and moral values on which Princeton had been founded.

Father Halton was particularly outraged in 1956 when Whig-Clio invited convicted perjurer Alger Hiss to campus. Not surprisingly, the Hiss speech became a major controversy, focused as much on freedom of speech issues as on the propriety of inviting a convicted traitor to the campus. Father Halton seemed to his flock to have become completely unhinged, to the point where a small group of us went to Trenton to petition the local bishop to have Halton removed. Unfortunately, the bishop informed us that Father Halton, as a member of a religious order, did not fall under his jurisdiction, and there was nothing he could do. However, word about Father Halton's eccentricities reached the appropriate ecclesiastical authorities, and he was removed several years later.

The center of my intellectual activities, beyond my Reformation thesis, was the Russian language. I took all available Russian-language courses. In addition, I worked as a research assistant for Princeton's leading Russian historian, Cyril Black, translating and analyzing for him articles on Soviet historiography. Between my junior and senior years, I attended the eight-week summer intensive Russian-language program at Middlebury College. This was a real challenge. One undertook not to speak English for the entire course. I quickly discovered that activities such as playing bridge in Russian were more difficult than they seemed. I enjoyed the classes and took part in Russian folk dancing, where I scandalized some of my fellow students by having an African American girl as my dancing partner. I also took part in yet another foreign-language play, this time Chekhov's *Kukharka zhenitsa*, or *The Cook's Wedding*. Among the participants on the course was a graduate student from Columbia University, Nathaniel Davis, who went on to have a distinguished Foreign Service career as a Soviet specialist and ended his career as director general.

I did not leave Princeton a confirmed Tiger. The university undergraduates were homogeneous, almost entirely white, and generally quite rich. Socially, my experience was largely negative. I did not fit the Tiger stereotype of the day: fun-loving, hard-drinking, oversexed. I held my own academically more than adequately but never really fit in. It was only in subsequent years, as I came back for regular five-year reunions, that I came to appreciate my fellow classmates. When I graduated I could not have imagined that so many of them, including the football players I so much looked down on, would have truly lived the university's motto, "Princeton in the nation's service."

In 1989 at a mini class reunion in Washington, Ralph Nader, the most famous, some would say notorious, member of the class, challenged his fellow classmates to give back to the university in some meaningful way some of the knowledge and experience we had acquired in the thirty-five years since our graduation. The result was the creation of the Princeton Project 55, public service fellowships in Washington, Chicago, and New York. Over the years that small seed grew into the modern Princeton Alumni Corps, continuing those fellowships but also engaging nonprofit leaders in training and providing the services of Princeton retirees on a pro bono basis to help nonprofits improve their performance. Twice I served on the board of the Alumni Corps, thereby maintaining regular contact with the university and its activities.

I confess that I, too, was much influenced by the university's long-standing commitment to "Princeton in the nation's service." That motto was subsequently modified to add the phrase "and in the service of all nations." That commitment reinforced for me Andover's similar commitment, expressed in its motto, *non sibi* (not for oneself), as a guiding principle. For all its elitism and sense of superiority, the Princeton legacy of service was to stay with me through almost forty years of government work.

6
Oxford Days

A return to England had not been in my plans as I approached my senior year at Princeton. However, as my grades held up, I belonged to the intellectually elitist Special Program in the Humanities, I had a fair range of extracurricular activities, and I worked as a research assistant to Professor Cyril Black, a distinguished Soviet and eastern European historian. My thesis advisor, Professor E. Harris Harbison, urged me to put my name forward as a candidate for the Rhodes, Marshall, and Keasbey Scholarships. I remember little of the process of writing essays and completing applications. The results were mixed. I was offered a Keasbey Scholarship, then relatively new and unknown, for study at either Oxford or Cambridge. I made the state-level finals for the Rhodes but was completely upended by a series of questions about science, including the work of Mendel, the Austrian monk. I did not pass on to the regional round.

For the Marshall Scholarship, then in its second year, I was invited to San Francisco for an interview by a committee chaired by Consul General Sir Robert Hadow, affectionately known in the British Diplomatic Service as "Shadow" Hadow. He was a gracious, courtly, and somewhat idiosyncratic British diplomat who insisted on focusing on my interest in Russia and the Foreign Service. I won the Marshall Scholarship, with Oxford as my designated destination. The scholarship then was worth only 550 pounds sterling, from which room, board, and tuition were deducted. I was certainly not going to be rich, but I was assured that this would be more than enough to cover my expenses.

My next problem was to choose a college. I consulted the British embassy in Washington and was told that the three "best" colleges were Christ Church, Trinity, and Magdalen. I assumed that best meant academically best, but in fact it meant socially best. Without really knowing what I was doing, I opted for Christ Church, the House, as it is still affectionately known by its members from its Latin title, Aides Christi, the House of Christ. In most respects for an American of that era, Christ Church was one of the least suitable colleges. Old Etonians seemed to make up a disproportionate percentage of its students. It appeared to me, as a rather naive and impressionable American, that there were peers of the realm and maharajahs on virtually every staircase. The most famous dining club in Oxford University, the Bullingdon, had its locus in Christ Church. Conscious of its social superiority, the House was unconcerned about its reputation for academic mediocrity. The world of Evelyn Waugh's *Brideshead Revisited* lived on, although elsewhere in the university the rather special social elitism of the interwar years was fast eroding.

The twelve Marshall scholars traveled as a group to England on the *Queen Mary*, much as the English-Speaking Union scholars had traveled as a group on the *Queen Elizabeth* four years before. We were a congenial group, anxious about our future, whether at Oxford or Cambridge, London, Birmingham, or Edinburgh. We played shuffleboard and bingo and took part in the daily competition to guess the number of nautical miles traveled since the previous day. We did not worry that we were traveling third class and denied access to the more elegant spaces above us in first and cabin class. I remember at one point climbing over the barriers and sneaking upstairs to see how the upper classes lived. Like all arriving passengers of those days, we traveled up to London from Southampton on the boat train, for most of us our first experience of a British rail carriage with doors opening to the outside from every compartment.

Once in London, we were given hotel accommodation. The Marshall Commission invited us to a reception at Devonshire House, near Hyde Park, the former home of the Duke of Wellington. We were most impressed by the elegance of the venue and by the eminence of the English officials and politicians who joined us. Our stay in London was short, and we were anxious to get to our respective universities.

Arriving at Christ Church, I was assigned a drafty room at the top of a staircase between the great Tom Quad and the more elegant *Brideshead Revisited* Peckwater Quad. My room, at the very top of the narrow staircase named Kilcannon, was three floors above the baths and toilets. The room, though sparse, was comfortable enough, at least until winter, when it was almost unbearably cold. A two-bar electric fire did little to dispel the dampness and the chill. My "scout," a college servant assigned to each staircase, every evening placed a jug of water inside my room to be used for morning ablutions. By morning the water had frozen. What distinguished Kilcannon was that one of England's most well-known detective writers, Michael Innes, had rooms two floors below me. Innes, a.k.a. J. I. M. Stewart, took little notice of the undergraduates around him, but I felt important to be located so close to a major literary figure.

In my second year I moved to large rooms on Tom Quad, the vast sixteenth-century quadrangle at the entrance to the college. My suite included an elegant sixteenth-century fireplace and the high ceilings of that era. I occasionally gave lunches in my room, ordered through the college and served with impeccable Jeeves-like ceremony by my scout. Every staircase had its scout, whose job it was to see to the comfort of the dons and students in residence. Oxford rooms were thought of as private sanctuaries. If one did not want to be disturbed under any circumstances, one could close not only the inner door to one's rooms but also the heavy outer door. This was known as sporting one's oak. It was a clear sign that one wanted to be left in peace.

I had informed the Marshall committee that I wanted to pursue a DPhil in history focusing on French intervention in the Soviet Union in the period immediately after the Russian Revolution. I was referred to the senior history don at Christ Church, Sir Hugh Trevor-Roper. Already famous for his book *The Last Days of Hitler* and his works on Tudor England, he quickly recognized that he was not the ideal person to supervise my doctoral work. He referred me to Max Beloff, a noted historian of Soviet foreign policy, who quickly agreed to take me on. I met regularly with Max, who had become a fellow in Oxford's most distinguished college, All Souls. He received me faithfully once a term, offered me dry sherry, and counseled me on sources for my work. We had a warm and congenial relationship, and he arranged for me to move academically from Christ Church to Nuffield College, a recently created postgraduate research college that focused almost exclusively on the social sciences. But my relationship with Max was ultimately not very satisfying for reasons that became apparent three years later.

One of the relics of a bygone day was the existence of moral tutors. Each undergraduate at Christ Church was assigned a moral tutor, in my case the aging and venerable classics scholar Robert Dundas. Early in my first term he invited me to his rooms in Tom Quad. I was not at all sure of the purpose, but it quickly became apparent. As I settled into my seat in his study, he rather nervously and with many characteristic Oxford harrumphs and stammers asked me if I knew about the birds and the bees. He said that he assumed that as an American student I did, but he just wanted to make sure. I assured him that I was familiar with the subject. (In fact, my mother, before sending me off to the dangerous moral climate of an eastern boarding school, had arranged for the doctor for whom she worked to have a private talk with me about those same birds and bees and to give me useful tips on safe sex.) Mr. Dundas expressed great relief and promptly offered me a glass of sherry. That is not to say that Oxford was a naive or innocent environment. Plenty of sex went on behind the shuttered doors, the "sported oaks," of undergraduate rooms or in punts on the Cherwell, but relationships still began with a cup of tea in the afternoon or a glass of sherry in the early evening.

Life in Oxford was as much social as it was academic. A ferocious joiner, I joined the History Society. I enrolled in the Oxford Union, where I learned to debate "Union style" and unsuccessfully sought election to its library committee. In the Cecil Sharp Society, I learned English country dances. Subsequently I joined the Scottish Society, although I had not a drop of Scottish blood. Because of my exposure to folk dancing during my summer at Middlebury in 1954, I was fascinated by country dancing. Its Scottish version was more complex and balletic. I eventually acquired a kilt and became a member of the society's dance team. I became president of both the History and Scottish Societies and enjoyed both the organizing role that this entailed and the opportunity, in the case of the History Society, to invite and dine with some of the great historians in England. The highlight of my Scottish dancing career was when Susan and I, already married, were part of the demonstration team that danced for the Duke of Gloucester at the Royal Agricultural Show in Woodstock in 1959. We were only bit players in a daylong series of "exhibitions." The Oxford Scottish team's performance was sandwiched between Boy Scouts pitching tents and elderly ladies demonstrating first aid. Still, it was a performance for the presiding "royals."

Oxford was the beginning of my six-decade-long love affair with Susan. We did not meet in entirely optimal circumstances. The venue was the House of Commons, the occasion a reception in honor of the newly arriving Marshall scholars. Although there are now over fifteen hundred graduates of the Marshall Scholarship program, at that time there were fewer than fifty in all, and well over half were at that reception. We older scholars were rather a self-satisfied and self-important collection of young men and women who had mastered the English way of life and were anxious to explain to those green newcomers "how it was done." I was the center of attention, having just returned from the Moscow Youth Festival. The speech I had given in Red Square had caught the attention of the international media.

It did not take me long to focus elsewhere and single out the very pretty and very bright Mount Holyoke graduate who was one of the stars of the new cohort. She and I immediately hit it off. Several days later the two of us joined several other scholars, including Warren Ilchman, who had already been in England for a year, to attend a performance of *The Entertainer*, starring Laurence Olivier. The play was on at the Windmill, noted as the only theater in England where the Lord Chancellor permitted frontal nudity onstage, on condition that the actresses did not move.

Pursuing Susan was no easy matter. She was very much focused on her English degree and in term time worked extraordinarily hard. However, she would often agree to a cup of tea or a glass of sherry in college (by then I had a room in Nuffield) in what was the standard Oxford social format. I introduced her to beagling, the pursuit on foot of a hare across muddy fields behind a pack of a dozen or more hounds. This very British sport was particularly popular in Christ Church, which had its own pack. On Saturday afternoons we would follow those hounds across the muddy fields around Oxford in pursuit of the ever-elusive hare the beagles sought. Today the Christ Church beagles remain one of only three remaining university-based packs in the United Kingdom.

In the spring break of 1958 Susan decided to travel to France and Italy with a college classmate, Robin Bovard. Her trip happily coincided with my own, and I finally caught up with them in Florence, where they were staying at the romantic Pensione Bartolini overlooking the Arno. We did an enormous amount of sightseeing together and immediately thereafter in Rome, where we spent Holy Week, including the Easter Vigil at Santa Maria Maggiore. I proposed shortly after our return to Oxford, despite Susan's worry that an engagement after little more than a six-months' acquaintance would seem hasty and socially incorrect. However, those concerns were overcome, and our respective parents responded enthusiastically. We announced our engagement in traditional fashion in *The Times* of London and married in August 1958.

My academic work proceeded normally, or so I thought. In my second year, I was elected to a studentship at Nuffield College. I beavered away in the Bodleian Library, the British Museum, and the Bibliothèque Nationale in Paris. As noted, I met once a term with my supervisor, Max Beloff, over a glass or two of sherry in his elegant lodgings at All Souls College. He asked how I was doing and, on being assured that I was more or less on track, encouraged me to keep up the good work. I was sustained by a collaborative friendship with George Kennan, who was spending 1957 in Oxford as the Eastman

Professor. He was working on his history of U.S.-Soviet relations in the same period as I was researching Franco-Soviet relations. Richard Ullman, an Andover classmate and longtime friend, was working on Anglo-Soviet relations in that same postrevolutionary period. We were a congenial triumvirate with common interests. The Kennans were particularly hospitable to us two young scholars, often inviting us for drinks and lunch in their college quarters.

I did not confine myself to Soviet history. Nuffield was filled with an array of scholars. One to whom I became particularly attached was Dame Margery Perham, one of the great Africanists of that generation. She was then working on a biography of Lord Lugard, the former governor general of Nigeria, with whom she was widely rumored to have had a romantic relationship. She put on a regular series of programs on postcolonial Africa, which I found fascinating, never imagining that some twenty years later I would find myself an ambassador in a postcolonial African country.

Dancing for the Duke of Gloucester was not in fact the highlight of my time in Oxford. Rather, meeting with the Duke of Edinburgh on the occasion of Nuffield's receiving its royal charter topped the list. The ceremony took place in the dining hall at Nuffield on June 6, 1958. I had invited Susan, by then my fiancée, to attend. It was a warm and humid June day, and Susan began to feel faint. We decided to return to my rooms on the ground floor of the main quadrangle. As she was recovering from her faintness, the door opened and the college's warden, Norman Chester, entered, accompanied by the Duke of Edinburgh. The duke affably made some polite remark about typical undergraduate goings-on. I don't recall if we formally shook hands, but Susan's friends, on hearing about the incident, were only concerned to learn whether she had curtsied or not. That she did not is the one thing of which I am sure.

◆ ◆ ◆

In the vacations between the short Oxford terms, I invariably traveled around Europe. Three trips in particular stand out: two long trips with fellow students to Turkey and Spain in my first two years and the 1958 vacation in Italy in pursuit of Susan. In the case of Turkey, I was joined by my former Princeton roommate Roger Lloyd and a colleague from Christ Church. After getting to Istanbul on the Orient Express, we went by bus to the southern coast and on to the east in small fishing boats, stopping at places such as Bodrum, Fethiye, and Antalya, which were at the time quite inaccessible. We went on from Turkey to Syria, visiting Homs, Hama, and Damascus, as well as the great crusader castle, the Crac des Chevaliers. We spoke virtually no Turkish beyond a few restaurant phrases and one politically relevant one that delighted the Turks: "Kıbrıs turktür" (Cyprus is Turkish).

At the end of my second year I wrote to the Marshall Commission summarizing my work to date. I indicated that I had done research in Paris and had written half of the thesis. I was confident I would complete it on time. However, I was critical of the DPhil program for what I called a "surfeit" of freedom. I had found my thesis topic stimulating, but "the mere drudgery of research" was sufficient to encourage me to seek every possible excuse for avoiding it. The result of this dissatisfaction was that I threw myself into extracurricular activities such as the university's History and Scottish Societies. At that point, I frankly expressed the view that I would have been better served intellectually to have done a BA or BPhil degree. Luckily, I was saved from a lack of intellectual challenge by my election to the studentship at Nuffield, where I found a small, closely knit cohort of intellectually curious and highly articulate young scholars in the social sciences.

By the end of my third year, I had completed my thesis and received Professor Beloff's approval to submit it. Shortly after submission in the early summer of 1958, I was summoned to my viva, or oral examination. The examiners were two of Britain's most eminent twentieth-century historians, A. J. P. Taylor and E. H. Carr. I remember the viva as having gone well, or at least without notable controversy or hostile questioning. To my very great surprise, a few hours later Professor Beloff notified me that I had failed without recourse. They had explained that there was not enough original material to justify awarding the DPhil degree. There was to be no rewriting or updating my work. I had failed outright, and instead of the anticipated DPhil I would be given a compassionate BLitt degree for my efforts. Beloff was apologetic, as well he should have been, but there was little either he or I could do. The examiners' word was final. The thesis was, in fact, not very good. George Kennan agreed to read it after its rejection and in early December wrote me a long and thoughtful letter full of comment. His summary conclusion was that the thesis was characterized by "lack of unity and structure in the presentation of material, imprecision of language, and a spotty use of sources."

I had recently been elected to a research fellowship at St. Antony's College to work with the warden, William Deakin, on the origins of the Italian Communist Party. I offered to resign the fellowship in light of the degree disaster, but Warden Deakin said it made no difference as far as he or the college were concerned. I should continue to plan to spend my last year in Oxford at St. Antony's.

My hopes for an academic career dashed, I concentrated on my work at St. Antony's and my pending application for the Foreign Service. During that year at St. Antony's, I studied Italian, read the impenetrable works of Antonio Gramsci, and delivered a series of lectures in the examination schools on the origins of the Italian Communist Party. This series of six lectures was my only foray into formal academic presentation until forty-five years later, when I resumed an academic career at American University in Washington. The lectures were poorly attended, since they did not fit very clearly into any of the subjects being taught for the degree either in history or in PPE (politics, philosophy, and economics). In fact, an initial audience of some twenty-five dwindled by the sixth lecture to a mere handful. I was not encouraged by my performance as an academic lecturer. In addition to lecturing, I also gave tutorials to students from Queen's and Jesus Colleges focusing on international relations in the interwar period of 1919 to 1939. I was young and inexperienced and savagely critical of the essays produced by my students, some of whom were only two or three years my junior. One of my first assigned pupils was a Rhodes scholar, who immediately asked to be transferred to another tutor, since he had not come all the way to Oxford to be instructed by a young, inexperienced Marshall scholar.

For all that, I remember those four years with affection. Life in Oxford was always intellectually stimulating, although for Americans, discussion could be somewhat rarefied and inaccessible. Nonetheless, one had the sense of being in a great university surrounded by intellectual stars in almost every field.

My final year at St. Antony's was particularly rewarding. I was no longer a mere graduate student but a member of the college's senior common room, one of the dons, although a very junior one. I worked closely with Warden Deakin, who had had a "good" war. He had been parachuted into Yugoslavia to work with Tito's partisans, and his bravery was widely acknowledged. He had subsequently written a well-regarded biography of Mussolini and was an authority on Italian politics. My work on the origins of Italian Communism fitted nicely with his interests.

St. Anthony's was a lively place, with a strong emphasis on European and Soviet politics. Among its fellows was David Footman, who had the dubious distinction of being Kim Philby's boss in the MI6 station in Beirut when Philby, unknown to his superiors, was actively spying for the Soviet Union. The college had been founded in 1950 by a Frenchman, Antonin Besse, who reportedly believed that French intellectuals needed the final polish of an Oxford education. He not only endowed the college financially but also gave it a substantial supply of very rare Madeira, some of which went back to the mid-nineteenth century, before phylloxera had destroyed the vines of France. Senior French politicians often graced the senior common room and high table. I remember in particular one especially lively evening with Pierre Mendès France, the former prime minister of France.

◆ ◆ ◆

The highlight of that year was our marriage. Not only did we have to go through all sorts of church formalities, but Susan was required under the statutes of the Marshall Scholarship to resign her scholarship, with the right to apply for reappointment. We were the first Marshall scholars to marry, and the Marshall Commission had no precedents to apply. Happily, on receiving Susan's application for reappointment, the commission's executive secretary, John Foster, referred the matter to the commission's chairman, Lord Coleraine, who rapidly approved her reinstatement. We were relieved, as there was always the possibility that a rules-bound institution would not change its procedures.

We were married in St. Aloysius Church on Woodstock Road on August 7, 1958. Because we were a mixed Catholic/Protestant couple, Susan had to receive formal marriage counseling. Through a network of friends, we arranged for her to receive counseling from Father Thomas Corbishley, the rector of Campion Hall, Oxford's Jesuit College. He and Susan immediately hit it off when Susan expressed interest in discussing the Petrine claims, not a normal subject for marriage preparation. Father Corbishley, learning that Susan could read Greek and Latin, suggested that she might want to read up on the subject. "Counseling" took the form of free reading in the Campion Hall library.

Father Corbishley performed the wedding, and our close American friend Bill Norgren, an Anglican priest who was pursuing an advanced theological degree at Christ Church, gave Susan away. The reception was on Boars Hill at the family home of Roger Lloyd, my best man and former Princeton roommate. We were a small group of fewer than thirty, mostly close Oxford friends. A Mount Holyoke classmate of Susan's, Mildred Nighswander, then on a Fulbright Fellowship in France, was able to cross the Channel to be her maid of honor. Our parents and we were both sad that distance and cost made it impossible for them to attend our marriage on that glorious English summer's day. We enjoyed Champagne on the lawn of the Lloyds' elegant house, and, following the reception, Dick Ullman drove us to the airport in his rather ramshackle vintage red convertible. We could not have asked for a more perfect day.

We flew to Paris and spent our first night in a small, elegant hotel on the Left Bank, the Relais Bisson, which family friends had recommended. It subsequently became famous as the hotel at which Kay Thompson's Eloise stayed in Paris. It no longer exists, and the internet regards it as fictional. We dined at a rather seedy African restaurant, the Baobab, an unusual choice. I had discovered it on an earlier research trip to Paris and wished to show it off to my new bride. The weather was foul, and on the next day, before taking the train to Venice, we wandered rather disconsolately around a rain-soaked Paris. We finally gave up and went to the movies, where we saw the now-famous black-and-white comedy *A Pig across Paris*, describing the wartime exploits of several men trying to smuggle a live pig from one end of Paris to the other.

Our six-week honeymoon was a series of adventures. In Venice I was most impressed to see the American consul general's launch cruising on the Grand Canal with the American flag bravely flying for the edification of tourists and locals alike. I easily imagined myself as a future consul general in Venice. Alas, the consulate was closed in 1963, long before I had risen to the point where I might have been considered for what I believed to have been a most glamorous post.

We boarded a Turkish steamer, the *Ege*, bound for Piraeus. We had tickets in third-class A, which meant that we were segregated in men's and women's cabins, each sleeping about twelve—a somewhat unusual arrangement for a honeymoon. On arriving in Greece, we went almost immediately to a ferry that was to take us to the island of Paros, famous for being the place where St. Helena had a vision of where in the Holy Land to find the relics of the true cross. We did not know that all the islands were sacred to the Virgin. We arrived without reservations and discovered to our horror that we had arrived on the eve of the feast of the Assumption, in orthodox terms the feast of the Dormition, of the Virgin. There were no hotel rooms to be found in the principal town, but a kind hotelier set up two cots in a breezeway for that night. The next morning he recommended that we try a small hotel on the opposite side of the island in a little village called Drios. There we found a hostel frequented mainly by intellectuals and writers from the mainland. We were well received and spent a happy and comfortable few days there. The food left something to be desired, as the staple dish seemed to be roast lamb and rice. On Paros, we visited the famous church of the 120 gates in the capital city, Parikia, built on the spot where St. Helena had had her vision. Subsequently, we went on from Paros to Kos and finally Rhodes, where we visited ancient and medieval monuments and the famous valley of the butterflies, which swarmed with literally thousands of brightly colored butterflies. We returned to Athens and went down to Marathon and Cape Sunion, then to Izmir and Istanbul by the same *Ege* on which we had arrived.

In Turkey, we marveled at the usual monuments, sailed up the Golden Horn to the café where Pierre Loti had written his famous novels set in the time of the Ottoman Empire. We developed a taste for Turkish food, rakı, and thick sweet Turkish coffee. In Istanbul we stayed in a rather scruffy hotel, the Cayaloğlu Palas. It too was fully booked, but we were given single beds in the hall close to the men's bathroom, to which throughout the night Turkish men went back and forth. As far as we could tell, Susan was the only woman in the hotel. We returned to England on the Orient Express, stopping for a day in Zagreb.

Susan and I lived in a small flat behind St. Antony's with the oddity of a bathtub in the kitchen. I had a small study, where I gave tutorials to a motley series of students from Jesus College, including that highly disgruntled Rhodes scholar who resented being taught by a Marshall scholar only two years older than himself. Susan was extremely busy preparing her final examinations in English, from which in the summer of 1958 she emerged triumphant with a brilliant first-class degree. We still had time to entertain friends, keep up our Scottish dancing, and enjoy the varied and numerous activities of Oxford life in term time. In our final month in Oxford we joined with Dick Ullman to give a garden party, complete with Champagne and strawberries and cream—a fitting end to our time in Britain.

During this period we made many close friends with whom we stayed in touch in the ensuing years. Anthony Levi, then a Jesuit and later a professor at St. Andrew's, was a good and close friend; it was he who had arranged for Susan to have marriage instruction with Father Corbishley. Trevor Lloyd, a fellow student of Nuffield, went on to be a professor of history at the University of Toronto; he had been my cicerone as I tried to advance into the hierarchy of the Oxford Union. William Norgren, who gave Susan away at our wedding, like me had the shock of failing his DPhil. I lived with him and Tony Harris, a fellow Christ Church student, during the year when I was courting Susan. I was also briefly on the fringes of a poetry group led by Peter Levi, SJ, later the professor of poetry. The group included Denis Bethell, a friend from my Sherborne days who went on to teach at Trinity College Dublin. Another member was Constantine Trypanis, a published poet and distinguished professor of Byzantine history. My efforts at writing were of little distinction, although Professor Trypanis seemed to think they were of some merit and recommended that I submit my poems to *The Spectator* and other publications. I never had the courage to do that, and they remain unpublished. My career as an aspiring poet lasted for little more than a decade, although I did continue to write sporadically in Australia and Pakistan.

In retrospect, those four years at Oxford seem a lifetime ago. Its rarefied social and intellectual atmosphere was unique. I was young and highly impressionable. Neither Susan nor I were ever completely at home there. Yet we traveled widely, made lifelong friends, and engaged in a wide variety of activities. Those years left an indelible mark on us both.

7
Meeting the Soviet Bear

Halfway through my academic studies at Oxford, I saw an advertisement on the college junior common room notice board offering an opportunity to attend the 1957 Moscow Youth Festival for a mere 100 pounds sterling, in effect the cost of the rail fare to and from the East German frontier. As someone studying the Russian Revolution, I did not want to pass up this offer. However, I had passed the Foreign Service written examination in my senior year at Princeton and remained an active candidate. I worried that a trip to Russia under Soviet sponsorship might affect the prospects of my getting a security clearance. I thus went up to London to consult the American embassy on the likely impact on my future career of a decision to go to the festival.

The embassy was then directly across Berkeley Square from its subsequent location. After a certain wait in the embassy foyer, I was taken to see an embassy official introduced to me as Mr. Kelly. We met in an office devoid of papers or any indication of official business. Mr. Kelly, hearing of my background and research interest, said that the embassy thought it might be a good idea for a loyal and patriotic citizen like myself to be part of the American delegation. My job would be to tell the truth in the midst of what was sure to be plenty of Communist propaganda. He urged me to return in two weeks for a last-minute briefing. I dutifully returned the week before my departure. When I asked for Mr. Kelly, I was informed that he was unavailable but that I could see Mr. Brown. In the same antiseptic room, I met my new contact. Unlike Mr. Kelly, he told me that the embassy thought it a very bad idea for me to go to Moscow. My participation would give credibility to the Communist organizers. When I expressed surprise, given my original meeting at the embassy, Mr. Brown informed me that Mr. Kelly had been transferred. When I asked about the likely impact on my future career, he rather darkly said that he could give me no assurances.

Reflecting on these two meetings and the opportunities to do a little thesis-related work, I decided that I would go, whatever the consequences might be. So in the last week of July, I set off with a small group of Oxford undergraduates for the long train ride to Moscow. I remember little of the journey beyond the delay at the Russian border at Brest-Litovsk, where we changed from the European standard gauge to the Russian gauge. On arrival in Moscow we were taken to a hostel on the outskirts of the city.

On the evening of our arrival there was a delegation meeting at which we were given guidance on how to get to the opening ceremonies the next day. The meeting got off to a rocky start when the organizers produced a banner, prepared in advance and which we were to carry into Lenin Stadium the next day, which proudly proclaimed: "American Delegation Salutes World Youth." Seemingly innocuous, it immediately drew the attention of several members of the group, who pointed out that we were not a delegation but merely private participants. The principal American youth organization, the National Association of Students, had formally boycotted the festival to protest the Soviet invasion of Hungary the previous autumn. After a heated discussion and in the best tradition of democratic centralism, the organizers allowed the issue to be put to a vote. It was agreed that the word "delegation" would be removed and that we would insert "participants" instead. So it was that the next day this crazily patched banner was carried into the opening ceremonies.

The opening ceremonies themselves were a further source of discussion. Some of us were worried about the optics of marching. We asked, "Did we all have to march behind this banner?" The organizers once again were flexible and said we could go directly to our assigned seats once we got to the stadium and need not march if that was our preference. The departure was set for 10:00 the next morning. We were told to assemble and be prepared to be bused to the stadium. Buses were in fact not available. Instead, we were shown to flatbed trucks with two raised tiers of benches. The trucks were decorated with painted peace doves and the words *Mir i Druzhba* (Peace and Friendship), the motto of that year's festival. At about 11:00 we were loaded onto our trucks and then, for something over three hours, driven slowly across Moscow through streets thronged with enthusiastic Muscovites cheering the presence of this group of young American anti-imperialists. At one point we passed the American Embassy, where we could see various embassy staff photographing us, we assumed for future reference and identification. Just as we passed the embassy, a group of Russians rushed forward and handed us live white doves, which we immediately released into the air. I felt annoyance at being exploited, but the image of peace-loving young Americans challenging their own embassy could not be undone.

On arriving at Lenin Stadium, now filled with tens of thousands of Russian youth, we were allowed to go to our seats as promised. Our more ideologically pure comrades marched into the stadium, where they saluted Chairman Nikita Khrushchev and the other two members of the ruling troika, Nikolai Bulganin and Kliment Voroshilov. Looking back on that day, I can only be impressed by the Soviet organizers' extraordinarily skillful planning and the impact the day must have had on the participants. A hundred thousand young men and women, over thirty-five thousand of them from every corner of the globe, shouting "peace and friendship" in unison projected a powerful message of solidarity, which the Soviet authorities were anxious to convey.

Much of our time in Moscow was taken up with sightseeing. Those of us among the American participants who were Christians were taken out to the famous monastery at Zagorsk. We toured the beautiful whitewashed, blue-and-gold-domed monastery and then met with Orthodox seminarians. They were woefully ignorant about America and asked whether it was true that all Americans carried guns and lived like the cowboys. This was the only image they had of Americans from the few western movies they had been allowed to see. We also toured museums, including the Tretyakov and the great

St. Basil's Cathedral in Red Square, then a museum of atheism. We visited the tomb of Stalin and Lenin—Stalin the field marshal in full military regalia, Lenin in his revolutionary fashion statement, a simple gray suit and no tie. I even managed to work in a few mornings of research in the Lenin Library, for which I was given a reader's card. The Russians were helpful, and I felt myself as welcome as I might have been in any major European library.

After our week in Moscow, we were taken to Leningrad, where we visited the Hermitage and the Russian Museum. We were allowed into the vaults and shown dozens of abstract paintings by Kandinsky and Malevich that Stalin had banned as degenerate and that had not been seen since the early days of the Revolution. We were also taken to the Smolny Institute for Young Noble Ladies, the former girls' school that Lenin made his first headquarters on returning to Russia in October 1917. I was impressed by the simplicity of his quarters, spare and monastic, a reflection of the personal austerity of the man, who visibly scorned bourgeois comforts.

◆ ◆ ◆

Three moments in Moscow stand out in my memory. One day while I was walking in Red Square a man came up to me with a letter for his relatives in the United States. He said that he was a member of the Jewish community and had no way to stay in touch with these relations. He asked me to try to see that the letter reached his family. In the course of my stay I was given many such letters, all of which I dutifully smuggled out. I gave the letters to the American embassy in London to use and reference and to forward to the addressees as appropriate.

Embassy staff translated one particularly articulate letter for me. It was not from someone who claimed to be Jewish but from a young Communist who described himself as a supporter of democracy. It was a passionate letter, claiming, among other things, that "Lenin led the people to the palace, to paradise—but we have arrived in prison." As a souvenir he also enclosed a twenty-five-ruble bond issued in

1955 and inscribed "a young champion of democracy (equality and freedom)." He concluded his message to me: "Forward to the end of dictatorship and long live civil liberties." Clearly not all the citizens of Moscow shared the overall spirit of fraternal goodwill toward Communism.

On another occasion, when walking through Red Square, I was surrounded by a fairly large group of Russians who wanted to know why there were so few Americans in Moscow for the festival. I explained that after the brutal Soviet invasion of Hungary the previous autumn, many young Americans did not want to have anything to do with the Soviet Union. All of this I managed in my somewhat inadequate Russian. A photograph of me making that speech in Red Square was carried the next day in the *New York Times* and many other American papers, giving me a certain notoriety with my fellow students when I returned to Oxford.

Perhaps the most fascinating moment was our group's fraternal meeting with the large North Korean delegation. This meeting was, I am certain, the first between Americans and North Koreans since the end of the Korean War. The Korean delegation was over a thousand strong. They presented us a program of music and dance set out in beautiful traditional Korean costumes. When they had finished, they asked us to present some aspect of American culture. Happily, Peggy Seeger, sister of the internationally known folk singer Pete Seeger, had brought a guitar with her (no doubt prompted to do so by the authorities). She suggested that we sing traditional American folk songs for our North Korean brothers and sisters. To their edification and applause, we sang that old favorite, "I'm going to lay down that atom bomb, down by the riverside."

Most of the American participants were young American leftists, children of members of the Communist Party USA, or sympathetic fellow travelers. However, a few of us saw ourselves as patriotic Americans, and we were extremely jealous of other delegations that had propaganda materials or national trinkets to distribute. We wanted to take advantage of the extraordinary openness of Moscow at the time to distribute similar American materials. We went to the embassy and met with a public affairs officer who stonily told us that it was a disgrace that we were in Moscow and that he would not give us even United States Information Service (USIS) pamphlets or pencils to hand out in our meetings with Russian and foreign students. Our pleas were unavailing; we were aiding the enemy.

Some of us had another encounter with the embassy, this time with the recently arrived ambassador, Llewelyn Thompson. The Chinese government, seeking to take advantage of the festival to entice youth to China, offered a free trip across Siberia to Beijing and a weeklong tour of China. Many of my fellow participants thought this would be a fascinating experience. Up to that time China had been completely closed to American visitors since we continued to recognize the Republic of China on Taiwan as the only legitimate government of China. The ambassador made it clear to us in no uncertain terms that we should not go to China. Many of us accepted his judgment, although a small group of Americans led by Shelby Tucker, a fellow Andover graduate and later a well-known travel writer, did make the trip, to the strong disapproval of the U.S. government.

On my return to London, I was debriefed by yet another embassy officer, who seemed particularly interested in my contacts with Russian Jews. I shared with him the letters I had brought out. Back home the FBI approached my mother, asking to see any letters I might have written to her about my experiences in Moscow. This was not their first concern about my Russian connections; when I was at Princeton I, like other students of the Russian language, subscribed to the *Literaturnaya Gazeta*. The FBI had spotted my reading habits and had asked my mother about them. In both cases she said it was none of their business. But she did give them copies of my letters from Moscow. In one of those letters, I gave my assessment of the Russian attitude to the invasion of Hungary, explaining that it was the same as that of American liberals about Guatemala, "a regrettable but inevitable mistake." My conclusion about my festival experience was summed up in that same letter: "There is no one who is going to return to his own country after the festival who will not say that the Soviet people want peace. It is only a short step in far too many people's minds to the statement that the Russian government wants peace. This, of course, by no means logically follows."

Interestingly enough, two years after my return from Moscow I was directly approached by the embassy in London. They asked if I would agree to go to the next Youth Festival, in Vienna, the first such festival to be held outside the Soviet Bloc. In a series of meetings on park benches in London, like scenes out of a John le Carré novel, I was asked to provide information about the goings-on at the Vienna festival. I was briefed on what to expect and what to look out for. Unfortunately, no one paid my way. Nonetheless, Susan and I decided to include Vienna in our summer holiday and spent a day at the festival. There really seemed little I could do. Even more than in Moscow, I was struck by the totalitarian nature of the event. Once again, tens of thousands of young men and women gathered under the auspices of the Communist sponsors, the World Federation of Democratic Youth. There was the same opening ceremony in a large stadium in Vienna, but instead of crowds shouting "Mir i Druzhba" they were shouting "Frieden und Freundschaft." To an American ear, the event seemed all too reminiscent of the videos I had seen of the great Nuremberg rallies in the early days of the Hitler regime.

My overall reaction to the Moscow festival was one of considerable admiration. I was surprised at the willingness of the Soviet authorities to allow outsiders seemingly unrestricted contact with their own citizens. I looked with amazement on the massive organization involved. Like most young people, I was shielded from the harsh realities of Soviet life and the brutalities of the regime. Moscow and Leningrad were clean and sunny, and subconsciously I think we were inclined to give the regime the benefit of the doubt, even though intellectually we knew full well that there was a darker side of Communist rule.

There was no follow-up to my visit by any American service. In retrospect, given the general paranoia about the Soviets, I often wondered how I passed the security clearance for entry into the State

Department. My hope at the time was that on entering the Foreign Service I would be able to put my Russian-language skills and historical knowledge to good use. When I left the service thirty-eight years later, however, I had spent only one night in Moscow and another in Leningrad as part of my travels as assistant secretary of state for security. The Cold War ended with little help from me!

On my return from Moscow, the *Washington Post* on September 4 published a long letter I had written headed "Moscow in Retrospect." I decried our failure to take advantage of the extraordinary opportunity the festival had offered to explain the American point of view to an information-deprived and information-hungry Russian audience. I argued that we had been hampered by the lack of a diversified delegation, with too few cultural representatives or students with "professional and working-class" backgrounds. Too few of us spoke Russian, and "the responsibility of defending America fell upon too small a group of students." I urged the American government to reconsider its "noncontamination" policy, which was "a shortsighted view of containment," and to prepare for the Seventh World Festival of Youth and Students, which I assumed would take place in some other place behind the Iron Curtain in two years' time. In retrospect, my views seem naive. I overestimated the degree of real influence a larger group of Americans might have had and the degree to which we could have become a real catalyst for change in Russia. In the end, the festival was a brief period of what would become known a generation later as *glasnost*. An opportunity, however small, had been lost.

PART 2
In the Nation's Service

8
Foreign Service Beginnings

Susan and I returned to the United States from England on a shabby German passenger liner, the ss *Bremen*, and I prepared to enter the junior officers' class, commonly referred to as A-100, scheduled for the beginning of November 1959. Getting into the Foreign Service had turned out to be something of a challenge. Although I had taken the written examination in the spring of my senior year at Princeton, I had postponed taking the oral examination because of my studies in Oxford. After waiting nearly three years for me to show up for the oral examination, the State Department in the spring of 1959 gave me an ultimatum: return for the examination or be dropped from the register of candidates. With my prospects very much up in the air, I elected to fly back to Washington.

While waiting to take the examination, I explored the possibility of a career in the CIA. I was interviewed in their interim personnel office in a temporary prefabricated World War II building on the National Mall. The more I learned about work in the clandestine service, the less it appealed to me. It was not a life I wanted to lead. I indicated to the recruiters that I would go forward with a Foreign Service career if that were offered to me but that I was not a candidate for the Operations Directorate of the CIA.

The oral examination then was as much about personal style as about substantive knowledge. I faced a panel of three male senior officers. They began by offering me a cigarette. I politely declined, since I did not smoke. Little did I know that this was a slightly malicious offer, as there were no ashtrays on the table (although I am reliably assured that Ivy League men taking the examination were unfazed and simply emptied the ash into their trouser cuff). I was then asked what I drank before dinner. I volunteered that I rather liked a dry sherry. Judging from the raised eyebrows across the table,

I realized that this was not the normal American diplomat's tipple. We then moved on to more substantive geographic matters: What would I see on a trip by boat from Pittsburgh to the sea? What rivers would I sail up if I were sailing on the Chesapeake Bay? I managed the first question with relative ease but was completely stumped by the second, volunteering the Potomac and the Delaware as the only two rivers in the East that seemed to fit the bill. The answer showed my ignorance. The examiners then tested my knowledge of international relations. What was NATO? Who were its members? What were the OAS, OAU, SEATO, and so on? I was going strong. However, when they asked me about RFD, I found myself stumped. I stammered, "Regional Federation . . . ?" What about COD, Mr. Quainton? "Council on . . . ?" I confessed myself completely at a loss by what I should have known were rural free delivery and cash on delivery. With gentlemanly courtesy they hinted that I should get to know my country better. Then to my surprise they told me that I had passed. I was added to the roster of eligible candidates for appointment as a Foreign Service Officer, class 8, at the princely salary of $5,390 per annum. I was one of only 150 officers appointed that year, and I entered the junior officers' class on November 12, 1959.

The junior officers' class to which I was assigned was composed of twenty men and five women, all but one under the age of thirty-five, the legal age limit for entry into the Foreign Service. We were in many ways a diverse group—though we were all white, we were not from any particular social class or elite educational background. In fact, I was one of only four with an Ivy League or Seven Sisters background. We came from all across America and were young, several right out of college, with one as old as thirty-five. We were a congenial group and quickly established close relations in our classes at the Foreign Service Institute (FSI), housed in a rather unattractive apartment building in Rosslyn, Virginia, just across Key Bridge from the District of Columbia.

The training was relatively uninspired and boring: endless lectures and presentations on the bureaucratic and administrative aspects of life in the State Department. We were taken out to the Department of Agriculture's Research Station in Beltsville, Maryland, where we were briefed on the latest research, including, to our amazement, the creation of parthenogenetic turkeys. Most of these poor benighted birds were deformed or blind. It was not clear to us how this would prepare us for our first post, only weeks away. We were also sent away for a long weekend to a site in Harpers Ferry, West Virginia, outside of Washington, where Joseph Campbell, the noted cultural historian, lectured to us. I was at my worst Oxford self, highly critical of what seemed to me his glib generalizations about culture and history. That contrarian streak, I regret to say, continued to haunt me as my Foreign Service career advanced.

On completing the A-100 course we were given our first assignments. To my dismay, I was assigned as vice consul in the Consulate General in Sydney, Australia. I had acquired the prevailing Oxford view that Australia was a rather barbaric place populated by former criminals with a culture that was but a pale imitation of that in the UK. In addition, since I had passed into the service with both Russian and French, I was disappointed at being sent to an English-speaking post and a consulate at that. (All five of us in the class with foreign-language competency were given English-speaking assignments.) Of course, I was completely ignorant about Australia, its magnificent outback, its rich cultural life, and the warm friendliness of its people. FSI made little effort to correct my uninformed impression. Before setting out for Sydney I was given an intensive introduction to consular work, focused on the intricacies of the Immigration and Naturalization Act, which I would be called on to enforce once I took up my post. I knew little of Australia's colonial or current history.

Thus we set out on what was to be a thirty-eight-year odyssey— Susan, who was by this point seven months pregnant, and I, armed with limited professional knowledge and a head full of prejudices. After stopping in California to see her parents, we flew to Sydney via Tokyo and Manila. As was customary in those days, even junior vice consuls flew first class, so we made the long trip in reasonable comfort. We stopped off in Tokyo, saw the principal sights, and went for a night to Nikko, where we nearly froze to death in a snow-covered Japanese inn. Sleeping on the floor was not my ideas of bliss, but it was even more difficult for Susan. But we found Japan fascinating and exotic in ways that we were sure Australia would never be.

On arrival in Sydney we were met by the head of the consular section, Orray Taft, the deputy principal officer and senior consular officer, who was to be my boss for the first part of my tour. Rather dour and acerbic, he was a formidable figure with a limited sense of humor and a rigorous demand for excellence in his subordinates. In my diary I described my first impression of him as "a slightly Conradian figure, in rumpled tropical suit, floppy straight hair, and sallow complexion." His face, I thought, "might also have been weakened by demon rum." That first night he and his wife and their two children kindly took us out to dinner at the American club, where Susan had her first oyster, a must in any Australian dinner. We were taken to temporary lodgings on Manning Road in Double Bay, a house where we were to stay for three months before moving to much more fashionable quarters on Yarranabbe Road on Darling Point. There we had a small but comfortable apartment with a "harbor glimpse," meaning that if one stood on the toilet seat and looked out the bathroom windows one could just catch a glimpse of nearby Rushcutters Bay.

Katherine, our firstborn, was brought to Susan in the hospital as a "fair dinkum Aussie." She came home to that first house on Manning Road, which, while reasonably comfortable, seemed somewhat primitive to American eyes. While there was indoor plumbing, that was not universal in the Sydney of the 1950s. I had a contact in the trade union movement who lived in the city and had an outhouse in his back garden. Instead of a washing machine, we had only a large copper kettle in which diapers and other items were meant to be boiled. Thankfully, a laundromat was only two blocks away, and generous grandparents gifted us a diaper service. Grandparents also gave us two weeks of a live-in Mothercraft nurse, a lovely young woman from the outback, to help us all adapt to the new routine of having a baby. Communications with our family back home were not without problems. When Katherine was born, the family in America did not immediately know that all was well. A telegram sent to them right after Katherine's birth came through garbled with the alarming sentence "not doing well." The original text had been "both" doing well.

On our first weekend in Sydney it was suggested that we "go to the dogs," in other words, attend greyhound racing in the nearby suburb of Randwick. Greyhound racing leaves much to be desired. The races are short and the animals indistinguishable from one another. However, there was a certain excitement in each race, and betting was furious. It was often said that Australians so loved gambling that they would even bet on the mechanical "bunny" after which the hapless greyhounds chased. (Each year when Australia's classic horse race, the Melbourne Cup, was run, traffic in the major cities literally came to a stop so that Aussies could listen to the race on their car radios.) I later learned from contacts in my consular work that greyhound races could be "fixed," but I naively assumed that they were as honest as Thoroughbred racing!

♦ ♦ ♦

Visa work was tiring. While I had a small cubicle in the consulate, I spent the entire morning on my feet behind an open counter interviewing nonimmigrant visa applicants. As I reported to my in-laws two months after our arrival, "Visa work has turned out to be more amusing than I had imagined, if only because the public is such a weird and disparate mob." The public I observed seemed incapable of filling out forms. In answer to questions on the visa application about race and ethnic classification, Australians invariably answered British and Protestant. I reported on our share of cranks—"the strange old men who want to tell us of a new secret weapon they have invented; the mad Irishmen, usually drunk as lords, who want political asylum; and the quarrelsome Russian émigrés from Shanghai and Harbin who believed they could shout or bully their way into the United States."

I spent a certain amount of time on animal matters. Early on in my tour I had to arrange visas for a group of owners and trainers who were taking their horses to race at Hollywood Park in Los Angeles. Unfortunately, their applications were delayed, and every delay made its way into the local papers, half of whose coverage was devoted to racing. (I had a similar challenge with the owners of a group of greyhounds going to race in Tijuana, Mexico, and who had to pass through San Diego first.) These cases were not very difficult. I learned the tricks of greyhound racing, which amounted to ways to make a good greyhound lose. Apparently, the best greyhounds would always win at very low odds, so the challenge was to have them lose several times before cashing in on a subsequent winning race. Two techniques were explained to me as I issued the necessary visas. One was to sprinkle dust in the eyes of the dog when it was put into its box so that for the first several seconds it could not see the bunny clearly. A second technique, more difficult to detect, was to take the greyhound swimming in the surf off Bondi Beach to tire it out before the evening's race. I was not a sufficient aficionado of "going to the dogs" to profit from this inside knowledge.

Consular officers were required by law, then as now, to ascertain whether applicants intended to return to Australia following their trip to America. We also had to assure ourselves that an applicant was not coming to the United States for immoral purposes, did not have a previous criminal record (meaning, had not been convicted of a crime involving moral turpitude), or was not a member of the Communist or some other subversive party. Candidates had to be asked orally in the presence of a roomful of waiting applicants questions designed to find the answers. It always seemed odd to have to ask a nun whether she was a Communist or going to the United States for immoral purposes, but that was the law.

On my very first day on the job, an elderly man presented himself seeking a visa to transit the United States with a group of veterans traveling to Europe to visit Gallipoli and the battlefields of the First World War. When asked whether he had committed a crime involving moral turpitude, he seemed surprised, but when the term was explained to him, he confessed that the answer was affirmative. I asked what the crime had been, and he calmly told me, "Murder." Needless to say, this young consular officer with no previous experience with criminals, not to speak of murderers, was taken aback. On returning from the Great War the applicant had killed a man in a bar forty years before and had served twenty years in prison. After his release he had led an unblemished life for twenty years, and I consequently sought a waiver of ineligibility. Alas, in the eyes of the Justice Department, once a murderer always a murderer, and my appeal on his behalf was denied. He traveled to Europe through Canada, which apparently had a more tolerant view of murderers than did the United States.

We often encountered, through our police contacts, cases of applicants who had been convicted of indecent exposure. The number of cases seemed abnormally high, but we soon found the reason. The convictions resulted when workingmen who had consumed two or more pints of beer before the pubs closed at 6:00 p.m. relieved themselves in local parks in the absence of public facilities. We did not consider these cases to be crimes involving moral turpitude. We also frequently denied visas to young women we suspected were going to the United States hoping to get married, although their ostensible purpose was tourism. Politicians and prominent lay and religious figures often appealed these cases to my boss. He seemed to take pleasure in the number of high-ranking persons who intervened and would only overturn my decision when some unspecified but critical number of individuals had approached him on a particular case. Equally difficult were the cases of American veterans who had married Australian girls and who had been persuaded by their wives to vote in Australian elections, since voting was compulsory. Unfortunately, American law at the time specified that such voting caused you to automatically lose your American citizenship. While the Supreme Court overturned this law in the 1960s, it was a terrible blow to these young men, who had fought in the South Pacific.

Early on in my time in the consular section, I was faced with trying to live by the State Department's gift acceptance policy. At one point a visiting actor and comedian came to the consulate for passport services. I handled his case, and in gratitude he offered me two tickets for his show that night, which he said I could pick up at the box office. Susan and I worried over whether accepting this gift was proper, but since the tickets were not expensive, we agreed to go. We found a babysitter and went. On arriving at the theater we found two tickets waiting for us, but alas, they were not free; we were expected to buy them. This we did and enjoyed one of America's well-known comics, Pat Henning, who told jokes about himself and his relatives who covered their baldness by combing their eyebrows up.

Although assigned to a consular position, I spent only my first year in the consular section. I had enjoyed consular work and the interaction with a broad cross section of Australians, though it was not what I had envisaged as my career focus. Happily, in my second year I was transferred to the commercial section, where I became an assistant commercial attaché. In addition, I was assigned by the consul general to do such political work as fell the consulate's way. For example, I was to report on the politics and elections in New South Wales, our consular district. Although the reporting load was light, I came to know a fairly wide circle of local politicians and labor leaders, including some such as Laurie Short, the famous president of the Ironworkers Union, who had a highly visible and distinguished career battling Communists in the labor movement at the national level.

As a commercial officer I was quite incompetent. I had scant experience selling anything: lemonade at the end of our driveway as a small boy and shoes in the University Store at Princeton. Commercial work essentially involved writing reports for the Department of Commerce describing the background, reliability, and financial position of local companies, usually ones with whom an American firm wished to establish a relationship. I also was assigned to do industry reports and traveled widely in New South Wales visiting steel mills and manufacturing plants.

To a more limited extent I was expected to help sell items or, rather, to obtain agents for a particular American product. I found myself engaged in pushing to local department stores American beach towels, provocatively emblazoned with the phrase "come play with me," and my one great and only triumph, onion harvesters. Through a stroke of good fortune, I managed to sell a couple of onion harvesters to the Sydney municipality, which, on studying the literature that I had provided, decided that the harvesters would be ideal for raking beer bottles off the beach after Saturday night parties to make the sand clean for the Sunday family crowd. I have never sold anything since.

◆ ◆ ◆

Susan and I traveled widely in the state of New South Wales. I was often asked to stand in for the consul general at up-country outback events. I would give talks on American foreign policy or preside over local events. I remember a visit to Mudgee, where I was to be the guest of honor at the local debutante ball. When I stepped off the plane in this small country town, there was evident surprise on the faces of my hosts. To them even a vice consul was a senior official, probably bald, fat, and fifty. Instead, they got a green and very young-looking twenty-six-year-old. They were good sports, and the debutantes were duly presented to me at the gala ball that evening.

We also traveled widely outside of our consular district. In 1961 we went by train from Sydney to Alice Springs in the Northern Territory. This was a long and arduous trip, as we had to change trains at the border with the state of Victoria (which did not share a common rail gauge with New South Wales at that time), then again in Melbourne and Adelaide and finally to a narrow-gauge line to Alice Springs. What linger in one's memories of that final section of the trip were the flies. They were everywhere, and most locals wore hats with netting that hung over their eyes and nose, much like that of a beekeeper. Alice Springs was a small oasis in the vast desert of central Australia, but it was the jumping-off place for touristic visits to Ayers Rock (now Uluru) and to mission stations in the hinterland. We visited a small

Lutheran mission some distance from Alice Springs, where in the idiom of the day the missionaries hoped to make civilized Christians of their Aboriginal clients.

Australia in those days was intensely racist, and little value was given to Aboriginal culture or values. The same could be said of Australia's relationship with Papua New Guinea, of which Australia became an international trustee after the Second World War. It was a national news story in 1960 when the first Papuan entered a university. Australia's culture was then decidedly paternalistic and colonial. Australia was proud to be "white" and hoped to remain so.

Everywhere we went in the outback we were received with the warmest hospitality. Americans were enormously popular, and memories of the Second World War and our efforts to protect Australia at the Battle of the Coral Sea remained strong. By the 1960s America had replaced Great Britain as Australia's leading ally. While the Sydney town hall still carried plaques commemorating Australians who had fought for the Crown in the Boer and First World Wars, the fall of Singapore in 1941 marked the end of Britain's ability to be the principal protector of Australia. We had taken over that role and would not lose it for several generations thereafter. As the "white Australia" of 1960 began to give way to the multicultural Australia of today, the reference to England as "home" faded from common parlance. Australia had become a Pacific power and was to remain one.

◆ ◆ ◆

Our time in Australia was one in which we learned the diplomatic ropes. I developed skills in reporting and began to reach out in the community to develop useful contacts. We also began to entertain officially, as well as serve as general dogsbody at receptions given by the consul general at Craigend, his beautiful residence at the end of Darling Point. Our most trying representational assignment came during the formal inspection of the post, when the consul general instructed each officer to give a dinner in the inspectors' honor and to invite his principal contacts. We had a tiny apartment and had little experience at this sort of entertaining. Susan, for the first time but certainly not for the last, rose to the occasion and produced an amazing meal centered on roast pigeon as the main course. Our guests included the speaker of the New South Wales legislature, Ray Maher, and John Ducker, who was to become a prominent trade union leader. All went well.

At some point in the spring of 1962 the State Department sent out a circular notice to all posts seeking junior officers who were willing to volunteer for a hard language. Members of Congress, having read or heard of the novel *The Ugly American*, concluded that the United States was losing the hearts and minds of the people in Southeast Asia to the Russians, who reportedly spoke Lao, Cambodian, and other seemingly esoteric languages of the region. The department was urged to remedy the situation as soon as possible. Thinking that assurances of more rapid promotion would result, I volunteered for Indonesian, Farsi, and Hindi. I was chosen for Hindi-language training, which I began in the fall of that year in Washington in the expectation that my next assignment would be in New Delhi, the only Hindi-speaking post in the service.

This language study became my first home assignment and the entrée to what was to be a fifteen-year romance and engagement with the Indian subcontinent. Our first encounter with Indian culture, beyond London's curry restaurants, was on the way home from Australia. We stopped for a night in Fiji, where half of the population had come from South India to work on the sugar plantations. After the ordinariness of Australia, Fiji's culture seemed romantic and exotic. We decided that we were ready for the Indian subcontinent.

I might have expected that India would at some point be in my future. My boyhood days had included listening to the headmaster of St. Michael's read *The Jungle Book* and *Kim* to the boarding students. I had collected the postage stamps of the Indian princely states, and the romance of the Raj was already in my emotional toolkit. When I got to Princeton, I became fascinated by Gandhi and his doctrine of *ahimsa*, or nonviolence. It led me to conclude, as I wrote at the time:

Certainly for far too long American foreign policy has been based on force and the belief that power and military considerations must be paramount. This, of course, has a certain limited adequacy when we are dealing with other European nations raised in the same tradition. But in our relations with Southeast Asia, we must make sure that democracy means more than a mutual assistance arms pact against communism. The social and economic aspects must be played up above all. For they, far more than political institutions, provide the substance instead of the illusion of democracy. To the Indians particularly, it seems far too often that we are presenting only a negative program of anti-communism based on force. With their new-found liberty this is not enough.

Such were the views that I carried into the next fifteen years of my career, devoted almost exclusively to the South Asian subcontinent.

9

The Raj and Beyond

In early August 1962, I returned to Washington to begin the study of Hindi. I quickly discovered on arrival that there were no Hindi-designated positions open in India the following year. I was asked to agree to study Urdu instead, a closely related language with the same sentence structure and grammar but written in the Persian script. The department promised me a job in the economic section of our embassy in Karachi the following summer.

I was pleased to be going to Pakistan, which had a strong and positive relationship with the United States as a member of both the Central Treaty Organisation (CENTO, originally known as the Baghdad Pact) and the South East Asia Treaty Organization (SEATO). They allowed us to conduct vital aerial intelligence-gathering operations against the Soviet Union from a base in Peshawar. In addition, we had a massive aid program. Together with the World Bank we were engaged in the major Tarbela and Mangla dam projects and an extensive investment in tube wells in the Punjab. There would surely be plenty of useful work for an economic officer backstopping this strong economic and political relationship between the two countries.

I came to Washington alone, as our son Eden was about to be born in southern California, and Susan could not travel immediately postpartum. When they followed soon thereafter, we found an apartment in Arlington, Virginia, a few blocks from the Foreign Service Institute. For the next ten months I spent six hours every day in Urdu class with two other students. In addition, we were expected to spend additional time listening to tapes and practicing our lessons in the language lab. We had three teachers: Hamid Naz, a charming poet from West Pakistan; Saeed Khan, a former Pakistan army officer and aide-de-camp to Pakistan's first governor general; and Uma

Grewal, an Indian Sikh from the Punjab. We were an exceptionally hard-working threesome, and by early in the new year our reading skills surpassed those of at least one of our teachers, Captain Khan. He was essentially an English speaker with a limited technical vocabulary in Urdu. He found it hard to keep up with our efforts. We all emerged from the year reasonably proficient, and I was pleased to receive recognition of professional competence.

However, that level did not convey our true proficiency. During one of my first calls on a senior Pakistani official, I used my newly minted Urdu. As an economic officer I had boned up on rather obscure technical terms. I remember trying to discuss currency issues with a joint secretary in the Ministry of Finance using the Persian word *zer-e-mubadila*, the gold of exchange. My interlocutor looked surprised and immediately replied to me in South Asian English: "You must be meaning 'foreign exchange.'" I quickly learned that the government of that period did all its business in English and that my rather ambitious effort to do my business in Urdu was doomed to failure.

Susan was able to take Urdu classes with two other spouses for the first three months, but when the other two spouses were assigned overseas, Susan would have become a private student. FSI would not pay for a spousal tutorial. However, by continuing her studies at home, she acquired enough Urdu to have a useful competence when we set up our households in Pakistan, India, and later even Kuwait, where she had to deal with Urdu-speaking servants.

We traveled to Pakistan by a combination of air and sea, by air to Europe and then by ship from Genoa to Karachi. As travel was still first class, we enjoyed the ten days it took to reach Karachi. We stopped off at both ends of the Suez Canal and in Aden. I remember a quick overnight trip to Cairo while the ship traversed the canal. Susan stayed behind nobly but somewhat unwillingly because we could find no one to look after the children. I have owed her a trip to Egypt ever since. The voyage was much like a modern cruise. There were games and competitions and even a costume party for the children. Katherine and Eden, now four and almost two, came as Alice and the White Rabbit. I performed in a shipboard production of *Hello, Dolly!*

On arrival in Karachi, we were assigned to a semidetached house in the Pakistan Employees Cooperative Housing Society (PECHS), half an hour's drive to the embassy. It was a small house with an ample garden. We shared the compound with the embassy security officer. While life in Australia had been remarkably similar to the life we had known at home in America, in Pakistan one immediately had to learn how to live in a world surrounded by servants. We were now sahibs, with all the rights and duties pertaining thereto. We had an ayah to look after the children, a bearer to serve at table, a cook, a gardener, and a sweeper to clean toilets and bathrooms. This was to be the pattern of all our posts in the subcontinent until we left for Africa a dozen years later.

Given the servants' distinct roles, they all required managing. This was one of Susan's challenges as a memsahib, as each servant was extremely conscious of his or her class and status. While there is in theory no caste structure in Islam as there is in India, the positions the servants held and the work they did determined their status. The ayah was preeminent and lived inside with her employer. Others lived in servants' quarters at the back of the house.

We lived not far from the American School, and shortly after our arrival Susan was offered a job teaching part-time. She also soon became director of English-language classes at the Pakistan American Cultural Center, whose students were young Pakistanis aspiring either to study abroad or to advance in their jobs in Karachi. Classes were mixed, although the women sat in front, removing their abayas to communicate with the teacher without contravening the modesty rules that precluded interaction with unrelated men.

This privileged life of sahibs and memsahibs had not greatly changed from the days of British India. We were only fifteen years from the partition of India, and the social institutions of the Raj still existed. We joined the Karachi Boat Club, picnicked on the beach outside Karachi, rode camels, and mixed almost exclusively with members of the diplomatic and expatriate communities. I played tennis with the ambassador and his chief of mission colleagues. Our third child, Margaret, was born in the Seventh Day Adventist hospital under the care of American doctors. We were in every way a privileged class.

Like the rest of the world, we were rocked by the news of the assassination of President Kennedy. I will never forget the blocks-long line outside the embassy of ordinary Pakistanis who came to sign the official condolence book. All Pakistanis were America's friends on that day. Two years later, when war between Pakistan and India broke out, we had become unreliable partners.

Having had a taste of public diplomacy as a vice consul in Sydney, I was not surprised when, shortly after our arrival, the ambassador, Walter McConaughy, asked me to represent him at a Karachi Rotary Club luncheon and to give a speech on his behalf. I received virtually no guidance on what such a speech should include, so I gave a quick overview of the history of U.S. foreign policy going back to Washington's Farewell Address, the Monroe Doctrine, and the open door to China. This last excursion into late nineteenth-century history got me into trouble. The next day, to my astonishment and horror, the leading Karachi English-language paper, *Dawn*, carried a front-page story announcing that the economic officer at the American embassy had come out for an open door to China. This was big news, since the United States, unlike Pakistan, did not recognize the Communist regime in Beijing. Ambassador McConaughy, a China hand himself, called me in and rather sternly admonished me not to give further speeches about American policy. I followed his advice for many years to come.

I was assigned to the three-officer economic section, where I did general economic reporting on trade and industry, work not radically different from what I had done as a commercial officer in Sydney. I wrote a lot of reports but had relatively little interaction with the economic ministries of the Pakistan government, which had already begun to migrate north to the new capital, Islamabad. Indeed, the need for interaction with these ministries led the embassy to consider sending an economic officer to the recently established ministry branch office in Rawalpindi in the Punjab. I was chosen, although this meant uprooting the family after only a year in Karachi.

Before going north, we had several opportunities to get outside of Karachi and had visited some of the ancient ruins in the Sindh between Karachi and Hyderabad. Our most notable trip was the one we took to the wilds of Baluchistan with the other junior officer at post, Grant Smith, and his wife, Renny. We traveled by jeep several hundred miles to the west as far as Turbat, then a fly-blown provincial town noted in those days for its dates and little else. We were accompanied for part of the way by a young Pakistani district officer, Hassan Baluch, an affable and knowledgeable official who did all in his power to make us comfortable, even though we had to spend the first night on the cement floor of the community center in Lasbela. He guided us on a rather rough journey along rutted tracks across what seemed to us an impenetrable wilderness. On our way home from Turbat we stayed in a "dak" bungalow, one of the hundreds of such buildings built across British India to accommodate visitors on inspection tours. This one was dirty and decrepit, but there were beds. A cook was found to kill a chicken and make dinner for us, enabling us to hang on until we could reach the comforts of Karachi.

◆ ◆ ◆

If Karachi was relatively modern and cosmopolitan, Rawalpindi remained what it had been throughout the period of British rule, a cantonment town, headquarters of the Pakistan army. The president of Pakistan, Field Marshal Mohammed Ayub Khan, governed from his headquarters in Rawalpindi, over a thousand miles from the bright lights of Karachi. Pindi, as it was generally called, was a relatively sleepy place, with tree-lined streets, a small Anglican church, and a charming hotel, Flashman's, which could have been taken from a Kipling story. It had a rather indifferent restaurant but solemnly served afternoon tea to anyone who so desired. Indeed, the local Lions Club met there regularly for what were described as tea meetings. The Rawalpindi Club had tennis and squash courts, a restaurant, and a bar. Built by the British, it retained much of its colonial charm. On Fridays at noon, expatriates and some Pakistani officers would gather for a Gin and It, gin and Italian vermouth, at what were affectionately known as Friday prayers. The Pakistan army is now completely dry, but in those days British traditions had not yet been snuffed out.

The American staff was extremely small. In addition to Principal Officer Harry Spielman, who had risen through the ranks of the Foreign Agricultural Service, there were only a handful of Americans. Spielman spent much of his time playing golf with the senior generals of the Pakistan army, who were useful sources of information about the goings-on in the military regime. I was the sole economic officer, charged with a broad range of responsibilities covering the full gamut of traditional economic reporting. The political officer, George Walsh, had had a checkered career long before Pindi as a ballet company manager in Beirut and a movie importer in Calcutta. Finally, there were a young administrative officer and two secretaries. Working outside of the embassy office itself were two U.S. Agency for International Development (USAID) public safety officers training the Pakistan police and a young military advisor. We socialized with them and their families but had no direct organizational authority over their work.

We were virtually the entire diplomatic corps in Pindi, although the British had a similarly small establishment with three officers. The Canadians had a single representative. The rest of the world was absent. From my perspective, both the embassy office and the diplomatic corps were ideally sized. Over the next two years this situation changed as other countries began to move their embassies to Pindi in preparation for a definitive move to Islamabad. During our last year in Pakistan the American office moved from its small quarters on the Peshawar Road to a much larger bungalow in Satellite Town, a suburb of Pindi closer to Islamabad. We remodeled this bungalow to be an embassy chancery.

Though the State Department had assigned me to Pakistan as an economic officer, when I arrived in Rawalpindi I became a jack-of-all-trades and was asked to do some political work because of my language skills. My boss asked me to cover the presidential election campaign in 1965 between President Ayub and Fatima Jinnah, the younger sister of Pakistan's founder, Mohammed Ali Jinnah. Although Ayub was a military autocrat, he permitted Miss Jinnah to campaign freely as a signal to the international community of his democratic inclinations. At the height of the campaign, as the office's only Urdu-speaking officer, I went to Rawalpindi's principal park to see and hear Miss Jinnah, a waif-like figure in a white sari, exhort an enthusiastic crowd many thousands strong to vote for her. It seemed at the time that there was hope for democracy in Pakistan. Because of the complex electoral college system, Miss Jinnah was not able to translate her broad popular support in Pakistan's cities into an electoral triumph. She received only 35 percent of the vote in the final tabulation.

There was much to do. Both the foreign and finance ministries had moved to Islamabad, as had the legislative assembly. Still, in some respects, Islamabad was little more than a vast construction site, with ministries and the president's house under construction. The three substantive officers at post were kept busy making démarches to senior officials and reporting on Pakistan's foreign and defense policy. Harry Spielman's contacts with the military turned out to be critical in the summer of 1965, when India and Pakistan became ever more hostile to each other. Events moved inexorably toward war, which eventually broke out in early September.

The war posed many problems for us. Notwithstanding all the aid we had provided in the previous years, the United States was extremely unpopular. The Pakistanis asserted that we had failed to come to their defense when India attacked. They claimed that, given their membership in CENTO, a mutual assistance treaty, we should have come to their help in time of need. For us, the only conceivable contingency that would have triggered action was a Soviet attack, not a war with India.

Responsibility for the outbreak of hostilities is still debated in New Delhi and Islamabad. Both sides claim they were provoked. Even from our perch close to the Pakistanis, it did seem as though Pakistan pushed hard against the Indians, first in the Rann of Kutch dispute and then on other border issues. Foreign Minister Zulfiqar Ali Bhutto was certainly a firebrand and made inflammatory speeches attacking Indian motives and responses. The war was relatively short, lasting a mere thirteen days, but long enough for us to install blackout curtains throughout our houses, smear our cars with mud as camouflage, and dig Z-shaped trenches in our backyards, into which we were expected to retreat during Indian bombing raids. Several such raids did occur, and a handful of Indian bombs did land on or near Rawalpindi's airstrip.

Only one bomb fell close to our house, on the night of the first raid, before our trench had been dug. Susan and I, together with the visiting political counselor, hunkered down with our backs to an interior wall, as Susan had been taught to do in school during the Second World War. The children did not even wake up. On one subsequent occasion all five of us did descend into the trench. During the war our life was transformed in many other ways. For example, we used only candles at home to avoid attracting the attention of Indian bombers. Our daughter Katherine remembers that on one night when there was a full moon, I read to the children on our front lawn by moonlight.

Two days before the end of hostilities, Washington ordered the evacuation of all family members from the embassy office in Pindi and consulates in Lahore and Peshawar. Susan and the children, together with all the other dependents except the principal officer's wife, were flown in a military C-130 to Tehran, which along with Beirut was designated as a suitable safe haven in the region. They remained in Tehran for three months, until finally, at our instigation, the State

Department permitted them to return in time for Christmas. I was able to visit them once in the rather cramped apartment they had been able to rent. Those of us who stayed behind were particularly outraged that the principal officer had determined it was safe enough for his wife to remain because, he argued, she was needed for representational work. It was particularly hard to endure this enforced separation when the Americans were the only ones to evacuate their dependents during this war.

I cannot say we managed the crisis with any particular skill. The embassy in Karachi, alarmed by the prospect of an Indian advance toward Pindi, ordered us to burn all our classified material. This we did in a barbecue-like drum on the roof of the office. Unfortunately, in our zeal to comply with Karachi's order, we burned our emergency plan, which we had only recently drafted. This was small loss, as we had erroneously assumed that the only serious threat we would have to face would be an invasion by Soviet forces through the Khyber Pass. Our evacuation guidance was thus to climb into our cars and drive to safety in India, obviously not very practical with Indian armored and infantry divisions moving across the border toward Lahore.

One of the skills I developed was that of control officer, managing various visiting groups, including one from the National War College, putting together their program of calls on senior Pakistani officials and looking after the logistics of accommodation. I also had to look after visiting Washington dignitaries. I remember in particular the visit of Ambassador William Handley, the deputy assistant secretary for South Asia. On arrival at the Pindi airport he told me that he needed some rather special help. The previous day the zipper in the fly of his best suit had jammed, and he urgently needed a new zipper. I said I was sure a tailor in the Pindi bazaar could arrange something. I dutifully took the trousers to a tailor, who assured me the trousers could easily be fixed in time for Mr. Handley's departure the next day. An hour before the departure, I picked up the trousers with the new zipper replaced. Unfortunately, the cloth to which the zipper was attached was a brilliant robin's egg blue, which provided a quite dazzling focus on the wearer's nether parts. Ambassador Handley was furious, as he had planned to wear his suit to the ambassador's residence for dinner that same night in Karachi. I never volunteered for sartorial duty again.

Ambassador McConaughy was a fairly frequent visitor to Pindi. He had a guesthouse where he could stay overnight and entertain senior Pakistani officials. This he did perhaps once a month. These visits were not always a great success. On one occasion he gave a dinner for the entire Pakistani cabinet. In order to please his guests, he had brought succulent filets mignons from the commissary in Karachi. Under normal circumstances such beef would have been a great delicacy for his Pakistani guests, as it was intended to be. When dinner was served, the ministers and other guests went to the buffet table, took their steaks and associated condiments, and returned to their assigned places. However, no sooner were they seated than they all arose and returned the steaks to the serving platter. Unfortunately, and unbeknownst to the ambassador, to suit American tastes the steaks had all been wrapped in bacon. The ambassador was appropriately apologetic, but the dinner could hardly have been called a success or contributed to Pakistan-American bilateral relations.

Life in Pindi was an active one. Security was not an issue, except for the brief period of the Indo-Pak War. We could travel widely, spending weekends in the hill station of Murree, traveling up and down the Grand Trunk Road to Attock, and then on to the military commissary in Peshawar to the north or southward to Lahore. We were able to make regular excursions to the famous Gandharan ruins at Taxila, a relatively short drive from Pindi. We managed one trip to Muzafferabad, the capital of Azad Kashmir (the portion of Kashmir occupied by Pakistan after the 1947–48 war with India).

Among our many activities, Susan volunteered in a local leper colony. I joined the Pindi Lions Club as a charter member after having been invited to one of their monthly tea meetings and having been presented, inaccurately and inexplicably, as a long-standing Lion who could speak to them about Lionism around the world. With that introduction, I formed a lifelong connection, leading me to join Lions Clubs in Nepal, India, Central African Republic, Nicaragua, and Peru. In every case, I found that I got to know members of the community usually completely unknown to the embassy. I enjoyed the fellowship and the opportunity to engage in community projects and to follow in some small way the Lions motto, "We serve."

We helped found a local theatrical group, the RATS, the Rawalpindi Amateur Theatrical Society, which put on play readings in private homes, produced *Arms and the Man* in the home of our political officer, and staged a full version of *The Fantasticks*, in which I had the complicated nonspeaking role of the Mute.

I served briefly on the joint Anglo-American school board. This effort at amalgamating two different educational philosophies and goals was a complete failure. The American parents chafed at what they saw as an excessively disciplined and inflexible British system. The British deplored the American lack of discipline and rigor. The school formally divided shortly after we left Pindi.

There was plenty of entertaining among the small but growing expatriate community. Costume parties were common, and shortly before we left post we hosted a Roman banquet, to which guests came in togas. We reclined on mattresses distributed about our living room, which had been cleared of all superfluous furniture. Even the servants dressed in Roman costume.

Although our time in Pakistan was in many ways happy and rewarding, our lives there were devastatingly shattered and forever marked in 1966 by the tragic death of our two-year-old daughter, Margaret. An electrical fire in her bedroom air-conditioner led to death by smoke inhalation. We struggle still not only with our loss but also with a sense of guilt. Susan and the children were all having afternoon naps in rooms adjacent to Margaret's and did not realize until too late that her room had filled with smoke. I was at the office and only knew of the tragedy after it had happened. The embassy staff rallied round us wonderfully and were supportive in every way during this terrible time. Margaret is buried in the Christian area of the Rawalpindi cemetery, surrounded by British graves, including those of many children. All had come to Pindi offering service to empire in the preceding century. Crape myrtle (*Lagerstroemia*) trees surrounded Margaret's grave, and her lovely simple tombstone is inscribed, at Susan's inspiration, with the words of Robert Herrick's beautiful lament "To Daffodils." The embassy moved us to a new house on the Peshawar Road immediately after the tragedy, but the move could not erase the memories of the smoke-filled room in which our lovely younger daughter had died.

By the summer our three-year tour in Pakistan was up. I received a posting to New Delhi in the external section of the embassy as its Pakistan watcher. We left on home leave in August 1965 and began to prepare for the second stage of our subcontinent journey.

NEW DELHI: DEMOCRACY AT WORK

We flew home from Pakistan on Pan American's round-the-world service through Bangkok, but we returned to South Asia once again by sea. After our home leave in Seattle and Los Angeles, we embarked on the ss *President Cleveland* for a twenty-one-day trip across the Pacific to Hong Kong, whence we flew on to Bombay and New Delhi. The voyage was notable not just for the usual shipboard entertainment but for the presence onboard of the famous bridge guru Charles Goren. For many of the first-class passengers this was a "Travel with Goren" cruise. There were bridge lessons in the morning, match play in the afternoon, and informal bridge in the evening, during which the great man went around the room playing four hands at each table. Conversation at meals tended to focus on the mistakes of the previous sessions. Susan, who did not enjoy bridge, quickly became fed up with problems such as how to make three no trump with only twenty-four points between two hands. I, however, rather enjoyed the opportunity to play a few hands with Goren and learn something about his system of bidding.

On arrival in New Delhi, we were assigned an unremarkable second-story apartment on a quiet maidan, an open green space, in

Jor Bagh, a modest residential area less than a mile from the embassy. I could bicycle to the embassy. A major park, the Lodi Gardens, was only a block away, where baby Elizabeth, who arrived in Holy Family Hospital some four months after our arrival, was taken daily by our ayah for an airing with other expatriate and Indian babies. We had air-conditioning in the bedrooms and felt ourselves to be quite comfortably housed.

New Delhi was a large and important post. India, though annoyingly a leader of the nonaligned movement, was also the largest functioning democracy in the world and a strong counterweight to China. Chester Bowles, former governor of Connecticut, congressman, and under secretary of state, was our ambassador. He had already served as ambassador to India in the Truman administration and had an encyclopedic knowledge of and unbridled affection for India. He had reorganized the embassy, breaking up the traditional political and economic sections and replacing them with internal and external sections. All officers in these two sections were expected to perform both political and economic work, depending on whether their focus was on the internal realities of contemporary India or on India's relations with the outside world. My job in the external section was to monitor Indian policy toward its neighbors: Pakistan, Nepal, Bhutan, and Sri Lanka.

Almost from my first day on the job it was clear that the ambassador regarded me with some suspicion as an alien interloper from Pakistan. Unfortunately, throughout the 1960s and 1970s, the embassies in Islamabad and New Delhi had become strong partisans for the positions of the governments to which they were accredited. Each regarded the rival embassy as biased and misguided. In the three years that I served in New Delhi, I was in the ambassador's office only twice, the first time to be introduced and the second to say farewell. Nonetheless, reporting on Pakistan was rewarding, since the Indian Foreign Ministry, South Block as it is known, spent much of its policy energy monitoring Pakistani (mis)behavior. I had frequent access to the Indian Foreign Ministry and was able to report on Indian policies with relative ease. I assiduously followed border conflicts in the Punjab and Kashmir and paid particular attention to the long-smoldering dispute about how the eastern waters of the Ganges and Brahmaputra Rivers should be shared between the two countries.

My portfolio also included India's relations with two Himalayan entities, Sikkim and Bhutan. Sikkim was under Indian control but not at that time fully integrated into the Indian Union; and Bhutan, though technically independent, operated under close Indian monitoring, as it had under the British in the preindependence era. I was lucky to visit both.

In the case of Sikkim, we had to be most careful not to stoke the aspirations of the ruling Chogyal for independence while at the same time not endorsing some of India's more heavy-handed efforts to maintain control. Sikkim was a charming mountain principality with a strong Tibetan culture and a ruler who was Western in orientation and whose wife, Hope Cooke, was distantly related to one of the embassy's officers. The Chogyal received us most hospitably, but I remember little of substance that was discussed, although he made it clear to Galen Stone, the embassy's external counselor who led the delegation, how unhappy he was with the state of his country's relations with New Delhi. Indeed, he had good reason to be concerned, as Sikkim's autonomy was formally snuffed out by New Delhi only a few years later.

I made two trips to Bhutan in delegations led by the external counselors, Galen Stone first and Herbert Gordon the second time. The Galen Stone visit was the first by an official American delegation to the Bhutanese capital, Thimphu, and to Paro, a town in the most prosperous of Bhutan's mountain valleys. In Thimphu we stayed in the rather spartan Indian government guesthouse. (There were no hotels.) We made a round of calls on ministers, including the finance minister, who graciously opened his desk, took out a tin box, and cashed Galen Stone's traveler's check, perhaps the first foreign banking transaction in the country's history. In the late 1960s Bhutan was incredibly isolated, its only formal external relations being with India.

It had virtually no foreign trade beyond the sale of exotic postage stamps and was completely dependent on its southern neighbor for all necessities. While we did not meet with the king, we did meet with several ministers and members of the royal family, including the queen mother, who gave us each a piece of cloth that she had embroidered. Bhutan is a beautiful country dotted with Buddhist monasteries and small villages in high mountain valleys. The road up from the Indian Terai, where we landed, was narrow, tortuous, and dangerous, but at least it provided access to the outside world.

In the early 1970s Bhutan sought to break out of its isolation by joining the United Nations. As the India (and Bhutan) desk officer in Washington then, I was tasked with the job of trying to keep Bhutan out of the UN. Our policy at the time was to oppose entry of all countries with a population of less than one million and annual exports of less than $1 million. Bhutan met both criteria. However, Under Secretary of State U. Alexis Johnson, when presented with the exclusionary policy paper I had drafted and cleared throughout the department, overruled his subordinates' advice and told a visiting Bhutanese delegation that we would happily support Bhutan's admission. Later that year, when the first Bhutanese delegation arrived in New York for the General Assembly session, I was the note taker for the bilateral meeting of the new Bhutanese delegation with Secretary of State William Rogers and Assistant Secretary Joseph Sisco. It was a friendly encounter, although I was privately embarrassed when the secretary naively asked the Bhutanese exactly where the country was located.

Halfway through our tour in New Delhi the embassy underwent an official inspection. I had some experience with inspections, as the consulate general in Sydney had been inspected on my first tour. This inspection seemed much more rigorous, with the inspectors looking into filing cabinets to find specific files. The deputy chief of mission asked if Susan and I would host a small dinner for middle-grade officers in the inspectors' honor. We agreed to do so and entertained them on the roof of our apartment, the *barsati*, where traditionally

Indian families slept in the hot premonsoon weather. The dinner went well enough.

Afterward the officers sat in a circle with the inspectors, who asked us what we thought of the ambassador. To the inspectors' amazement and our collective surprise, one officer spoke up, telling the inspectors that while the ambassador was a fine man, he unfortunately lied. A stunned silence ensued until the officer went on to explain that, contrary to the advice and expertise of the economists on his staff, Ambassador Bowles was transmitting unrealistic data about India's commitment to fertilizer production. The Indian government had made a commitment to produce a large amount of fertilizer over the next five years, in return for which India would continue to receive large aid transfers in support of what came to be known as the Green Revolution. The economic officers in the internal section knew the Indian figures were false and had tried to convince the ambassador, to no avail. But Bowles was not about to challenge the Indian government on this score.

While Bowles was a great and dynamic man, at that point he was beginning to show the first signs of Parkinson's disease. He passionately believed in India as the only viable democratic alternative to Communist China. The Indian government admired his support but was also unsure about the extent to which he spoke for his government or just for himself. When the Soviets intervened in Czechoslovakia in 1968, the ambassador went immediately to call on Prime Minister Indira Gandhi to ask that the Indians condemn the Russian intervention, in accordance with Washington's policy. However, shortly after the ambassador's meeting with Mrs. Gandhi, the Indian foreign secretary, T. N. Kaul, called the deputy chief of mission to ask whether in his démarche to Mrs. Gandhi the ambassador had been speaking for himself or his government. The fact that the question was asked reflected the wariness the Indians had of Bowles's unabashed enthusiasm for all things Indian. Even in the embassy there were worries. Cultural events at Roosevelt House, the ambassador's official residence, tended to feature Indian rather than Western music. Mrs.

Bowles always dressed in a sari, and many embassy wives followed her example, although it must be stated in all fairness that she made no attempt to influence anyone to do so.

We used our three years in India to travel as widely as we could, although family travel was somewhat constrained by the birth of Elizabeth in April 1967, less than six months after our arrival. In the best traditions of the British Raj, we did try to get away from Delhi's relentless and oppressive heat in the summer. One year Susan and the three children went to Mussoorie, a relatively nearby hill station, where the family rented a cottage for a month. The following year we had an idyllic holiday in the Vale of Kashmir in a small cabin in Gulmarg and on a brightly decorated houseboat on Lake Nagin. We tobogganed down glaciers, rode through the hills on horseback, fished and swam in the lake. We felt entirely safe, even though the most recent Indo-Pakistan war over Kashmir was only a few years in the past.

The highlight of our travels was a two-week train trip through Rajasthan. An old friend, Warren Ilchman, who had been a Marshall scholar with Susan and was now in India with the Ford Foundation, arranged the entire complicated itinerary. His wife, Alice, one of Susan's closest friends and a classmate from Mount Holyoke College, was working on her PhD in village development. They were traveling with their toddler son and a nanny, while we took our two older children. An embassy couple, Don and Margot Born, completed the party. We hired a railway inspection car that slept ten in relative comfort. We took our cook with us, who shopped at each stop and provided all our meals in the dining section of the carriage. We went first to Bikaner, where we called on the maharajah. His palace was a veritable museum of hunting trophies, with mounted stuffed animals adorning the walls. Keeping up his shooting skills, the maharajah was engaged on our arrival in skeet shooting next to his palace. He invited us to join him and graciously offered us tea and small cucumber sandwiches, almost as though we were in England. We went on across the Thar Desert to Jaisalmer and then back through Jodhpur, Udaipur,

Ajmer, and Jaipur and then on to Delhi—an incredible adventure to the major cities in the region.

In some ways our posting in New Delhi occurred in a time warp. We had a great deal of unapologetic fun. Security concerns were almost nonexistent in the embassy. The Marine Security Guards' primary responsibility seemed to be to catch officers in security violations. I managed to acquire almost all possible versions of documentary security violation. I left my safe open, left classified material on my desk overnight, and forgot to destroy or secure typewriter ribbons and used carbon paper. With advancing technologies, many of these violations are no longer possible. However, they piled up in my case, and the department eventually formally reprimanded me. Thereafter, I must admit, I became much more careful.

Diplomatic life itself was remarkably relaxed. I appeared in a variety of theatrical events—first as Paul in *My Three Angels* at the British Embassy; then as Roger Spelding, the TV broadcaster, in Gore Vidal's *Visit to a Small Planet*; and later as the young blond Italian immigrant Rodolfo in Arthur Miller's *A View from the Bridge*, produced on the embassy's own small stage. I grew a rather Hitlerian mustache for the first and colored my hair a golden blond for the third. Finally, I appeared in *A Thurber Carnival*, playing a drunken customer on a Macy's Christmas shopping spree. Susan played the double bass in the small jazz combo that accompanied the actors. Susan had taken up the bass again after many years in response to an advertisement in the *Hindustan Times* seeking players for the Delhi Symphony Orchestra. She found this a congenial orchestra in which to play. It was made up primarily of musicians from the Indian army band. The orchestra's director was a demanding and distinguished Brazilian musician, Hans-Joachim Kohlreutter.

Perhaps the theatrical highlight of our tour was an in-house production of *The Stone Age Follies*, a series of skits put together by officers in the internal and external sections to honor Galen Stone, the outgoing external counselor. A group of us, including the future deputy director of operations at the CIA, Clair George, dressed up in skins and skirts and danced and sang our way through this lighthearted tribute. The Bowleses allowed us to use the official residence, Roosevelt House, for the occasion. It was a memorable send-off for the Stones.

We left India in 1969 with some regret. We were anxious to return home after six years in the subcontinent, marked by exposure to the fascinating legacies of the Raj and the richness of the Muslim and Hindu cultures, for which India and Pakistan were justly famous. The subcontinent is often described as a land of contrasts. Certainly we found this to be true in our own lives. During those six years there, we had the joy of Elizabeth's arrival, but sadness as well. We were to leave behind the daughter who had been born and died in Pakistan. We welcomed the prospect of three years of tranquility in our own home and country.

THE INDIA DESK

My career seemed to be moving in a logical and predictable direction. After two tours and three posts in South Asia, my assignment to the India desk in Washington made eminently good sense. I started as the junior political officer for India in an office that covered not only India but also Nepal, Bhutan, and Sri Lanka. David Schneider, an experienced South Asia hand, was director, and he became my guide and mentor over the next three years. These were tumultuous years in South Asia, culminating in the Indo-Pak War of 1972 and the creation of an independent Bangladesh. The India desk turned out to be a critical perch in a year of extraordinary challenges for U.S. South Asia policy.

I found myself at the heart of these challenges. The office was kept busy with the usual stream of requirements: briefings for high-level meetings between senior Indian and American officials, taking notes at meetings, and routine support of our mission in New Delhi. In my work analyzing and summarizing the situation in the region, I was often required to be in close touch with colleagues on the Pakistan desk. One of the constant challenges was dealing with the partisanship of our embassies in Islamabad and New Delhi. Both ambassadors and, by extension, their missions tended to see the policies and actions of their respective countries through rather rose-tinted lenses. This tendency became particularly acute in the spring of 1971, when, in the aftermath of national elections, the Pakistan army brutally put down demonstrations in Dacca. There was widespread protest over the exclusion of the East Pakistan leader Sheikh Mujibur Rehman from the position of prime minister, even though his party had won a clear majority of the national votes in the recent election. The Pakistan army's actions resulted in enormous loss of life, worsened by a vast refugee flow from East Pakistan into India of both Hindus and Bihari Muslims numbering in the hundreds of thousands.

The embassy in New Delhi pressed the State Department to take a more critical stand about Pakistani abuses, which to outsiders appeared to be something close to genocide. Many of us on the India desk shared that view. On April 6 our consul general in Dacca, Archer Blood, authorized a telegram to the department in which virtually all the officers of the consulate general called for strong and clear condemnation of Pakistani actions in East Pakistan. All the junior members on the India and Pakistan desks in State and USAID joined in supporting what came to be known as the Blood Telegram. The telegram was an extraordinary group rejection of established U.S. policy and our seemingly laissez-faire attitude toward Pakistani brutality. Consul General Archer Blood shared the views of his subordinates but did not formally join their protest.

Our superiors, notably Assistant Secretary for Near Eastern Affairs Joseph Sisco and Deputy Assistant Secretary Christopher Van Hollen, were sympathetic, but they did not want to go against the White House, which was clearly unwilling to criticize the Pakistanis. We on the desk were completely unaware of the negotiations then going on with China and the intermediary role Pakistan was playing. From President Richard Nixon's and National Security Advisor Henry Kissinger's perspectives, this initiative trumped everything else. The Blood Telegram had the effect of estranging the State Department from the White House. Kissinger at one point asked Secretary Rogers why he couldn't keep his troops in line. There was some fear among the signers that what some saw as a rash act of defiance would ruin their careers. But the department respected our dissent, and several who signed went on to senior positions.

It is fair to say that the Indians were not always the best advocates for their cause. While the Pakistanis consistently supported American positions internationally and were facilitating the China initiative, the Indians would preach about the errors of American global policy. India also led the nonaligned movement, which was openly hostile to the United States and its allies, the former colonial powers. As the crisis advanced and increasing numbers of refugees fled East Pakistan, the Indian demands for help and understanding became increasingly shrill. The Indians compounded our fears by signing a peace, friendship, and cooperation agreement with the Soviet Union in August.

The Pakistanis fueled the White House's fears by suggesting that India's real motives were not humanitarian but rather were designed to bring about the breakup of Pakistan, the separation of its two wings, and ultimately the fragmentation of West Pakistan itself. Raw intelligence, seen at the highest levels of the U.S. government in the later stages of the crisis, indicated that India indeed had plans to invade West Pakistan. That intelligence led to a hardening of the U.S. position and a deepening of U.S. suspicions of India's motives. We were blind men confronting an elephant. We could see some parts of the puzzle but not all of it. We tended to assume that the Indians exaggerated their case and had ulterior motives in their demands for external intervention to end the killing in East Pakistan.

In July I was at the very center of the policy debate. I drafted a forty-page paper on contingency planning in South Asia, which was approved within the department on July 9 and summarized by National Security Council (NSC) staff five days later. A most comprehensive paper, it went through many iterations within the department. (The NSC staff characterized it as "by far the best paper so far produced on the situation.") The paper summarized the current U.S.

strategy and its limitations and then presented a series of options for senior-level decision, including engaging the Soviets and the Indians, and it proposed that there be a speech by the secretary of state outlining our policy. All options were presented with appropriate pros and cons.

I followed this effort with a paper entitled "Scenario for Action in the Indo-Pakistan Crisis," which was discussed at a meeting of the Senior Review Group a day later. The constant theme of our policy was restraint: restraint by the Pakistanis inside East Pakistan and restraint by the Indians in confronting the refugee crisis. The vital interests of both sides were at stake, and neither side was willing to put those interests aside. For Pakistan it was a question of maintaining the unity of the country. For India it was the challenge of managing the refugee flow, which eventually numbered as many as nine million. The White House became so concerned at the possibility that the Indians would act unilaterally against Pakistan that it ordered the aircraft carrier *Endeavor* into the Bay of Bengal as a warning to the Indians. The Indians saw this step as threatening, and a rapid and deep coolness in our relations resulted.

In early November in the midst of the crisis, Indira Gandhi, the Indian prime minister, came to Washington. We drafted briefing papers urging restraint on the Indians. The visit went badly. President Nixon and Prime Minister Gandhi disliked each other personally, and each regarded the other as duplicitous and unreliable. Those of us on the India desk did not participate in any of the formal meetings, but Susan and I, along with other relatively junior officers, were invited to the White House for dessert after the official dinner.

The end of the story is well known. India did invade East Pakistan. An independent Bangladesh was proclaimed, and most of the refugees returned to their homes. Long-term damage was done to our relations with India and with Mrs. Gandhi, who carried a deep grudge against the United States throughout her period leading India.

It was an unhappy time for us on the India desk. We were persuaded that U.S. policy was morally flawed and politically shortsighted. The

Indians, difficult and sanctimonious though they were, deserved our support, not our threats. In the end, my dissent and support for the Blood Telegram was not held against me. The American Foreign Service Association (AFSA) gave me the William R. Rivkin Award for constructive dissent. Assistant Secretary Sisco himself arranged for me to be assigned to the Near Eastern affairs position in the political section of the embassy in Paris. Consequently, after long service in the dustier corners of South Asia, we looked forward to enjoying four happy years in France.

My entire participation in the Indo-Pak crisis of 1971 almost didn't happen. As I approached the end of my first two years on the India desk, I had begun to look for another job. I was offered a position in the United States Mission to the United Nations to handle Middle Eastern affairs in the political section. Though tempting, it was also expensive. As we looked at our finances, we realized it would be difficult to manage the New York cost of living, notably finding housing and private schools for our three children. I indicated that if I were promoted that year, we might just swing it. Happily, as it turned out, I was not promoted. The Soviet desk offered to send me to Moscow to head the internal political unit. In preparation, I would serve in the department working in the internal unit of the Soviet desk. As someone who once thought of himself as a Soviet expert, I would normally have jumped at the job, but with so much South Asia under my belt, I declined and remained on the India desk for the historic events of 1971–72.

From the family's perspective, this time in Washington was a quiet and happy one. In retrospect this seems somewhat surprising. America was going through the trauma of the Vietnam War, which I passed through unscathed. I was not asked to serve there and so was spared the moral and ethical dilemmas of my colleagues. My professional life was focused on India. There were moral dilemmas there, too, as my engagement with the Blood Telegram testifies, but Vietnam was an alien world from which I remained apart. Through it all I bicycled serenely to the department in the upright posture of an Indian civil servant en route to work, parking my cycle in one of the rare racks set aside for bicycle commuters.

My private life focused on family and friends. The children were successfully enrolled in our local parochial school. Susan found a job teaching at the National Cathedral School. I cycled to the office. We played tennis on the weekends on the cathedral courts and enjoyed Scottish country dancing once a week. Susan resumed playing the double bass in the National Cathedral School / St. Albans School orchestra. There were none of the strains of official entertaining, caring for high-level visitors, or late-night summonses to the Operations Center. All that lay ahead in future assignments.

10
Paris Interlude

Paris seemed an unlikely assignment after three long years on the India desk. The personnel system of the State Department was inscrutable, but there were still a few pocket boroughs of personal privilege left. The assistant secretary in the Near East and South Asia Bureau had in his pocket a job in the political section in Paris to cover French Middle East and Africa policy, a power he shared with the assistant secretary for Africa. They exercised their control over this position alternately. As a result of this tradition, the assistant secretary for Near Eastern affairs would appoint every other incumbent. In 1972, when it was Assistant Secretary Joseph Sisco's turn to choose, he called me up and said, "As a reward for three years in the trenches, how would you like to go to Paris?" Being his man in Paris seemed a wonderful idea. I spoke French, and Susan and I were anxious to move to a post in the first world. So off we went to Paris, expecting to stay for four years. I was to work in the embassy's political section.

Paris was everything we had hoped it would be. We lived in a beautiful apartment on the rue Jean Mermoz, only a two-block walk from the Champs-Élysées and half a mile from the embassy. It was an easy walk down the rue Saint-Honoré past the president's residence, the Élysée Palace, to our then unfortified embassy next to the Crillon Hotel on the Place de la Concorde. We were lucky to get this apartment when its previous owner, Allen Holmes, was promoted to political counselor and became eligible for embassy housing. We rented the apartment from a French couple, Madame and Conte de Bertier (a Napoleonic baronetcy, we were informed with some disdain by our upper-class French friends). They did not interfere in our life, and we were able to furnish this elegant apartment with our own furniture and things left behind by previous occupants. It was ideal for entertaining, and we made good use of it in the short time we spent in Paris.

In the political section officers were divided up by geographic regions, with a political counselor in charge of it all. I had both the Near East and Africa portfolios. Paris, like London a megaembassy, had a huge political section consisting of ten officers, of whom six or seven were doing external work.

It was assumed that the French and the British retained global interests. Indeed, the French at that period had as many embassies as we did around the world and certainly played a critical role in Francophone Africa. In the Middle East, where the French had historical relationships with Syria, Lebanon, and North Africa, they were important players. We cared about what the French were doing. Other officers followed their policies in Europe, vis-à-vis the Soviet Union, and in South and Southeast Asia, while the rest focused on internal politics. Half a dozen of us did full-time external work. Nothing went on in the world on which we didn't want to know the French position. My job was essentially one of going back and forth to the Quai d'Orsay inquiring about French policy in Gabon or Lebanon or in places where our interests intersected with those of France. I was expected to maintain contact with the French African and Middle East establishment, journalists, academics, and so forth. I also stayed in touch with the Élysée Palace, because the French presidency had a separate department dealing with Africa under Jacques Foccart, who over the previous twenty years had managed intelligence throughout French Africa.

It was an exciting and rewarding job because it brought me in touch with professional diplomats in the French Foreign Ministry and with the presidency, leading French newspapers, and academics. So for a young second secretary it was both interesting and challenging. I had a lot of reporting to do on a wide range of countries and the French interest in them. My job was clearly defined, and I was quite autonomous. The political counselor, Allen Holmes, was interested in what I did, but he was not a micromanager. The members of the section had a great deal of latitude in defining their own turf based on instructions from Washington, requests for démarches, and need for reports. It was a traditional Foreign Service job in a large embassy with lots of other agencies represented. Both the political and economic sections in Paris at that time had an importance that does not exist in smaller embassies.

The greatest challenge of working in Paris was the French. Like the Indians, they have an extraordinary capacity to patronize and infuriate the United States. There was also the problem of language. Of all the places where I served, Paris was the one where the ability to communicate in the local language was the most difficult and most important. The French did not want to speak to anyone in English, although many of the leading figures could and sometimes did with the ambassador, who for most of this period was former under secretary of state John Irwin. He succeeded Arthur Watson, the former head of IBM, who had been removed from his ambassadorial position after being caught pinching a stewardess on a Pan Am flight. Watson spoke good French, unlike Irwin, who did not. As a result, senior French government officials were constantly putting Irwin down.

I remember accompanying him to discuss some important Middle East question with the secretary general of the Quai d'Orsay, Geoffroy de Courcel, an extraordinary French diplomat who had served as ambassador in London for over a decade. He had been educated in England and spoke perfect English with the fruitiest of Oxford accents. Irwin made the required démarche, and de Courcel looked at him and said in his very British voice, "Mr. Ambassador, I regret to say that I regard the policy of the United States as pusillanimous. I may have the wrong word, you know, but then English isn't my native tongue." I always suspected that Irwin had no idea what pusillanimous meant, and so the comment sailed over his head.

The first time I went to the Quai d'Orsay was to see a rather senior *sous-directeur* (the equivalent of a State Department deputy assistant secretary), Fernand Rouillon, later to be French ambassador to Syria. My task was to inquire about French policy in the Middle East. He listened to my démarche, which I had prepared with some care. I had looked up all the appropriate words and got through the démarche without too much difficulty. He smoked Gauloises and kept one lit between his lips throughout his entire response, moving it from one side of his mouth to the other without opening his lips while talking at the same time. It was a technical tour de force and left this young diplomat absolutely spellbound. I was like a deer in the headlights of an oncoming truck. I understood hardly a word he had said and returned to my office knowing I had to write a cable on the French position. I consulted the political counselor, asking him what he supposed the French position was. We cobbled together an anodyne report based on past French positions. Washington happily did not know that their man in Paris was making up his reporting out of whole cloth. However, Rouillon never played that game again, and I found it increasingly easy to communicate both with him and with other French officials and to understand what they were telling me. Nonetheless, this first meeting at the Foreign Ministry was a good and chastening lesson to a young diplomat.

The tour in Paris turned out to be a prelude to a later stage in my career, in Africa. In December 1972 Washington authorized me to take a familiarization trip to Africa to attend a West African chiefs of mission conference in Ghana. In addition to a three-day stay in Ghana I managed to go to Niger, Mali, and Senegal to consult with our embassies. In Mali the embassy arranged for me to visit Timbuktu. I was fortunate to get this long-sought opportunity then, since the security situation in future years would have made this trip impossible.

One of the things I did in Paris was to take Ambassador Irwin to call on President Jean-Bédel Bokassa of the Central African Republic (CAR) in his hotel room. The president wanted American astronauts to visit the CAR, a request we faithfully conveyed to Washington. I later learned that his request was received positively, and two astronauts went and were received with all the honors of a head of state! Little did I know then that I would spend almost three years under Bokassa's watchful eye.

The French were deeply engaged in both regions of my portfolio, Africa and the Middle East. They considered Africa as their backyard and believed that American ambassadors were pursuing policies everywhere designed to undercut French influence, which greatly concerned them. In the Middle East, they were less concerned, although French relations with North Africa were clearly equally privileged. I must say I always found the French the most professional among all the diplomats with whom I dealt. They were quite open in describing French policies and interests. I felt I had a good relationship with them in Paris, as well as with the French ambassadors with whom I subsequently dealt as colleagues and friends in Africa, the Middle East, and Latin America.

French diplomats are extremely well educated and highly intelligent. I regularly met with three *sous-directeurs*: Fernand Rouillon, with whom I had my first encounter, handled the Middle East and was the crustiest of the three. The second, Jose Paoli, who dealt with Algeria, a separate portfolio of its own, was the son of a Corsican farmer and had risen to senior levels in the Foreign Ministry by virtue of his evident intelligence and talent. The third was Lionel de Warren, an aristocrat whose family at one point controlled a sizable chunk of Ireland after the Norman Conquest. At a dinner at his home he proudly showed me his family tree, going back to the eleventh century. All three were open and accessible. By the end of our first year we had been invited to their homes, and they would come willingly to dinner at our apartment. Toward the end of my stay I also dealt with Hubert Dubois, recently returned to Paris after a tour as the *viguier*, the French viceroy, in Andorra. He was a colorful character full of stories of his life in the Pyrenees.

One of the assumptions of diplomatic work in Paris was that one would entertain one's contacts, whether official or private, at lunch in a suitably rated Paris restaurant. The level of information acquired seemed to be closely linked to the culinary rating of the restaurant to which one went. A one-star Michelin restaurant, a three-course, two-wine lunch, was sure to be productive. I returned from such events badly in need of a nap but confident that a good and informative reporting telegram would result.

One of the unanticipated responsibilities of the job turned out to have nothing to do with the Foreign Service per se. My predecessor, Andrew Steigman, had called from Washington to tell me that diplomacy was not my only responsibility in Paris. He informed me that I would be the next secretary of the Princeton Club of France. Andy was a Princetonian, as was his immediate predecessor, Robert Oakley. Since I was also a Tiger, the Princeton Club of France wanted to continue the tradition and have me take on the job that my two predecessors had held. I agreed after being assured the responsibilities were minimal.

In fact, they turned out to pose a specific challenge when John Irwin arrived in Paris as the new ambassador in 1973. He, too, was a Princetonian, and the president of the club immediately called to ask if I could arrange for the ambassador to speak at one of the club's monthly luncheons. I duly extended the invitation, and the ambassador was happy to accept. Several days before the luncheon he called me in and asked what he should talk about. I suggested a general theme about the administration's foreign policies. He then asked me to write the speech for him. He reviewed my text, made some marginal changes, and in due course delivered it at the club's meeting in the elegant Georges V Hotel. Irwin was not a good public speaker and delivered my text in a rather dull monotone. About halfway through, an elderly Princetonian at my table leaned over and asked me, "Who do you suppose wrote this god-awful speech?" Taken aback, I said I assumed that a junior embassy officer had written it. I was mortified at his reception of my rather lofty and sententious speech. I vowed never to write a speech for someone else again. It was a promise I faithfully kept throughout the remainder of my career.

For the family, this was a halcyon time. The children prospered at the École Active Bilingue. We traveled every weekend to the many cathedral towns, châteaus, and historical monuments within easy reach of Paris and picnicked in the Forest of Fontainebleau or one of the many beautiful parks in the Île-de-France. The kids went to summer camps run by the Touring Club of France and rapidly became immersed in French culture and life.

It was thus a terrible shock when, in the summer of 1973 as the family and I were preparing for our summer holidays, I received a phone call from William Cargo, who had just been named ambassador to Nepal and for whom I had worked in the economic section in the embassy in Karachi some years before. He asked if I would be willing to be his deputy chief of mission (DCM), a big step up for me. It was a blow to my family. The children were becoming comfortable in France. Susan had become a successful Parisian hostess, and Paris had been a dream that we expected to last for four years. Reluctantly, we agreed that I should take the job, given my previous South Asian experience and the opportunity for greater responsibility. So in the summer of 1973 we returned once again to Washington for briefings and preparations for our new post.

11
Nepal

As the chance to be a deputy chief of mission (DCM) was an important career opportunity, I gratefully accepted the offer of my former boss in Karachi. William Cargo, the new ambassador to Nepal, had just finished three years as head of the State Department's Policy Planning staff, following his tour as DCM in Karachi. He was an experienced and considerate boss who helped me learn the ropes as a novice DCM, particularly important, as I was totally unprepared for the job. I had had no management training and no leadership experience. I had never supervised anybody in my fourteen-year Foreign Service career. I knew absolutely nothing of interagency management. I had shared a secretary at several posts but had never supervised one. With no DCM course at the Foreign Service Institute at that time, I received virtually no advice on what a DCM was supposed to do other than act as the ambassador's alter ego. I read up on our policies and programs on the Nepal desk. Luckily, I knew many of the Washington players from my time spent elsewhere in South Asia and on the India desk and was familiar with the political and economic agenda. Although I had never been directly involved with policy toward Nepal, I had visited Kathmandu when assigned to New Delhi and had the responsibility of supporting Ambassador Carol Laise from New Delhi. The interagency aspects of the job were a complete mystery, and I was forced to learn by doing.

We arrived in Nepal in late 1973 and left in early 1976, roughly two and a half years, not completing the usual three years. (Lightning had struck again when I was asked to go to the Central African Republic as ambassador.) In Nepal, a country of relative isolation and seeming insignificance, we had a relatively large embassy, with a big AID mission, a substantial Peace Corps presence of over a hundred volunteers, and the usual array of political and economic officers. So it was an interesting and challenging job. The ambassador allowed me to do most of the managerial work, although that was not always easy, in part because I was quite junior. I was not in the senior service at the time and was only the equivalent of a lieutenant colonel in the military, whereas the ambassador and AID director were both three-star diplomats.

The AID director, Carter Ide, was a career minister who took directions from no one, certainly not from me. This was always a problem. Ide was able and experienced and managed the AID mission skillfully. Nonetheless, there was always a certain amount of tension with the embassy both because of the autonomy that the AID director insisted on maintaining and because of his access to high levels of the Nepalese government. He was one of the leaders of the American community.

An example of his influence came when the security officer approached me to ask that I underscore the responsibility of all mission personnel to wear their identification badges in the embassy. That seemed a sensible idea to me, and I duly put out a memorandum to all mission staff reminding them of their obligation. The next day the AID director arrived at the chancery for the weekly country team meeting without his badge. The Marine Security Guard politely explained the DCM's reminder of the requirement that staff wear their ID at all times. Ide was outraged, since everyone in the mission, including the Marine Security Guards, knew him. He retorted angrily that if the ambassador ever wanted to see him at a country team meeting in the future, an exception to the rule would have to be made. I reported the problem to the ambassador, who, I regret to say, agreed to allow the director to come to the embassy without his badge. I was completely chagrined. Development assistance was at the core of our relationship with Nepal, so the AID director had unusual clout and authority. In short, if you had resources and programs, you had access. The AID director always had access, while my notional authority as the ambassador's deputy was entirely ephemeral.

Even in those far-off days, security was a growing issue. There had been several high-visibility terrorist incidents in the Middle East, and embassies were urged to make security a priority. The Israelis had already done so, and their embassy was something of a fortress, unlike other missions in Kathmandu. Not only were we lax in wearing our badges, but we were also not rigorous in controlling access. At one point after the badge incident, the Israeli ambassador paid a formal visit to Ambassador Cargo and criticized the embassy's security posture. To make the point quite clear, he pulled a loaded pistol from his belt and placed it on the coffee table in front of the ambassador. After that rather embarrassing incident the ambassador ensured much greater attentiveness to the use of our installed metal detector and to the screening of embassy visitors. However, by contemporary post-9/11 standards our efforts were quite primitive and limited.

At that time, the United States was primarily interested in Nepal as a buffer between India and China. Nepal is situated on the border of Tibet, and large numbers of Tibetan refugees had fled to Nepal. Our programs working directly with the Tibetans gave other members of the embassy privileged access to the highest levels of the Nepalese government. At the time, Nepal was an absolute monarchy, though with some limited self-government through local councils, or panchayats. Since the king took all important decisions, officials at the palace were our principal interlocutors. The only other Nepalese player of any significance was Bhekh Bahadur Thapa, the finance minister, with whom the AID director dealt on a daily basis. The minister had been educated at Claremont College in California and subsequently became ambassador to Washington and later to India.

Neither Washington nor the mission made any significant effort to promote democracy in Nepal or to persuade the king to be more liberal in his policies. The ambassador may have raised such issues from time to time, but they certainly did not form a main feature of our policy. We were much more concerned with preserving the independence of Nepal from what we saw as the predatory intentions of its two large neighbors and with helping Nepal, one of the least developed countries in Asia, to achieve momentum in its economic development.

USAID had developed a broad spectrum of programs over the years. We had done a fair amount of road building to try breaking down some of the country's isolation. We had agricultural development projects in various parts of the country and were particularly concerned about deforestation. We also had family planning and population programs. Nepal's high rate of population growth created serious economic problems, particularly in the hills. Although no religious or political leaders opposed family planning, it required a fair amount of education to introduce these ideas into the culture. I am not sure how successful our programs were, but there was no official resistance to them.

We were much engaged at the grassroots level through the Peace Corps and the many AID programs we had in place. Our political agenda focused on ways to strengthen Nepal vis-à-vis its neighbors and to mitigate tensions with India in particular. The Peace Corps was engaged in rural development and English-language teaching. Rural development was primarily in the Terai, the lowlands bordering India. In the mountains we focused on small water projects, cooperatives, and the like. As it did in other countries, the Peace Corps made a considerable effort to teach English as a second language. Nepal was a particular challenge for the volunteers because of the extraordinary terrain and the lack of roads. It was Peace Corps policy at the time not to post a volunteer more than a twenty-four-hour walk from the nearest road. It was important to be able to get Peace Corps volunteers out because of the risk of accidents and illnesses. We had a helicopter on lease that was always available for possible rescue operations.

At the time, the Peace Corps sought to maintain the maximum distance from the embassy. The Peace Corps director was a member of the embassy's country team, but the volunteers didn't see themselves as working for the U.S. government. In 1970, at the swearing in of a new batch of Peace Corps volunteers, they refused to take the standard oath of allegiance to the Constitution, insisting on writing their own oath based on the ideals of the Peace Corps and the government of Nepal. This caused the ambassador some considerable concern, so instead of being present at the taking of the oath, he sent me, his deputy. The volunteers had to sign the constitutional oath if they wanted to get paid, but they refused to take it in an open, public setting. Despite the tension between the Peace Corps and the embassy, individual volunteers whom we got to know were personally very friendly.

A much greater set of problems arose from world travelers in Nepal. Large numbers of young Americans came to Kathmandu for the drug scene, the Buddhist scene, and life in "esoteric Asia." They often got into difficulties with the authorities by overstaying their visas or by getting into scrapes with the police. The consular officer was kept busy dealing with the problems of these travelers, though very few ended up in jail. The Nepalese were fairly tolerant of drug consumption if those involved were not unruly and did not commit other types of illegal acts. Usually, drug problems were medical problems. Young Americans who fell ill would have to be repatriated and their families informed. That was a greater problem than dealing with the Nepalese authorities. Many of the world travelers looked for jobs, including as teachers in our cultural center, where the United States Information Agency (USIA) sponsored an extensive English-teaching program. Susan ran this program for USIA throughout almost our entire time in Nepal. Getting visas for these world-traveler teachers was a constant challenge.

Ambassador Cargo used me to supervise the reporting of the substantive officers. I also did a fair amount of internal coordination, although he did most of the direct coordination with the AID director. I was certainly expected to maintain good relations with all the agencies at post, because, as at any embassy, the DCM becomes chargé d'affaires when the ambassador is on leave.

I didn't see a great deal of King Birendra, but once a year the king traditionally would come to dinner with the American ambassador. (He also had yearly dinners with the British and Indian ambassadors.) These were highly contrived and stylized affairs. The guests were limited to two or three embassy officers, usually the ambassador,

DCM, and political officer, their spouses, and the king and his two brothers with their spouses. The king was young and not entirely self-confident. His father, Mahendra, had been king for quite a long time and a strong figure in Nepal. During the final years of his reign he had begun to move the country toward democracy, but full parliamentary democracy was still far away on the horizon. These dinners were rather stilted affairs and caused considerable anxiety for the ambassador and his wife, who wanted to make sure the event went off without a hitch.

The Nepalese, obsessed with India and fearing Indian domination and hegemony, always tried to play the Chinese off against the Indians. They dreaded the possibility that they would be overrun if India's population were allowed to come across the border and settle. The highly capable Indian ambassador, Krishna Rasgotra, had already been India's DCM in Washington and was later to be ambassador to the United States and foreign secretary of India. He acted every inch the proconsul, regarding India as having a special relationship with Nepal. He was not averse to squeezing the Nepalese in economic and trade terms if necessary to assure that Nepal did not stray too far from the Indian path or develop overly close relations with the Chinese.

India was heavy-handed in its dealings with the Nepalese. In their annual trade negotiations, the so-called access negotiations, the Indians always took a hard line, and the Nepalese always complained to us about the Indians. In New Delhi, our embassy tried to persuade the Indians to be somewhat softer in their position in order not to push the Nepalese in the direction of the Chinese. The Indians were not susceptible to advice on relations with their neighbors, particularly the Nepalese, any more than they had been regarding Pakistan and Bangladesh. They were not going to have the United States tell them how they should comport themselves. Ever since the crisis of 1971, in fact, they regarded our policy as being hostile to Indian hegemony in South Asia. They believed that we failed to recognize India's legitimate, privileged relationship with its neighbors and that we were always trying to undermine Indian influence. The Nepalese, on the other hand, tried to maximize their relations with the Chinese as a counterweight to India. Nepal remained important to us to the degree that it was an important buffer against Chinese encroachments in South Asia. Accordingly, Nepal got rather more attention and resources than other countries of comparable size in the third world.

Nepal was then, as now, a haven for mountain climbers. There were a couple of Everest expeditions during the time we were there, along with less visible expeditions to other major peaks such as Annapurna. These expeditions always caused the embassy great worry. In several cases Americans lost their lives on expeditions, and although the mountain climbers were highly professional and skilled, accidents still happened. World travelers were an even greater anxiety, as they hiked the mountains without equipment or training.

During school holidays in 1975 Susan and I, together with our two older children, had planned to fly to Lukla and trek to the Everest base camp. We arrived at the airport to find that our flight had been canceled because an earlier flight that same morning had crashed shortly after takeoff. That was the flight in which the wife of the famous New Zealand mountaineer, Sir Edmund Hilary, met her death. Rocked by this tragedy, we almost abandoned our idea of trekking. Ultimately, we substituted a trek to the north of Kathmandu. The embassy was prepared for fatal accidents to trekkers and even maintained a kind of morgue on the embassy property to be used while families back home made decisions concerning the disposition of remains. Local burial was a problem, since the small local British Christian cemetery was full, and cremation according to Hindu rites on the banks of the Yamuna River was unappealing to most American families.

Trekking was a great embassy pastime, and almost all the embassy officers did some trekking. The ambassador and I strongly encouraged officers to get a feel for the country, and the only way to see the country was on foot. I did some trekking with my family and with the embassy's local employees. You slept in the open or in villagers' huts, but trekking was not exceptionally strenuous except when one got to altitudes over ten thousand feet. Sherpas carried your supplies, cooked for you, and looked after your safety. They made sure you did not do anything too foolhardy, although the family remembers one horrifying night when we had to sleep in tents on a narrow ledge high in the mountains in what was a brief but blinding snowstorm.

The highlight of our tour was the coronation of King Birendra Bir Bikram Shah. President Gerald Ford sent a rather large delegation, led by personal friend and White House counsel Philip Buchen and composed of several other friends and dignitaries, including a woman who subsequently became ambassador to Nepal, Marquita Maytag. The Nepalese set a limit to the number of people who could attend the actual coronation. Our delegation exceeded that limit by some order of magnitude. Ms. Maytag and several others were not able to attend the coronation, and it fell to me as the DCM to entertain the disgruntled members of the president's party. The lucky ones who attended were overjoyed by the exotic nature of the coronation. The not-so-lucky others were less happy with the embassy's performance. As a result, the ambassador got a great deal of criticism in Washington for his failure to produce invitations for all those in the president's party. There wasn't much we could do except implore the Nepalese over and over, telling them how important it was that all these people attend, but to no avail. We explained to the American delegates that the palace courtyard where the coronation was to take place was very old and small and located in the center of the city. There was literally no extra space. Eventually they understood, although they felt much aggrieved at having been dragged halfway around the world without being able to attend the coronation. Though not a substantive problem, for the ambassador it was a major crisis.

Among the several members of Congress who came for the coronation was a southern congressman who insisted on teaching Sunday school while he was there. He said he had never missed teaching Sunday school in thirty years and wasn't going to miss it in Kathmandu. Finding such an opportunity was not easy, since there were not many Christians in Nepal. Some American missionaries, both Catholic and Protestant, had a presence in Kathmandu. Luckily, one

Protestant church had an English-language Sunday school, and we were able to put him in touch with them.

My only contribution to the coronation beyond hosting the "second team" lunch had been to prepare for the great event through a Lions Club service project. As a club member, I worked on a crew that painted in royal purple all the major bus stops and bus shelters around the city in the weeks leading up to the coronation.

As at earlier posts, theater was one of the few activities in which the entire expatriate community took part. We had a small group, the HAMS, or the Himalayan Amateurs, that mounted productions once or twice a year. Our most successful effort was a production of Arthur Miller's *The Crucible*, which I codirected with the director of the British Council in Nepal. The production was so successful that King Birendra asked if we could put on an extra performance for him. We were overjoyed to comply with this request. The royal family sat solemnly in the front row as we went through our paces.

The cast party that followed led to a family disaster. We decided to serve rabbit stew, a dish featured in the play. Our cook, Ratna, from the Nepali butcher caste, undertook to purchase live rabbits and prepare them for stewing. That seemed sensible, but we discovered that many Westerners do not like rabbit stew and refused to eat what had been prepared. Alas, the next morning our younger daughter, who was then only eight, discovered to her horror that we had eaten Updike, her pet rabbit. The cook, finding one of the purchased rabbits to be pregnant, had sacrificed the family rabbit instead.

Shortly after the coronation, I received a phone call from the director general of the Foreign Service, Ambassador Carol Laise, asking if I would be willing to accept an assignment as ambassador to the Central African Republic. I was stunned. It was a country about which I literally knew nothing, an area of the world with which I was unfamiliar, and a major break from the thirteen years I had spent working in and on South Asia. But when the gold ring came by, I grabbed it and said I would be honored to go, little imagining that the decision would take me away from South Asia for the remainder of my career.

12
The Heart of Darkness

Africa was largely a mystery for me. My childhood reading of Sir H. Rider Haggard and lectures with Dame Margery Perham at Oxford on British colonial rule in Nigeria did not in any way prepare me for this remote backwater of the French colonial system. Oubangui-Chari (or Ubangi-Shari), as the Central African Republic (CAR) was called before independence, was the most isolated and least desirable of all French colonies. It was a large country, equal in size to France, with only two million inhabitants. The French still played a significant role in the life of the country, providing a substantial part of the national budget. French citizens still ran most of the businesses in the capital, Bangui, including the supermarket, the hairdressers, the hotels, and almost everything else of significance. The French ambassador was the big gun in town and ruled with proconsular authority. The language of government was French, not Sangho, and the tastes of the ministers ran heavily to French food and drink. Champagne, not coffee, was offered to visitors at ministerial offices, even on morning calls.

It was a surreal atmosphere into which I was about to enter. The ruler, Jean-Bédel Bokassa, had been brought back from the French army to be commander in chief of the small Central African army shortly after independence in 1961. He soon seized power from the country's first president, his cousin David Dacko. By the time I arrived, Bokassa had steadily promoted himself to the rank of field marshal and president for life. He ruled with an iron hand and did not admit of any opposition.

Bokassa was proud of his past service in the French army. He had achieved a rather notable success for an African, rising through the ranks to become a captain in the regular French army. He served both in North Africa during the Second World War and in Vietnam. While in Vietnam, he married a local woman, with whom he had a child.

He later brought this child, the "real" Martine, back to Bangui as his acknowledged daughter when documentary evidence of his paternity was produced. Earlier, another Martine had come forward to claim that she was Bokassa's daughter, and she too had been brought back to Bangui. Only later did the "false" Martine lose her status as Bokassa's real daughter.

During our time in Bangui, Bokassa had multiple wives, two of whom vied for official recognition as his chief wife. Catherine, a beautiful young African woman, had already given him several children by the time she was twenty-five. She took her official title from Bokassa's political one and was known as La Présidente. Her rival, a Romanian folk dancer, had come to Bangui as part of a cultural troupe sponsored by the Romanian government. Bokassa, who was known for his love of the ladies, reportedly worked his way through the corps de ballet, one per night, and kept one permanently. Her official title was La Maréchale, in keeping with Bokassa's military rank.

Both autocratic and temperamental, Bokassa was capable of great charm. Astonishingly to outsiders, he became a friend of French president Valéry Giscard d'Estaing, who visited him annually to hunt elephants in the remote eastern part of the country. They were apparently congenial comrades, and Bokassa gave Giscard an elegant and expensive diamond necklace. The gift became a scandal for Giscard with the French press.

Nothing prepared me for my arrival in Bangui. I had had the usual briefings at the State Department, the Peace Corps, USAID, the CIA, and Commerce. En route I stopped in Paris to confer with the French Foreign Ministry. It was an accepted fact that the French underwrote the country's budget and that their ambassador functioned as a kind of proconsul in what was originally one of the most remote outposts of the French colonial empire. I had met President Bokassa four years earlier when he visited Paris and gave Ambassador Irwin a letter to President Nixon, asking the United States to send an astronaut on an official visit to Central Africa. As I was the junior political officer who focused on Africa, I had accompanied the ambassador to his meeting with Bokassa. From that meeting and from the briefings I had received, I realized that I would be dealing with a mercurial, unconventional, and unpredictable ruler of a country with which we had very few mutual interests. The CAR's cardinal virtue was that it always voted with the United States in the UN General Assembly. Our economic interests were extremely limited. Only one American company operated in the country, Diamond Distributors, a New York firm importing alluvial diamonds.

In several ways I got off to a difficult start. While on prearrival consultations in Paris I was informed that there had been an assassination attempt on Bokassa in which his nephew had thrown a hand grenade at him at Bangui airport. The perpetrator and several of his friends and acquaintances had been rounded up and summarily executed. Among this group was the embassy's general services officer, Mark Caldo, an Iraqi citizen serving as a third country national in our embassy. We learned later that he had been a business partner of the assassin. Together they had run a movie theater in the African quarter of the capital. Needless to say, the embassy staff was deeply shaken by Caldo's execution. He was a popular and, in many ways, indispensable member of the administrative staff, operating as the embassy's general factotum and local problem solver. Today it is unlikely that the ambassador would be allowed to proceed to post, at least until a protest had been made and a formal apology received. However, I was sent on without formal instructions.

Susan and I arrived in Bangui late in the evening, expecting to be greeted by the DCM and other members of the embassy staff. However, on landing we were greeted by a large troupe of bare-breasted Central African women, singing and dancing on the tarmac. Naively, I assumed that this was the typical way to celebrate the arrival of a new American ambassador. I quickly realized that this was not the case. On the plane was a far more important dignitary, the French minister of cooperation, the equivalent of our AID administrator. On entering the terminal, we found no arrival party and went through the usual customs and baggage checks without benefit of normal diplomatic immunities. We felt not only lost and ignored but rather angry at the lack of welcome. It was only after the formalities had been concluded that the DCM and other embassy officers found us and apologized profusely for their failure to find and greet their new boss.

Even before my arrival I had been a little apprehensive about what my working relations with the DCM would be. When my predecessor had left post the previous year, Bokassa had written to President Ford asking that the DCM, Bill Swing, be made ambassador. The department had ignored this unorthodox request, and my appointment went forward. Still, knowing that the DCM had a close personal relationship with the ruler was daunting for me, a new and totally inexperienced ambassador. As things turned out, Bill and I worked well together, and as a neophyte in Africa, I profited from his experience and understanding of what made things tick in the CAR.

The first order of business for me was to present my credentials to Bokassa. The Central African desk in Washington advised me that I would get off to a good start if, in addition to my letters of credence, I also brought a personal gift for Bokassa. After a certain amount of searching, I found at the Decatur House gift shop in Washington a porcelain bowl created for the Bicentennial. It had George Washington's arms engraved on it, as well as the Bicentennial dates. The bowl was elegantly wrapped by the department's protocol office. I presented this package to Bokassa with what seem in retrospect to have been unduly profuse expressions of friendship. As he unwrapped and gazed admiringly at the bowl, I explained with a straight face its significance. He and George Washington were both the founding fathers of their countries, both were generals, and both were historic symbols for the peoples of their respective countries. Bokassa beamed in pleasure and then, after reading the inscription, 1776–1976, observed, "Quelle longue vie!" (What a long life he had!) I felt I had gotten off to a remarkably good start.

The U.S. embassy, with only eight American staff plus a Peace Corps contingent of twenty, was still the second largest diplomatic mission in Bangui. The French embassy, whose presence was felt at all levels, was substantially larger. We occupied space in a former two-story commercial building, with the embassy offices on the ground floor and a small USIS reading room and library on the second floor. The quarters were cramped: all the windows had been blocked for official security reasons. We had no Marine Security Guards, but we did not feel ourselves threatened in any way. Terrorism in those far-off days was unknown in the CAR, as was communal strife. We were busy enough but certainly not overworked. I called on ministers, who invariably offered me Champagne rather than coffee. We traveled widely to every corner of the country, usually staying with missionaries. Two American Protestant denominations had divided the territory in half at the beginning of the century, with the Independent Baptists going west and the Grace Brethren taking the east. Although both were much more conservative theologically than I was, I greatly admired their fine work running clinics and health posts and providing literacy training through their Bible schools.

The Baptists were the more conservative. I discovered just how conservative when, to my astonishment, they refused to come to an embassy Christmas party at the ambassador's residence because the carols and other songs were to be played by a young Bahá'í missionary. As the senior Baptist pastor told me before the event, they had prayed about coming but had concluded they could not in good conscience attend when the music was to be provided by someone who "did not profess the Lord Jesus." For all that, they were good people and enormously hospitable to the Roman Catholic American ambassador. They were also wonderful sources of information about the conditions outside of Bangui, *en brousse* (in the bush), as we called it.

Although within the CAR we occasionally traveled by air, we made numerous long trips on the rutted laterite roads that joined the major cities. Since at the time there were only about one hundred miles of paved road in a country the size of Texas, the missionaries led surprisingly isolated lives, often staying as long as ten years at a stretch in a remote outpost. Home leaves are now much more frequent, but in those days families went to the mission field for life. Economic conditions outside of Bangui were quite desperate. Farmers engaged in subsistence farming, producing the staple of the Central African diet, manioc. Entire villages moved at regular intervals when the land within walking distance of the village became completely depleted.

"Bangui, La Grande Coquette," as a banner over the road into town from the airport proclaimed, was quite a charming town. It had all modern amenities, including a French supermarket to which twice a week arrived French necessities such as Breton oysters, French cheeses, and French cuts of meat. (Fish, mainly the large white *capitaine*, were caught locally.) Social life occurred exclusively among the expatriate, mainly French, community, although we did see a lot of other diplomats, some European and many African. The principal event of each week was a *grande bouffe* on Sunday at someone's house. Beginning shortly after noon and lasting all afternoon, these lunches involved multicourse meals with French wines and Champagne, excellent food, and long animated conversations about the state of the country and the world. Because Central Africans were not permitted to socialize with foreigners without the ruler's personal permission, the diplomatic corps led a remarkably sequestered and in-grown life.

Central Africans came rarely to the ambassador's residence, although Bokassa and other ministers would attend formal embassy-sponsored events held in other venues. An occasion for special hospitality involving Central African officials was the visit of the director of Central African affairs in the State Department, Thompson Buchanan. Bokassa had been pressing me for some time about his desire to make an official visit to Washington or about the possibility of Dr. Kissinger, now secretary of state, making an official visit to Bangui. I repeatedly reminded him how crammed everyone's schedule was in Washington and how unlikely it would be that he could make an official visit or that a reciprocal one to Bangui would take place. Eventually in response to this repeated importuning, the department decided to send Tom Buchanan as a special emissary with a personal letter from Dr. Kissinger. I sought and received an audience for the two of us with Bokassa, who read the letter with evident pleasure, since it contained Dr. Kissinger's assurance of our friendship for Bokassa and the CAR. At the end of the meeting he told me he had instructed his government to attend the dinner we were giving in Director Buchanan's honor that night.

Alas, we had not invited the government, knowing that under normal circumstances, they could not come. Susan was horrified at the prospect of a large, unspecified number of guests. In the end, only three ministers came. But along with them came national television cameras and crew, who had been instructed by Bokassa to film the dinner for the national TV viewing audience, happily a rather small percentage of the population. So it was that as each course was presented, the klieg lights went on, and the dinner was recorded for history. The evening went off well, not marred as one had been a few weeks earlier by a monsoon downpour, which had filled the living room with water to the depth of about six inches.

Relations did not always have such happy outcomes. While we were on home leave in the summer of 1977, two American journalists were arrested. The first, Jonathan Randall of the *Washington Post*, was held for a week, beaten, and eventually released. He had been charged with writing defamatory stories about Bokassa and his government. More serious was the arrest of Michael Goldsmith, an Associated Press reporter. After spending a few days in Bangui, he had filed his stories to his bureau in South Africa. Not surprisingly, the texts of his reports, all highly critical of Bokassa and his style of government, were seized and shared with Bokassa, and Goldsmith was immediately arrested. Since I was away on home leave at the time, it was left to the chargé, Grant Smith, to protest both arrests. He succeeded in getting Randall released, but Goldsmith lingered on in the imperial dungeons. To make matters even more pressing, Goldsmith was Lady Bird Johnson's nephew, and she and the Johnson family brought considerable pressure on the department to get Goldsmith out. Our ambassadors in various African capitals whose rulers were known to have close ties to Bokassa were asked to inter-vene, but to no avail.

Eventually I was pulled away from my home leave in California and sent back to Bangui. I immediately sought an audience with Bokassa, which was granted, and demanded that Goldsmith be released. Bokassa flew into a rage, denouncing me as an agent of the CIA. He said I had been plotting his overthrow since my arrival the previous year. He threatened me with his presidential cane. But whether because of my démarche or the other approaches that had been made to Bokassa from outside, Goldsmith was released. Before being put on a plane in the middle of the night, he was brought to Bokassa, who apologized profusely for the way the journalist had been treated, offered him numerous glasses of Champagne, and pro-fessed his friendship. Goldsmith, who had been living on bananas and water for over four weeks, found this behavior not only strange but alarming, as Bokassa had also gone to some pains to denounce the American ambassador for plotting against him. When Goldsmith returned to America to tell his story, he urged the State Department to bring me home, as in Goldsmith's view my life was in imminent danger. I assured Washington that this was not so. In fact, at my next meeting with Bokassa, he kissed me on both cheeks and told me how much he enjoyed working with me and the United States.

Despite Bokassa's efforts to make amends by being personally friendly to me, the State Department in September initiated a review of our policy toward the CAR out of concern for the journalist inci-dents and one involving the mistreatment of a Peace Corps volun-teer who had been arrested for loitering in front of the presidential palace. President Jimmy Carter decided to eliminate new aid to the country and instructed me to convey that information to Bokassa personally. However, I was to do it in a way that would not lead to further attacks on American citizens. When I did so in early Octo-ber, Bokassa took the news with uncharacteristic equanimity and accepted the new realities.

Notwithstanding his many eccentricities, Bokassa was seen as a friend of the United States, and we went out of our way to stay on good terms with him. The embassy had access to $150,000 in "self-help" funds, which the ambassador could allocate (with AID's consent) to small development projects. Prior to my arrival, a substantial part of that money had been allocated for construction of a health post outside the presidential palace in Berengo, some thirty miles west of Bangui. Unfortunately, as often happened in such cases, the funds turned out to be insufficient, and the minister of health asked for another $100,000 to complete the project. We realized that this was probably throwing good money after bad, but the minister had made it quite clear to me how attached the president was to the project. I asked the newly arrived economic officer, Donald Steinberg, to draw up an aid program based on the available funds. He demurred, saying he could not possibly do the job without macro- and micro-economic data to justify the proposed allocations. I assured him that the allocations were largely political, and I would be happy to do his work for him. I wrote the report and approved the additional funds for the health post. Ironically, Steinberg went on to become deputy administrator of USAID!

When the project was finally finished and equipped, we organized a ceremonial opening. President Bokassa agreed to participate and reviewed the immaculate health post, with its well-stocked pharmacy and impressive staff of doctors and nurses. We toasted this symbol of American–Central African friendship with some enthusiasm. Unfortunately, our enthusiasm was short-lived. Everything in the dispensary disappeared within days. The doctors and nurses were recalled to Bangui, and to the best of my knowledge the health post never treated a single patient. But Washington's relations with Bangui and its ruler were on the upswing.

Bangui was not in the mainstream of USIA cultural programming in Francophone Africa. Prior to my arrival, the public affairs officer position had been abolished, but a small information center remained, staffed by locally hired employees. Nonetheless, we did get our share of programs. The first was a paper exhibit about the American space program, which came with a series of panels and a mockup of a Gemini space capsule. Bokassa came and admired the show. (He liked to think of himself as something of a science buff.) We were also sent a small jazz trio from Paris led by Mickey Baker, a jazz saxophonist. As there was no stage in Bangui, he performed in our back garden for a substantial audience of diplomats and expatriates. We put the embassy Ping-Pong table to use, which was all we could do to create a stage for him.

Official visits to Bangui by foreign dignitaries were comparatively few. When these visits occurred, the diplomatic corps was summoned to the airport to greet the arriving dignitary. We regarded these events with horror, as they often involved standing in the broiling Central African sun waiting for the official to arrive. One visitor, however, stands out: the president of Libya, Muammar Gaddafi. His visit transformed this sleepy corner of Africa. Within hours of his arrival, President Bokassa and the leading ministers announced that they had converted to Islam. Jean-Bédel Bokassa became Salahuddin Ahmed Bokassa. Ministers chose equally Arabic names. Reportedly, the president and his ministers received a handsome cash bonus for their decision to convert to Islam. Gaddafi brought with him a film entitled *The Message*, starring Anthony Hopkins and describing the life of the Prophet Muhammad. It was shown to the leading lights of Bangui, including the diplomatic corps, in a movie theater in the African quarter. Unfortunately, the film was in English. Projection was started and then stopped until a translator could be found. The film was repeatedly interrupted with cheers when Bilal, the first convert to Islam and an African, rode forth on his camel to kill infidels. Every time an Arab was killed the crowd burst into cheers, to the amazement of the diplomats in attendance. However, it was subsequently explained to us that Arabs had carried out the slave trade in Central Africa and that in the minds of local citizens, the best Arab was a dead Arab.

That evening at a sumptuous state dinner Islamic strictures prevailed. Instead of the usual whiskey, we drank orange juice. (This abstemious practice continued at official functions for some time thereafter, until Bokassa lost interest in the dictates of Islam and returned to his normal drinking habits.) The women of Bokassa's political party, MESAN, put on a song-and-dance routine for Gaddafi using the words "salaam alaikum" as its theme. They were dressed in brightly colored Central African cloth and included in their routine several simulated prayer inclinations. The next day Gaddafi gave a two-hour speech, exhorting his audience to condemn Christianity as the religion of the colonial oppressors and praising Islam as the religion of their oppressed victims. Gaddafi even managed to squeeze in a brief tea meeting with the diplomatic corps, at which he spoke in slightly broken English. The meeting gave him a chance to meet with the small group of ambassadors resident in Bangui. I found him charming and gracious, if not particularly substantive in his remarks to us.

It is often said that the buck stops with the ambassador, as was brought home to me in a very real sense in the summer of 1977. Early one morning the visiting AID director, normally resident in Cameroon, called me urgently to say that one of his contractors was in the local French-run clinic with appendicitis. I expressed sympathetic concern, which turned to alarm when the director told me that the French physician at the clinic had said our employee would have to have an appendectomy that day. The problem that immediately emerged was that the qualified French surgeons at the principal Bangui hospital were all on home leave in France. The patient would have to be evacuated by air to Europe or another African country.

Alas, the embassy administrative office informed me that this was one of the days when there were no outbound flights to Europe. There were flights to Brazzaville, but the United States did not at that time have relations with the Congolese government. We then explored a charter medical evacuation, but that could not be organized until the next day. We became increasingly desperate.

The AID director went back to the clinic and returned with the startling information that there was in Bangui an African who had done a parasurgical course at Montpellier University in France. Although he was not a qualified doctor, he reportedly had successfully performed many appendectomies. The clinic's doctor spoke highly of his work. After a brief reflection I concluded that we had no choice: the employee would have to accept this alternative. The AID director was horrified at the risk and said the choice was up to the ambassador. The buck stopped with me. Happily, the operation was a success. A trained French anesthetist assisted, and all went well.

♦ ♦ ♦

The highlight of our time in Central Africa was the president's coronation. In early 1978, Bokassa decided that his status as a seven-star field marshal and president for life did not give him sufficient recognition in the world of postcolonial Africa, so he proposed to make himself emperor. The first indication we had of that intention was when his Romanian wife gave birth early in 1978 to a little girl named Anne, and the local press announced her as the Princess Anne, implying royal parentage. There were many rumors about the coming empire, particularly what kind it might be. It was assumed early on in 1978 that Bokassa would try to model his empire on one of the great medieval empires in Africa—emulating the tradition of chiefly rule but dressing it up in a more modern kind of royal framework. In fact, what he wanted to be was the successor not to any African chief but to the pharaohs and Napoleon. So the style of the empire was Napoleonic; the pedigree of the empire was pharaonic. Bokassa announced that he had traced his ancestry back to the pharaohs. When the empire was established, it did not look at all Egyptian. Rather, it was a Black version of Napoleon's empire. To create such an empire was an expensive proposition, as the French government, which paid the bills for its establishment, was soon to find out.

On the last day of the republic, President Bokassa organized a splendid dinner in the courtyard of the presidential palace. All ministers, senior government officials, and the diplomatic corps were required to be in attendance. Zaire's president, Mobutu Sese Seko, a distant tribal cousin of Bokassa's, was the guest of honor. We were served filet mignon and other delicacies flown in from France. In front of every seat was a bottle of Dom Pérignon Champagne. The party did not really get going until well after midnight, when Mobutu had left. The palace gates were then locked, armed guards were posted, and guests were obliged to stay at the pleasure of the soon-to-be-crowned emperor. He decided with typical African enthusiasm that he wanted his last night as a simple citizen to be spent dancing. So it was that the ambassadors and ministers and their wives were asked to join a large circle on the dance floor. Bokassa placed himself in the center and with exaggerated bows and flourishes danced in turn with all the wives present. By dawn we were exhausted, and at last the gates were opened and we were allowed to return home to await the arrival of the empire.

The French were most reluctant to back the imperial project. They disapproved of Bokassa's Napoleonic ambitions but did not insist that he be an African-style king. They ultimately agreed to pay the full costs of his imperial coronation—costs that ran, according to some accounts, to something on the order of $45–$50 million. The French had no alternative to Bokassa. He had a claim to French nationality by virtue of his service in the French army. He had been a loyal friend of France on all African issues. He was a great admirer, publicly and otherwise, of Charles de Gaulle. He was a regular hunting partner of the president of France, Giscard d'Estaing. That Bokassa had such success in getting the French to underwrite his coronation also testifies to his personal qualities. He and the highly intellectual French president would spend two weeks on safari together sharing war stories, comparing reminiscences, and discussing the affairs of the world in a way that the French visitor apparently enjoyed.

Bokassa had been a loyal member of the French army; he had a château in the Sologne in the central part of France; and the French felt a certain loyalty to him, notwithstanding his quite extraordinary idiosyncrasies. Not that they approved of everything he did, but they saw no reasonable alternative to him at that time. That changed in 1979, when they brought about his overthrow with the introduction of French paratroopers. But this came only after another bizarre set of incidents involving the suppression of demonstrations by high school students in the center of Bangui. After Bokassa personally ordered the shooting of these young protestors, the French could no longer support the erstwhile emperor.

Bokassa's decision to crown himself emperor was thought in Washington to be the most extraordinary piece of foolishness. On the other hand, Washington remained cautious, since we did have some limited interests in Bokassa's support for us at the United Nations and our few economic assets in the country. The embassy tried not to make fun of Bokassa in the messages and cables we sent. I consciously tried to describe events with as straight a face as possible. It was easy to make cheap and rather amusing comments about this exotic regime, but the result might have been to put individual Americans, Peace Corps volunteers, missionaries, and businesspeople, in peril. We tried to avoid too many quotable quotes, although at times we did allow ourselves to describe the political evolution of the Central African state with a bit of tongue in cheek.

It took some months for the republic to die and the empire to be born, during which Bokassa prepared for the coronation. He invited the pope to crown him, since the pope had been invited to crown Napoleon. As he had on that earlier occasion, the pope declined, and the new emperor crowned himself. In developing a new court protocol for the empire, he consulted a number of ambassadors, not including the American ambassador. We were not thought to have any particular wisdom about imperial practices. Instead, he asked the Greek ambassador resident in Yaoundé about the court procedures in the period of Constantine XI Palaeologus, the last of the Byzantine emperors in the fifteenth century, someone Bokassa thought might be an appropriate model for his own empire. The Greek republican government had some difficulty coming up with anything useful for this new empire.

Nevertheless, court protocol was developed. We received instructions in diplomatic notes on how to comport ourselves in the presence of His Imperial Majesty. We had to learn how far we should stand from him, what kind of bow we should make, how we should answer questions from the imperial personage. (The answer to any question, we were instructed, was always to be "Yes"; if that answer left something to be desired, you were permitted to say, "Yes, but.") It was announced, although never enforced, that all those who went into the presence of His Imperial Majesty would retreat backward. Bokassa took all this as a great joke. I think he had great fun writing it all up and sending instructions around to bemused governments as to how they should behave in his presence.

A question arose as to how the United States should be represented at the coronation. Bokassa invited President Carter, as he did the pope and the president of France. A certain exchanging of views took place among the diplomatic corps about the level at which we were going to be represented at this solemn occasion. At the end of the day, the French decided to send a minister, Robert Galley, who was then the minister of cooperation, the French aid minister, and his wife. Most other governments, including our own, were represented by their resident ambassadors, although some African states sent ministerial delegations. President Mobutu came from Zaire to be present at the coronation.

Having decided on the level of representation, our government next had the problem of what ceremonial gift should be given on the occasion. The office of protocol had only a limited supply of gifts for coronations, and they were generally not suitable. I had started my tour in Central Africa with a gift for President Bokassa that had referenced a great American president. With that as background, the protocol office in Washington came up with a creative solution. At some point in the 1970s, the Franklin Mint in Philadelphia had produced a series of elegant silver plates engraved in gold with portraits of the presidents of the United States. Some of them had long since been given away: John F. Kennedy, George Washington, Abraham Lincoln, and others. But Chester Arthur and Millard Fillmore were still in stock, so I received two plates to give to the emperor on the occasion of his coronation. He kept me waiting for some hours to present our official gift because I was way down the protocol list of coronation delegations. Ministers got in first, but eventually Bokassa got to me. He expressed enormous pleasure, real or feigned, and said that the plates would have a prominent place in the imperial state museum when it was created. Alas, it was never created, and the plates have long since disappeared.

The coronation was a splendid event indeed. It took place at a sports palace built by the Yugoslav government some years before as part of their aid program. It was a rather handsome basketball stadium seating several thousand people. At one end stood a great golden throne in the shape of an imperial eagle. Bokassa wore a Roman toga embroidered with an estimated hundred thousand pearls. He entered wearing a gold laurel wreath in his hair and carrying an imperial staff. Like Napoleon, he crowned himself in the presence of his family, visiting delegations, and selected guests. He then drove in a golden coach pulled by the eight white horses that had been flown from Paris to draw the new imperial coach from the sports palace to the cathedral. The cathedral was a rather charming brick church built before the Second World War. Bokassa's first cousin, Joachim N'dayen, the archbishop of Bangui, celebrated a solemn mass in honor of the coronation. Archbishop Domenico Enrici, who had been sent to represent the Holy Father on this grand occasion, also graced the mass. The walls of the lofty cathedral apse had been decorated from floor to ceiling with what must have been tens of thousands of flowers flown in from France. Archbishop Enrici sat on his throne to the left of the altar attired as a seventeenth-century prince of the church. On the throne to his right sat Bokassa, wearing an ermine cape of Napoleonic proportions decorated with *B*'s for Bokassa. The children of the empire sang Mozart's coronation mass in high shrill voices, unaware of the irony that the coronation for whom the mass was written was that of the Virgin Mary. It was all rather splendid. The irony of it all was that Bokassa was not a devout Catholic, having briefly become a Muslim some months before during Gaddafi's visit to the republic.

The protocol office had prescribed the dress for the coronation. Men were to wear top hat and morning coat, which, luckily, I had already acquired for presenting my credentials. The requirements for women were rather more elaborate: full-length, long-sleeved dress in a pastel color, with a broad-brimmed hat to match. Thinking that this description sounded like something for the mother of the bride, Susan acquired an appropriate dress from a bridal shop in southern California while we were on home leave. Unfortunately, the French delegate's wife arrived in a short dress, and it was rumored that she had to be sent back to her hotel to change into something more suitable for an imperial coronation. Needless to say, the French were not much amused.

In the early spring of 1978, I received a cable summoning me back to take charge of the department's recently created Office for Combating Terrorism. I was told that I should report in two weeks' time. I protested that for family reasons that would not be possible, and I was allowed to postpone our departure until the middle of the summer. On the occasion of our departure, the diplomatic corps presented us with a bowl of ornamental fruits in ivory and ebony. Bokassa conferred on me the order of Central African Merit. At least, he gave me the decoration, although I have no document to prove that the CAR government ever formally approved it or that my acceptance was permitted by Washington's own prohibitive rules.

It had been an extraordinary three years, but I was not sorry to leave. Had I had more experience in Africa, I might have been more effective in my mission. Although I never returned to Africa, the Bangui years had left their mark on me.

13
Counterterrorism

In April 1978 I received a telegram from Secretary of State Cyrus Vance telling me that I was his choice to be the director of the Office for Combating Terrorism and instructing me to be back in Washington the following week. That was not only personally but also physically impossible. After some negotiations it was agreed that I would stay on in Bangui until June or July. As a result, I didn't take up my job until early August. I took thirty days of home leave. I was surprised to have to make this move, as I had not been in Bangui for the scheduled three years.

I was in charge of the office from 1978 until the late summer / early autumn of 1981, when I entered Spanish-language training in preparation for an assignment as ambassador to Nicaragua. The Office for Combating Terrorism hadn't been around terribly long, in total less than five years. There had been four previous directors, the first being Armin Meyer, who came out of Turkey, where he had been ambassador. He held the job for a very brief period and was followed by Lewis Hoffacker, Douglas Heck, and Heyward Isham. They all moved through the office fairly briskly. Isham was there less than a year, having incurred the wrath of Secretary Vance for reasons that I never fully understood—hence the vacancy to which I was called. The office was created after the series of hostage incidents that began in the late sixties with the kidnapping of Ambassador John Gordon Mein in Guatemala. Assassinated in August 1968, Mein was the first ambassador to be killed by terrorists. Other ambassadors were killed in the 1970s—in Sudan, Lebanon, Cyprus, and one on my watch, Ambassador Adolph "Spike" Dubs, killed in Afghanistan in 1979.

The office was designated D/CT and originally reported to the deputy secretary of state, who at the time was Warren Christopher. Later it was thought that the deputy secretary didn't have sufficient time to devote to supervising the office, and in 1981 it was moved to the under secretary for management, when the office became M/CT. I reported to under secretaries Ben Reed and Dick Kennedy. We were a small, autonomous operation with only six officers—me, a deputy, and four other—and two secretaries. This compact organization subsequently grew after my departure to the rather large bureau that it became following 9/11.

The job had four distinct elements to it. First, the director chaired the interagency working group on terrorism, which brought together some twenty-five federal government agencies that had an interest in terrorism. They included everything from the Postal Service and its concerns about letter bombs to the CIA and the other members of the intelligence community. There was hardly an agency in government that did not have some part of the counterterrorist agenda: the Federal Aviation Administration (FAA) for hijacking, the FBI for domestic hostage situations, the INS for keeping terrorists from crossing into the country, for example. The M/CT director had no authority over those agencies but was able through regularly scheduled meetings to coordinate and get information shared among the agencies that were developing programs and plans relating to counterterrorism.

The director's second function was to be the U.S. focal point for the negotiation of international counterterrorist agreements. That became a highly active part of the office's agenda when in July 1978 the Group of Seven (G7) met in Bonn and agreed on a declaration on terrorism. The G7 called for greater coordination with respect to international terrorist hijacking and made an undertaking to prosecute or extradite those guilty. It was not always easy to get the G7 to agree on the basic principles for handling terrorist incidents or on drafting principles. I was much involved in the negotiation of several declarations and their follow-up. Representatives of the G7 held regular meetings in various capitals, and I usually led the U.S. delegation. That gave me a more traditional diplomatic role. Some of that work also took place at the United Nations, where we succeeded in promoting a series of conventions making various terrorist acts—

hijacking, hostage taking, aviation bombing—criminal offenses that would require punishments by governments or extradition to another concerned country.

The third aspect of the director's role was contingency planning, making sure that our diplomatic establishments had appropriate guidance and policies so that if a mission were faced with a terrorist incident and were itself attacked, it could act in an expeditious way with minimum guidance from Washington. Emergency plans were updated around the world to take possible terrorist incidents into account. But busy embassies with more currently pressing issues were most reluctant to conduct exercises to test their emergency plan, notwithstanding our office's exhortations to do so.

The job's fourth aspect and the one that was the most taxing and for which none of us were particularly well prepared was crisis management. Whenever there was a hijacking or a kidnapping, the department established a task force in the Operations Center (commonly referred to as the Ops Center). The Office for Combating Terrorism directly ran the task forces and provided a substantial part of the crisis staff. The six of us in the office were often present around the clock. We got some help from the geographic bureaus and sometimes from the Diplomatic Security and Consular Affairs bureaus, but at that time we did not benefit from the highly organized task force mechanisms that later shifted the crisis management responsibility to the geographic bureaus.

To prepare myself for the crisis management side of my job, I sought to learn something of how other governments managed the hostage rescue function. There had already been two dramatically successful rescues: by the Germans in Mogadishu in 1977 and by the Israelis in Entebbe in 1976. At a time when we were beginning to stand up our own hostage rescue capability, the Delta Force, I decided to visit the other major rescue forces in Britain, France, Germany, and Israel. I was welcomed in Hereford, England, by the British Twenty-Second SAS, in Bonn by the German GSG 9, in Paris by the GIGN, and in Tel Aviv by the head of Israeli special operations.

All were most willing to show off their technologies and techniques. The German force, under Ulrich Wegener, was intensely proud of its success at Mogadishu. They had an extremely high-tech force and apparently unlimited resources. Colonel Wegener was a national figure and the first German military hero since the Second World War. For reasons of domestic politics and constitutional limitations, the German force was part of the police structure and not part of the military, as in many other countries. In France the GIGN put on a splendid display for me, rappelling into an abandoned apartment block and forcing their way in through the windows of the building. It was clear to me from those trips that we were lagging behind in the development of appropriate response capabilities, but I also became convinced that highly trained, specialized units could be important elements in a terrorist incident response capability. Only when the Delta Force came into operation in November 1979 did we have a comparable capability. I visited Fort Bragg to view the Delta Force's training in the months leading up to its formal commissioning and was impressed by the extraordinary physical and technical abilities of our own unit. Although I was mildly surprised to see that our soldiers affected the mustachioed style of their British counterparts, I had no doubt that we were creating an equally formidable counterterrorist force. As it turned out, in the next several years they were not called on to intervene in any of the incidents that we managed in the counterterrorism office.

There were many incidents over this three-year period. Some of them, hijackings, were of very short duration, while others went on much longer. A case in point was the incident in Bogotá when our ambassador to Colombia, Diego Asencio, along with other ambassadors and guests, was taken hostage at the national day reception of the Dominican Republic.

The Asencio case was significant because it put to the test the basic U.S. policy, then as now, no substantive negotiations, no concessions, and no ransom. The basic philosophy behind these policies was that if we made concessions, terrorists would be emboldened to repeat their violence in order to profit from the willingness of the government to meet their monetary and substantive demands. However, in Bogotá we were not in control of the situation. There were other countries to deal with, some friendly and some not friendly, including the Cubans, the Israelis, the Mexicans, and the Colombians. The outcome was a pacific one. I received a lot of criticism from people who were not responsible for the outcome, including Ambassador Asencio, who felt I had thwarted his effort to get a negotiated outcome. In fact, the Bogotá incident posed a number of real-world problems. Ambassador Asencio, though being held hostage, believed he was still in charge of the embassy. However, we regarded the DCM as being in charge during this time. The DCM was caught in the middle, since he often received conflicting instructions. We tried to stick with the official policy of no negotiation and no concessions. Ambassador Asencio wanted to find a negotiated outcome that would not do too much violence to the policy. Much to our consternation, he and his Mexican colleague became informal advisors to the terrorists inside the Dominican residence. Each day before the formal negotiating sessions in a trailer in front of the residence, Asencio would meet with the terrorist negotiators and advise them on the day's strategy for dealing with their Colombian interlocutors. In fact, at the end of the day, the hostage-takers managed to broker a deal that allowed the terrorists safe passage to Cuba with assurances that their compatriots in Colombian jails would get a fair trial with international observers. Ambassador Asencio and the other ambassadors organized a $5 million ransom payment, put together by the wives of the hostages without our knowledge.

After his release, Diego Asencio wrote a book describing the Bogotá incident entitled *Our Man Is Inside*. In it, he comments rather pejoratively about the management of the crisis from the Washington end. We felt, however, that as the incident dragged on for over two months we developed a suitable strategy for consultation with the Colombian government, for discussions with other governments who had ambassadors inside, and for coordination with our embassy on a very regular basis.

Looking back on this incident, I am aware of its bizarre features. It began on February 27, 1980, at a celebration of the national day of the Dominican Republic at the Dominican ambassador's residence. The terrorists, who were playing football in a park outside the residence, broke out weapons from their sports bags around noon, seized the residence, and took all the guests hostage. They let most of the guests go except for fifteen ambassadors and a journalist who managed to stay inside taking pictures of the unfolding crisis. The terrorists whittled down the number of hostages to a manageable one, keeping only the ambassadors they thought were important, including our ambassador but also those of Israel, Egypt, the Vatican, and a few Latin American countries. Halfway through the incident, the Uruguayan ambassador escaped through a bathroom window, causing great consternation among the remaining hostages, who regarded him ever after as a traitor who had put their lives at risk. The standard view then, as now, is that one hostage should not try to escape unless he can get everybody out at the same time.

We were loath to press the Colombian government to make concessions, but the hostages had a different point of view. They believed that with a little flexibility on the part of the Colombian government they could all be gotten out safely. Negotiations were eventually set up under the auspices of the Red Cross in a trailer outside the front door of the residence. The American and Mexican ambassadors became the lead advisors to the terrorist negotiating team. They, of course, were very keen to negotiate an outcome with concessions on the part of the Colombian government. This caused a great problem for us because we did not want to see a negotiated outcome that would result in concessions being made to the terrorists. Yet our man inside was quite enthusiastic at that prospect. The instructions that he was given to stand back a little bit were ill received by him. We gave these instructions to him through the DCM, who was running the embassy. The ambassador took the view, however, that he was still ambassador, and since he was still in the country, he could give the DCM orders and not the other way around. We regarded the situation, as one might expect, as one in which the ambassador was operating under duress, was not a free agent, and hence could not be in charge of the embassy. Settlement was finally reached after sixty days. The ambassadors were released after their wives were able to raise something on the order of $250,000 each for a package deal of $5 million, which was given in cash to the terrorists prior to their departure to Cuba. Again, this was not something that American counterterrorist policy favored, but events moved outside our control in terms of managing this aspect of the negotiations.

Not all governments shared our tough no-negotiation stance. In the Bogotá case, the Israelis, through a special envoy they sent from Tel Aviv, pressed the Colombian government very hard to make concessions. The Israelis do not have a no-concession policy and have made concessions and released prisoners when their own officials have been taken hostage. The two countries most keen on concessions were Israel and the Vatican. The Vatican was very anxious to get its nuncio out. They also sent in a special envoy, their nuncio from Argentina, Pio Laghi, who subsequently became the first Vatican diplomat to hold the title of nuncio to the United States. He joined the Israelis in urging the Colombians to make concessions.

There were many unexpected and surprising twists to this story. The journalist who was inside managed to get some of his photographs out in the food containers that the Red Cross was sending to feed the prisoners inside. Among the pictures that were shown in the Bogotá press was a picture of the nuncio cleaning toilets. The Vatican exerted considerable pressure on the Colombian government to get the photo suppressed. Archbishops, in the Vatican's view, were not to be seen cleaning toilets, particularly in a Catholic country. This, in Rome's view, was not an appropriate way to display the pope's representative in public. What had happened was that the hostages developed a system under which everybody shared responsibilities to keep the place clean and get the cooking done. There were no first-class citizens in this regard. It was humorously rumored that when the captive nuncio celebrated mass each morning, even the

Egyptian and Israeli ambassadors attended, as that was the only wine available as the siege went on.

Whenever there was an incident, our office always set up a crisis team and, depending on the nature of the incident, kept in touch with the appropriate agencies involved and with the White House. I had an excellent relationship with Colonel Bill Odom, then in charge of terrorism on the NSC staff. That helped, because by staying in touch with the person who had the responsibility in the White House for terrorism, we were able to mitigate the pressure to achieve rapid results.

The only crises of any length during my tenure were the Asencio hostage incident and the kidnapping of a Peace Corps volunteer, Richard Starr, who was held for a year and a half in Colombia. He was also ransomed, not by the U.S. government but through the good offices of the columnist Jack Anderson, who used his personal foundation to raise money for Starr's release. There was relatively little political interest in Starr's case. His mother tried hard to create interest and to stir up the government to take more vigorous action. Her pressure was manageable, at least until Jack Anderson became involved. We were quite skittish about Anderson's involvement, since his intention to pay the demanded ransom ran counter to established U.S. policy. However, Anderson wrote passionately about the case in his column, suggesting that the department was not sufficiently engaged in getting Starr released. In the end, after consulting Deputy Secretary Cristopher, our office agreed to facilitate the entry into Colombia of Anderson's envoy, who was carrying the ransom money in his personal luggage. The payment was duly made, and Starr was released. However, the case ended on a surprising note. Starr emerged from his captivity in the jungle with his pet parrot. He insisted that he would not return to the United States without it. Unfortunately, the parrot belonged to an endangered species, and U.S. regulations prohibited the importation of such parrots. The military, which had sent a plane to bring Starr home, was persuaded to fly to a base in Florida where there would be no customs inspection of Starr and his accompanying feathered friend.

In hijackings, the Office for Combating Terrorism was almost always secondary because the incidents were usually under the jurisdiction of the FAA or the FBI or both. In one case, we were able to provide a critical piece of information that reduced the U.S. government's concerns. An Irish airliner was hijacked flying from Dublin to Paris. On board were a lot of people with names such as O'Neill, Donovan, and the like who might or might not have been Americans, so we took an immediate interest in this case. The plane was forced to land on the French coast at Le Touquet. The hijacker claimed to represent the Third Secret of Fátima, a group utterly unknown in our counterterrorist files. The CIA did research to figure out if this was a terrorist group but could come up with nothing. By chance, one of the members of my task force, Richard Higgins, said he thought he knew the answer. He said that the terrorist had to be a crazy Catholic, because the Third Secret of Fátima was the third of the three messages given by the Virgin Mary in 1917 to three children in Fátima, Portugal. The third secret had never been revealed and had been sealed and held by the Vatican ever since. Dick's insight turned out to be true. The hijacker was a deranged former monk who was trying to hold the Vatican to ransom in order to get the Third Secret of Fátima released. He was easily persuaded to surrender by the French authorities.

The hijackings were all fairly routine affairs and were invariably resolved peacefully. In each case we set up a task force in the Operations Center—the office that was responsible at the time for all terrorist incident task forces, which, as the director, I led. This practice later changed, and the responsibility passed to the geographic bureaus for managing incidents in their region. We slowly developed a crisis-response capability, drawing on the resources of other government agencies. In the course of 1979, one of the major concerns of the interagency counterterrorism working group was the adequacy of our response capability to deal with terrorist incidents. The Germans had already had a notable success with their counterterrorism force at Mogadishu using the GSG 9. The Israelis had prevailed at Entebbe using their dedicated force. The United States at that time did not have any such qualified counterterrorism unit. An ad hoc group, Bluelight, had been set up at Fort Bragg, but it was just that, an ad hoc group. It was quite proud of what it could do, but it did not have the same qualities and experience as the international units. At some point in 1978 or 1979, the Defense Department decided to create what has since become known as the Delta Force to replace the ad hoc group. The commissioning exercise for the Delta Force ironically took place on the same night in 1979 that the hostages were taken in Iran. I was the State Department's representative at that commissioning exercise.

Our own capability came online just when we were for the first time faced with a major hostage rescue situation. Individual Americans had been taken hostage before, and some of them had died in a variety of situations. In Lebanon, Sudan, and Guatemala, our ambassadors had been kidnapped and killed. At the time and indeed for some considerable time afterward, the U.S. government did not acknowledge that anything called the Delta Force existed, although so much had been written about Colonel Charles Beckwith and his men that it was hardly possible to say there was no such unit. I was the principal point of contact for the Department of State with the military planners on the Joint Staff at the Pentagon and with the counterterrorist group at Fort Bragg. Almost immediately after the Iran hostage incident broke out, senior levels at the Pentagon contacted me asking whether I could be of help by getting photographs from department records of all the hostages. This was something that I could quite easily have done, but I was quickly told that for the duration of the crisis the secretary of state would handle all contacts directly with the Pentagon, with the deputy secretary acting as his deputy. This was a considerable shock to the military planners, who had been used to dealing at the working level with me and others on my staff. They were reluctant to take routine requests for information up through the cabinet level to get decisions. However, as the crisis unfolded, it became an increasingly visible political issue for the president; and for decisions about negotiations and a hostage rescue attempt, planning was handled by a small group, not including the Office for Combating Terrorism. We were not participants in the planning in any way, either diplomatically or militarily. We were somewhat involved with the task force that was created at the very start, for the first twenty-four hours under my direction, but the issue quickly developed into a political crisis of such importance that a whole separate team was brought together, which operated around the clock for over 440 days until the hostages were finally released in early 1980.

My colleagues in the office and I discussed the rescue option without being privy to the details of the planning. We agreed that a rescue would be enormously difficult and would depend to a very substantial degree on the intelligence that could be obtained about the location of the hostages within the embassy compound. In all successful hostage rescue attempts, the key has been the ability to identify, with great precision, where the hostages were located. The United States never got to test its intelligence because the rescue force never got to Tehran.

During the year of the Tehran crisis, there were two other major incidents for which I had lead responsibility. One was the kidnapping and subsequent execution of Ambassador Spike Dubs in Afghanistan on February 14, 1979, during which I chaired the crisis task force. The incident did not last long: less than six hours from the time Ambassador Dubs was captured in his official car en route to a meeting in the center of Kabul until the Soviet military units stormed the hotel room in which he was being held. We did what the textbooks recommended. We opened a line to our embassy and remained in contact with the embassy staff. They in turn were in constant communication with the hotel. There was a minute-by-minute dialogue with the embassy on what was going on and what could or could not be done to persuade the Russians and the Afghans to use restraint. In the end the Russians, whom we tried to contact at a senior level in Moscow, did not use restraint. We were never in control of the situation. The Russian motives remain under debate. To my surprise and dismay, it was subsequently alleged by Deputy Assistant Secretary Steven Pieczenik in an opinion piece in the *Washington Post* that I, as the task force director, had ordered the Soviets to assault the room in order to free Ambassador Dubs. That accusation was entirely false, as a department investigation concluded after interviewing those who were part of the crisis team in the Operations Center.

Dr. Pieczenik's accusations did, however, focus our attention on a real problem: the relative lack of training and expertise in the department for counterterrorism crisis management. He had charged that we were untrained amateurs. Dr. Pieczenik had been in the crisis team as an advisor to the under secretary for management. He was a trained psychiatrist with a PhD in international relations, an extraordinarily able man who constantly chivvied the department for its failures to develop a truly professional crisis response capability. He believed the Dubs case was an example of bungled crisis response. It is hard for me to be dispassionate on this point. We did what we could, but we were not, it is fair to acknowledge, highly trained professional crisis managers. Although embassy personnel were at the hotel where Dubs was being held, they had no influence when the Soviets went in with force. The actual circumstances under which Ambassador Dubs was killed will always remain obscure. The incident did lead to greater awareness of the need to have better internal coordination. We began to develop systematic crisis management exercises. We emphasized that embassies ought to be prepared for hostage taking and other kinds of crises and be ready to organize themselves to deal with them.

We also had other lessons to learn. When our embassy in Pakistan was assaulted and burned in November 1980, by chance neither the ambassador nor the DCM was in the embassy when the mob tried to take it over. It was not clear who was in charge or who was to manage the internal defense of the embassy. Was it the senior military officer, the political counselor, or the security officer? Various aspects of the embassy's defense were the responsibility of different people. This issue was of great importance once the staff withdrew into the vault and were in danger of being fried to death in a building that was burning around them. In the end the political counselor took charge. The incident was resolved peacefully. It is now an absolute requirement that there be a chain of command that goes beyond the ambassador and the DCM so that it is understood in advance who will give orders and who has the authority to do so.

Terrorism in those years was already a global problem. We were dealing with the Baader-Meinhof gang in Germany, the Red Brigades in Italy, and the Japanese Red Army—not to mention an array of Marxist terrorist/revolutionary groups in Latin America. They were all extreme radical groups bent on destruction of the modern capitalist bourgeois state. International terrorism in that period really had three dimensions that we worried about. The first was Latin American terrorism, largely Colombian and Central American. There we presumed that the terrorists were supported by the Cubans through the Soviets. They hoped ultimately to become the government of the country. Second, there were the three radical groups mentioned above. They were highly disciplined but had no pretensions to take over the government, unlike the Latin American terrorist groups. A third element was Palestinian. It was composed of many groups: the Popular Front for the Liberation of Palestine, the Democratic Front for the Liberation of Palestine, and Fatah, the militant branch of the PLO. The purpose of all these groups was to gain a homeland for the Palestinian people. They believed that their cause would be advanced by taking violent action against those states that supported Israel, notably the United States.

A fourth group, which had a specifically American connection at the time, was the Irish Republican Army. It did almost all its fundraising in the United States, most notably in South Boston. The United States was reluctant to take any action to control this fundraising, even though the British repeatedly pointed out to us that the money obtained was used to purchase weapons being used in terrorist acts against British forces in Northern Ireland. We stood back for domestic political reasons. The IRA never targeted us as all the other groups had.

Two other aspects that gained great attention were the vulnerability of our infrastructure and the possibility of chemical and biological terrorism. We had a number of exercises, scenarios developed by the Centers for Disease Control (CDC) in Atlanta, designed to get the U.S. government thinking about how to handle these very difficult issues. These issues had become more salient as senior policymakers had become increasingly aware that developing chemical and biological weapons was very much easier than anybody had previously thought. This was apparent to us in the counterterrorism world in 1981 when several ineffective efforts were made by criminals to poison food and bottled drinks. Another area where there was concern was offshore oil. Oil platforms were known to be vulnerable, as were electric power grids. You didn't hear much about either of those at that time, but the navy developed Seal Team Six with the capability of dealing with hostages taking oil rigs or ships at sea. Some thought was given to problems of electric power grids, although protecting them turned out to be extraordinarily difficult, because a few rifle shots in the right places could do an enormous amount of damage. We exercised our response capabilities with such scenarios in mind.

We not only conducted exercises among ourselves but also participated in several major exercises involving more esoteric threats in the realm of chemical and biological terrorism. These would typically involve an array of agencies. Counterterrorist exercises took place in many countries. I attended one in New Zealand in which the New Zealand Special Air Service took part in a hostage rescue assault scenario. The prime minister personally took part, as did his close associates. Counterterrorism had become a subject of global interest and concern.

One of the perennial questions was this one: Should we spend time thinking about the causes of violence? Could we anticipate situations that would lead to violence and find solutions to the problems that promoted it? In most cases there was no easy answer. The demand of the Basques, the Corsicans, and the Palestinians for the creation of political units out of existing states was one that we could not support. It was equally unlikely that we would support the radical groups whose antipathy was to the whole concept of modern capitalism, even though they had no territorial agenda.

Another question always on the table was whether this violence was being orchestrated from Moscow. Were the Soviets behind it all? There were profound differences of opinion on this point. Claire Sterling, in her 1981 book, *The Terror Network*, demonstrated to her satisfaction that virtually all these groups were agents of the Soviet Union. This book had a serious impact at senior levels of the Reagan administration, including on William Casey, the director of the CIA. Claire Sterling and I often clashed in academic settings. She clearly thought that I was both naive and soft on Communism. The evidence for systematic Soviet backing was, in my view, circumstantial. There were very few groups about which you could convincingly argue that they acted at Moscow's direction. Certainly, there were many groups that received financial assistance from Moscow or from the German Democratic Republic or from other eastern European states. Broadly, these groups had objectives that were consistent with the foreign policy of the Soviet Union. There were training bases in Yemen, Syria, and Iraq for some of the Palestinian groups. It was clear that the Soviets supported the Syrians and the Iraqis and were sympathetic to groups that could be described as national liberation movements. The Soviets took the position consistently that struggles of national liberation were not terrorism. They were wars, and in wars violence was one of those things that one might deplore but that couldn't be escaped, particularly in a cause that was "just." For the Palestinians, there were no innocent Israelis, whether they were in uniform or not. We, of course, never accepted that all Israelis were therefore acceptable targets for terrorist violence.

Whether or not the Soviets were behind all the violence in the world, we always tried to take the position that if innocents were being targeted, it did not matter what the cause was. Civilians had to be protected even in circumstances where the underlying equities of justice were not necessarily clear. The whole concept of innocence is a very tricky one. Almost all our successful international efforts focused on aviation terrorism. We succeeded in getting the international community to endorse a series of conventions, such as The Hague and Montréal conventions, explicitly stating that hijacking and bombing of aircraft were not legitimate under any circumstances. We did achieve a fairly wide consensus on this point, even from countries that otherwise supported terrorism.

Against this background, we focused on Libya as one of the principal patron states of terrorism. I was sent on a mission to Tripoli, where our embassy had been besieged by an angry mob. Two years later, in 1980, the State Department closed the embassy in part because of Libya's support for terrorism. When I was there, that closure lay ahead. In 1978 the foreign minister, Ali Treki, assured me that the government of Libya had no interest in terrorism and had a policy that it would not allow hijacked aircraft to land in Libya and would not make concessions to terrorists. However, he made clear that Libya's support for the liberation struggle of the Palestinians would not stop and that in Libya's view, their struggle was not terrorism.

Following the failure of the rescue attempt of the hostages in Tehran, increasing attention focused on the political dimension of military rescue. The military regularly hosted planning exercises in which the State Department players stressed the difficulties in getting host government authorization for military use. In one joint exercise with the Canadians, we simulated a takeover of our consulate general in Toronto. The Canadian crisis management structure, composed of very senior officials, participated fully. Cabinet members operated out of the cabinet crisis room in Ottawa with the full participation not only of the Royal Canadian Mounted Police but also of the provincial police in Ontario. As we played this incident on the American side, questions arose about whether we could use our military capability. The Canadians were horrified that we would even consider doing such a thing in their country. But the whole Special Operations command structure that we had created presupposed, if not the use of our military capability, then the prepositioning of it. The worst-case scenario always led to military deployment to the nearest possible site.

At the State Department, we were constantly in the position of raising red flags and saying deployment wasn't going to be so easy, given the political constraints of other countries. In general, the State Department was very skittish about the use of the military and always felt, with the legacy of the failed Iranian rescue attempt in mind, that the risks of failure were very high and that the political costs of failure would be equally high. So typically, our counterterrorist philosophy was to play for time—more time, and more time—until such point as the terrorists themselves gave in or began taking lives. The killing of hostages always provided a basis for the use of force.

President Reagan's team put that question about the use of force to me in February 1981. One Saturday shortly after the administration had taken over, Secretary of State Alexander Haig called and told me that on Monday at one o'clock in the afternoon I would be briefing the president and the National Security Council on the state of our readiness. The president wanted to find out whether we were better off than we were before and what progress we had made in developing a policy and structure for dealing with terrorism. The secretary then asked me what I was going to say to the president. So I told him. I emphasized that we had come a long way in terms of improving our military capability and that we had in place a pretty good coordination mechanism that defined crisis roles in a variety of scenarios. Before I went to the White House for the briefing, the secretary told me that I might be met with some suspicion by the president and others because I would be seen as the Carter counterterrorist, and the Carter administration was felt to be weak on terrorism. I do not think it was weak, but certainly the incoming administration had a negative perception of Carter.

Although nervous to be standing at a podium in the cabinet room, I gave the briefing to the president, who was joined by the vice president, the director of the CIA, the head of the FBI, and a number of National Security Council members. They seemed reasonably satisfied. The person who took the greatest interest in the briefing was Counselor to the President Ed Meese, who asked several pertinent questions. After eating a couple of jellybeans, the president dozed off, which was quite unnerving. However, his team was genuinely interested in what could be done to improve the quality of our coordination and response capabilities. In fact, although the administration wanted a tougher approach in general, they kept me on for another six months and made no dramatic changes to our policy.

One of the things that did change was that almost from the first day he took office, Secretary Haig announced in a message to all our ambassadors that counterterrorism would become a major priority of the administration. The interesting result was that we were inundated with messages from our ambassadors around the world explaining what good things they were doing in terms of counterterrorism. It was reminiscent of the arrival of the Carter administration and the announcement that human rights were the major foreign policy concern of that administration, when ambassadors immediately sent messages on what they were doing on human rights. Looking back over those years, one of the things that is most striking to me is the desire of career ambassadors to be highly responsive to political leadership. The day that political agendas change, career officers do the maximum to show that they are on board and that they are not fighting the new administration's agenda, although many in the new administration think of career people as wedded to the agenda of the predecessor administration.

Early in the summer of 1981, Ambassador Robert Sayre, former assistant secretary of state for Latin American affairs, was chosen as my successor. I briefed him over breakfast in the State Department cafeteria and urged him to develop close working relations with the NSC's leading counterterrorist, an army major general. He bristled at my suggestion that he call on him at the White House, retorting that ambassadors did not normally call on major generals. I thought that interagency relations were in for a nasty shock. As for me, I was about to embark on an entirely new endeavor, one that I never imagined would take me to revolutionary Nicaragua.

14
Life in Revolutionary Nicaragua

I was an unlikely choice for the role of ambassador to Nicaragua. I was not a Latin Americanist and had never served in the region. When selected, I did not speak Spanish and could read it only at the level of a high school sophomore, the last level at which I had encountered the language. For the previous three and a half years I had been the Carter administration's director of the Office for Combating Terrorism. As Secretary Haig had put it to me in his own inimitable style early in the Reagan administration, I had been "pushing the wet noodle of terrorism uphill" for the past three years. A new face was needed to confront the terrorist menace, which Haig had identified as the principal priority for the new administration. Clearly a limp-wristed Carterite was not the man for the job.

The department's solution to the problem was to suggest that I go to Rome as deputy chief of mission. After several positive meetings with the incoming political nominee for ambassador, Maxwell Rabb, I was chosen. And so in the first months of 1981 I began to study Italian to prepare myself for a welcome assignment in Europe after having spent twelve years in a series of hardship posts in Africa and South Asia.

The Fates were not to be so kind. I do not know how my name came to the attention of the assistant secretary for Latin America, Thomas Enders, but in May 1981 he called me to his spacious office on the sixth floor of the department and offered me the ambassadorship in Nicaragua, saying that my experience in counterterrorism would be a useful preparation for the growing conflict in Central America. I was gratified by the offer but politely turned it down, noting that I did not have the right qualifications for the job and, in any case, was already going to Rome, a post of which I had been dreaming for a very long time. I assumed that my refusal put an end to the matter. Alas, that was not so. Enders was not a man to take no as a final answer. Several weeks later I encountered Enders as I was walking out of the C Street entrance of the department. He waved me over and said he had been meaning to call me. He told me that he had talked to the secretary, and they had decided that I would be going to Nicaragua. Protests were of no use; Rabb had been informed that he would have to find another DCM. As graciously as I could and knowing the deep disappointment this would bring to my family, I said, of course, I was honored to have been chosen.

One of the most engaging features of the Reagan administration was the president's personal interest in his ambassadors. While I was studying Spanish at the Foreign Service Institute (FSI), I was told that the president would be calling me the next morning at ten o'clock to personally ask me to be his ambassador in Managua. I was told to be at my desk to await the call. Unfortunately, the management of FSI had decided to hold a fire drill at the same time. I explained my dilemma to the FSI administration, and with their blessing, I remained in my cubicle awaiting the president's call while the other employees streamed into the street. The president graciously asked me to be his representative in Nicaragua, and I expressed my pleasure at being his ambassador. The call was brief, but it was reassuring that the president had taken the time to call. He was again generous with his time as we were going out to post. He met with me, Susan, and our two daughters in the Oval Office. After the ritual exchange of cuff links and pins, I ventured the thought that he was sending me to a hot spot. With characteristic cheerfulness the president replied, "We'll see if we can't cool it down." Little did I know how hot it would actually get.

Being chosen was one thing; getting me there was another. It was clearly essential that I upgrade my limited Spanish. I knew a few words, having lived for a year in Mexico City in the mid-1940s when my father was an exchange professor at the Colegio de México, but I could not speak the language and had a minimal reading knowledge. The personnel department was accommodating, and Susan and I plunged into what was to be almost six months of intensive Spanish at the Foreign Service Institute while the paperwork for my nomination made its slow progress through the White House, State Department, and congressional bureaucracies.

The FSI experience was intense. I had studied Urdu at FSI twenty years before, but the pace had been relaxed and the stakes less high. In the case of Spanish, Susan and I were the only two students, and we sat in class six hours a day and several more in the institute's language lab, working our way through the increasingly complex dialogues that formed the basis of the audiolingual method then in vogue at FSI. When we became more fluent, we listened to and transcribed the daily news on the Spanish-language service of Voice of America. We made steady progress and at the end of six months were certified to have reached advanced professional competence, the much-desired 4 level. But I was far from confident that I would be able to handle the complexities of our policy in Nicaragua.

These many months of language study allowed me to begin to immerse myself in the political and economic issues on the administration's current agenda. Since my appointment had not been publicly announced, nor had my name gone forward to the Senate, the more sensitive briefings I would later receive were not then available to me. However, I did meet regularly with the office director for Central American affairs, the feisty and hard-working Craig Johnstone, and began to get a feel for the intense debates raging within the department and with the White House about the direction of U.S. policy in the region. Cold War hawks at the White House were arguing for a tough confrontational policy vis-à-vis the Sandinistas, backed by a vigorous CIA-led covert action program designed to force them from power. The State Department, under Enders's crafty and controversial leadership, pressed for a tough but creative negotiating stance designed to limit the Sandinistas' depredations in the region and their hostile policies toward their internal opposition. These two tendencies persisted throughout my tenure, with the White House view gaining ascendancy. Our covert programs led to a hardening of the Sandinista position and an even less responsive approach to our negotiating initiatives. In 1982, while the State Department retained the upper hand, Enders was authorized to carry a comprehensive package of proposals to Managua in September, while I was still at FSI. I was not a part of the planning for this effort, but the Central American desk kept me informed of its details.

At some point in November, my appointment became official inside the administration, but the formal announcement was not made until January. I had completed all the required paperwork detailing my assets, setting out my past record, and certifying to all interested parties (including Congress) that I had no ethical or other questionable problems in my past. Since the White House had blessed the appointment, and even though I was not yet announced, I was eligible to attend the Ambassadorial Seminar in early December. Known somewhat derisively in the service as little more than a charm school, this three-day seminar was designed to introduce new ambassadors to the intricacies of the Washington bureaucracy and the obligations and responsibilities of a chief of mission. Only two of the twelve new ambassadors in the course—Walter Cutler, who was going to Tunisia, and I—came from the career service. Not only was I a participant in the seminar, but since I had been the coordinator for counterterrorism, I was asked to make the presentation on terrorism. The highlight of the course was not any of the State Department presentations but rather the trip on the third day to the Central Intelligence Agency. There we were briefed by the deputy director for operations, Clair George, an old friend from India days, and offered a dinner hosted by the CIA deputy director, Admiral Bobby Inman. George's presentation before the dinner enthralled his audience as he set out in considerable and frank detail the role and modus operandi of a CIA station chief and the agency's expectations for close cooperation between the chief of station and the chief of mission. We were captivated. Little did I know at the time how fragile that relationship between the agency and the department was going to be in the special context of the "secret war" in Nicaragua.

The White House announced the president's intention to nominate me on January 13, 1982. The local press in Managua immediately picked up on the story and viewed my selection at first as positive, contrasting me with my colleagues in San Salvador and Guatemala, whose "awful facets" the press decried. Subsequent commentary would prove less favorable, as the press began to speculate on the role a former counterterrorist would play in dealing with the Sandinista revolution. Indeed, the Soviet press picked up on my appointment and made sinister references to my counterterrorist background. *Pravda* alleged in mid-January that I was a well-known expert in crushing national liberation movements, and the Sandinista press in turn replayed these reports.

My hearing before the Senate Foreign Relations Committee, together with that of Otto Reich, named to be the new assistant administrator of the Agency for International Development for Latin America, was scheduled for February 9. At the hearing, only the chairman, Senator Jesse Helms (R-NC), and Senator Edward Zorinsky (D-NE) were present. Otto Reich went first, stressing to the committee his moving personal history as a Cuban refugee exile committed to promoting the president's vigorous anti-Communist freedom agenda. As a graduate of the University of North Carolina (Senator Helms's wife's university), he had a very easy time of it during the hearing.

When my turn came, I did not make a formal statement, limiting myself to noting that Nicaragua was an "extraordinarily difficult" country where U.S. interests were being challenged in a fundamental way. I had met earlier in the day with Senator Zorinsky to go over my assessment of the situation on the ground, and he was satisfied that I would bring a balanced approach to the job. Helms was relatively gentle with me, noting both my "impressive" background and my lack of experience in the region. In my answers to questions I tried to keep my options open, noting that we wanted to maintain relations with the Sandinistas on the "basis of equality and mutual respect" but that we also had serious concerns about their internal economic and political policies and the military buildup that was taking place.

I underscored the implications of this buildup for the projection of Sandinista and Cuban influence in the region. As is often the case, I then had to answer in writing an extensive series of questions, most of which focused on our past and present economic assistance program to the government and private sector in Nicaragua and our assessment of the military buildup. I was confirmed without opposition several days later. My swearing in as ambassador took place before a small group of colleagues and family members in the Jefferson Room on the eighth floor of the State Department just outside the larger Benjamin Franklin Room, usually reserved for such occasions. Walter Stoessel, the under secretary of state for political affairs, presided.

Final preparations for departure included seemingly endless briefings at all agencies with programs in Nicaragua and with all offices in the department with some responsibility or oversight. The briefings also included outside bodies such as the Council of the Americas and, in New York, the Business Council for International Understanding. While only a few American companies were doing business in Nicaragua at this point, considerable interest in and support for the private sector continued, and the companies repeatedly encouraged me to maintain as many private sector contacts as possible.

Recognizing that I was a relative neophyte in all things Latin American, the department arranged through the Bureau of Intelligence and Research for me to meet with a panel of Latin American experts drawn from Washington think tanks and universities. They represented a broad ideological and intellectual cross section of the community and included Mark Falcoff of the American Enterprise Institute and Bob Leiken of Georgetown University. They introduced me to the history, political culture, and dynamics of Latin American revolutions in ways that I greatly valued. Many of those scholars and commentators remained sources of advice long after I left Nicaragua.

One somewhat unusual stop on the briefing circuit that I arranged myself was to the United States Conference of Catholic Bishops. I knew the Catholic Church was an important player in Latin American politics, and I wished to have the church's assessment. At the conference's modern headquarters in northeastern Washington, a highly articulate young priest, Bryan Hehir, described some of the ecclesiastical dilemmas I would encounter in Nicaragua. He noted the church's sympathy for some of the social goals of the Sandinista revolution but also concerns about efforts to manipulate the media in ways often critical of the church. He emphasized the Vatican's concerns about priests active in the revolution who held posts of official responsibility, most noteworthy being the Sandinistas' foreign minister, Maryknoll priest Miguel d'Escoto.

Of all the official briefings I received, the highlight was my meeting at the CIA, where I had a long discussion with the chief of the Latin American Division, Duane "Dewey" Claridge. Something of a legend in his own time, he epitomized the can-do spirit for which he was famous. Dressed in cowboy boots and a safari suit, he radiated optimism about the prospects for the anti-Sandinista forces as a result of his initial contacts with the Nicaraguan opposition. He had just returned from a secret meeting in Mexico City with Eden Pastora, the famed Comandante Zero, who had recently taken up arms against the Sandinistas from bases in Costa Rica. Claridge had come back much impressed with Pastora's ability to mobilize internal opposition to the Sandinistas. Knowing little of the reality on the ground, I remained largely silent, although I found his exuberant optimism exaggerated and somewhat naive, as indeed it turned out to be. No mention was made of the presidential finding that was to lead to the events of March 15, the day of my arrival.

At this point I had been well briefed and felt as prepared as any ambassador for a post in new and unfamiliar surroundings. In some important ways, I was wrong. By the time I got to Managua, I had held a wide variety of jobs in the Foreign Service, including ambassador in a small African country. But I was ill prepared for the special position of an American ambassador in revolutionary Nicaragua. Having inherited the proconsular image of my predecessors, I found myself living in a fishbowl. Everything I did was news. Everyone knew my face. I could not go out without being greeted by people on the street, usually with friendly smiles and welcome. Although in the Sandinista press I was taunted as "Mr. Cuentón," the storyteller or liar, I was always treated with personal respect, perhaps on the assumption that I had special power and influence. This constant attention and publicity, in some quarters bordering on adulation, was not healthy. I had been thrust into a political role as the agent of regime change for which I was unprepared and unenthusiastic, and I was ill prepared for this high-visibility role. Many Nicaraguans, both Sandinistas and anti-Sandinistas, tried to take advantage of that fact by playing up to my vanity and increasing fascination with publicity and image.

◆ ◆ ◆

Nothing prepared me for my arrival in Managua on March 15, 1982. Six years earlier I had arrived as a first-time ambassador in the Central African Republic to the beat of African drums and the sight of dancing half-clad native women. It was not so in Managua. Although our arrival was in the same tropical humidity, the atmosphere was totally different. As we emerged from the plane bringing us from Miami, a crowd of reporters, both foreign and local, and a forest of microphones and TV cameras besieged us. All were there, together with senior embassy staff and Sandinista protocol, to greet the new American ambassador.

Clearly, expectations ran high on that hot, sultry March evening. The embassy had been without an ambassador for over six months. My predecessor, Lawrence Pezzullo, had left the previous summer. I had been briefed about the difficulties I would face in the highly charged context of our strained bilateral relations, and I had prepared an optimistic and slightly sententious arrival statement. I quoted Nicaragua's national poet, Reuben Dario, to the effect that the Eagle and the Condor would have to live together in "the plenitude of harmony and strength."

I was totally unprepared for the first question put to me: "Mr. Ambassador, while you were flying from Miami to Managua, Comandante Ortega has imposed a state of emergency, because this morning the CIA blew up the bridges connecting Nicaragua and Honduras. What do you think about this start to your mission?" Like a deer caught in the headlights of history, I was stunned and almost speechless. I had been briefed before departing Washington on a presidential "finding" authorizing limited harassment operations against the Sandinistas, but no one had thought to tell me of the planned destruction of the bridges or the fact that the operation was to be carried out on the very day of my arrival. Still uncertain of my Spanish, which I had been studying intensively over the previous six months, I gulped and muttered something about my intention to discuss all the difficult outstanding issues between our two governments with Comandante Ortega as soon as possible. The Sandinistas had already proclaimed 1982 as the Year of Unity against Aggression, and this was my introduction to what was to be my two-year exposure to the diplomacy of regime change.

I presented my credentials not to Ortega but rather to the junior member of the ruling junta, Rafael Córdova Rivas, a portly cattle farmer with little political influence who was relegated to the relatively unimportant ceremonial role of welcoming new ambassadors. Our meeting was uncontentious. I assured him that we sought "a sincere dialogue" based on considerations of mutual respect and "the totality of our preoccupations." The English press inaccurately reported that I had agreed to "revise" our policies, a mistranslation of the Spanish *revisar*, which means only to review.

In a sense, this arrival was symptomatic of much that I was to experience over the next twenty-seven months: the conflict between two Washington policies that differed in both strategic objectives and tactical imperatives. On the one hand, we sought a reasonable accommodation with the revolutionary government on condition that it cease its export of revolution to its neighbor El Salvador and that it live up to its original commitments to a pluralistic political system and a mixed economy. This was the State Department's view. The alternative policy, championed in the White House and at CIA headquarters in Langley, was that nothing short of regime change would satisfy America's long-term interests in the region. As it turned out, there was not to be room in the Central American nest for both the republican North American eagle and the revolutionary Latin American condor.

THE CHURCH AND THE REVOLUTION

Of all the clichés about Latin America, the most prevalent in the 1980s was that Latin America was Catholic. I started with the assumption that the cliché must be true about Nicaragua, even revolutionary Nicaragua, although I did not fully comprehend what it meant to be Catholic in the Nicaraguan context. With that assumption in mind, I had consulted Father Bryan Hehir of the Conference of Catholic Bishops in Washington prior to my confirmation hearings. Liberation theology was in its heyday, and the Sandinistas had embraced the preferential option for the poor. From the point of view of the American church, much that the revolution was doing had positive aspects, particularly its efforts to eliminate illiteracy and promote the social and economic welfare of the marginalized lower strata of Nicaraguan society. But the church worried about such aspects of the revolution as its efforts to limit the church's role, particularly its media and educational outreach, and signs of the antidemocratic outlook of some leading comandantes.

After we had explored these complex issues, Father Hehir said he would like to ask me an impertinent question. Was I Catholic? I said that I was. He followed that question with several others. Where did I plan to go to church in Managua? The local parish church, I answered. Was I living in the ambassador's residence? Naturally, I replied. Did I know who my parish priest was? With some exasperation I replied that of course I didn't, since I had never been to Nicaragua and knew no clergy there. Following this brief catechism, Father Hehir said that if I decided to do what I said I was going to do, I would be making a large political statement.

My parish priest in the little Church of Santo Domingo in the neighborhood of the residence had as its pastor Archbishop Miguel

Obando y Bravo. When the Managua Cathedral collapsed in 1972, the archbishop had moved his residence and office to the parish of Santo Domingo. Obando, later to be made a cardinal by Pope John Paul II, had originally been a supporter of the revolution but had emerged in the course of 1980 and 1981 as a severe critic of the Sandinistas. While extremely careful in his public statements, he was seen to be one of the leaders of the opposition. If the American ambassador went to his church, it would be a strong message as to where the U.S. government stood.

I was initially skeptical of Father Hehir's analysis. It hardly seemed possible that my private faith and mass-going habits would be of interest to anyone. They certainly had not been in past assignments. I was quickly to be proven wrong. We arrived on March 15, only a few days before Holy Week, and, as was our custom, we decided to go to the usual services beginning on Holy Thursday. For convenience and perhaps to test Father Hehir's admonition, we went to Santo Domingo, where the mass was to be celebrated by the archbishop, whom up to that point I had not had time to meet. Television crews were present to cover the mass and in particular the archbishop's sermon, in the hope that he would make some new criticism of the revolution. To my consternation, I found that I was an equal source of interest. I was filmed receiving Communion and on coming out of the church was embraced by parishioners, mainly elderly ladies of the upper middle class who proclaimed that they now had the kind of ambassador they had always dreamed of. Perplexed, I asked why. The answer: Because you are *here*!

It was quickly apparent that if I wished to keep my faith private, I would have to find another church. That turned out to be more difficult than one might have supposed. The church in Nicaragua by 1982 was deeply divided. Many parish priests, including foreign missionaries, were enthusiastic supporters of the revolution and its social and economic agenda. The foreign minister was a priest; so too was the minister of culture. Both had been educated in the United States. Born and raised in Los Angeles, Father Miguel d'Escoto, the foreign minister, was, in many ways, more American than Nicaraguan. On the other hand, many priests were deeply suspicious of the revolution and its Marxist rhetoric. They feared the decimation and oppression of the church along the lines of what had happened in Cuba twenty years before. They were skeptical of the revolution's commitment to religious tolerance and scornful of its leftist rhetoric. Susan and I spent several Sundays searching until we found a lower-middle-class parish run by the Salesian fathers, who scrupulously stayed away from anything directly political (no mean feat, given the relevance of almost every Gospel text to the highly ambiguous situation prevailing in the revolution). We continued going to other parishes as well so as not to be allied with any particular one.

There was plenty of ambiguity to go around. One of the favorite stops of visiting delegations was the office of Comandante Tomás Borge, one of the three original founders of the Sandinista movement and minister of the interior. Notwithstanding that Borge was in charge of the secret police, the Directorate General of State Security, and its undercover operations against the opposition, he was also a poet of some renown and an amateur theologian. His principal office in the ministry, where he usually received visiting delegations, had one vast wall covered with a truly remarkable collection of crucifixes in metal, wood, stone, ceramic, and glass. He was quick to assure visitors that the revolution had its roots in Christianity and in the Christian commitment to the poor. In his inner office, which he reserved for special visitors or sensitive conversations, his desk was notable for the two books on it: the Bible and *The Fundamentals of Marxism-Leninism*. Borge did not claim to be a believer, but it was clear that at some level the Christian message had formed part of his social ideology.

The same was true of many leaders of the revolution, including Daniel Ortega, its leading figure, who had been educated in Catholic schools and at the Catholic University of Central America. The two priests who served in ministerial positions in the original Sandinista government, Foreign Minister Miguel d'Escoto and Culture Minister Ernesto Cardenal, were later joined by Ernesto's brother Fernando, a Jesuit priest, who became minister of education. All were drawn to the revolutionary cause by their personal commitment to liberation theology, which was much in vogue in Latin America following the Second Vatican Council, and to the writings of Peruvian priest Gustavo Gutierrez. The Vatican made strenuous efforts to persuade or force these priests to give up their ministerial functions, but to no avail.

Christ the worker and carpenter was the central figure of revolutionary folk art and popular liturgies. In accordance with liberation theology, Christ was portrayed as a spiritual leader who would free an oppressed people from the chains of superstition (represented in the revolutionary lexicon as the dictatorship of the previous regime). In this climate, religiously themed folk art flourished, and music written for the mass reflected the revolutionary fervor of those priests and nuns in the People's Church, as it came to be called. It was to this cultural world that the poet Ernesto Cardenal was drawn before the revolution.

The revolutionary leadership, whatever Christian ideals it shared, was not about to allow itself to be undermined by opponents in the church. One of their particular bêtes noires was Father Bismarck Carballo, the archbishop's private secretary and public spokesman and the director of Radio Católica, one of the few organs of public communication not controlled by the Sandinista government. He was widely known for his antirevolutionary views. Somewhere in the Ministry of the Interior it was decided to discredit Father Carballo. The means chosen were truly bizarre. On August 11, 1982, Father Carballo was lunching in the home of a pious Catholic woman who was the leader of a charismatic prayer group of which Father Carballo was the spiritual advisor. In the middle of lunch, an armed man broke into the woman's home and forced Father Carballo into the street totally naked. By "chance" a TV crew from Sandinista-controlled state television happened to be passing the house at that very moment and filmed the priest fleeing naked into the street. The official explanation was that an outraged husband had broken into his own house to find the priest in flagrante delicto, in bed with his wife. He was so enraged that he forced Father Carballo at gunpoint out of the house into the waiting arms of the Nicaraguan media. The scene was broadcast nationally on the evening news. The public's sense of shock and outrage was palpable. To put a priest, even an opponent of the revolution, on television nude was unthinkable and almost universally condemned. Even Sandinista supporters, who were willing to believe that the monsignor had indeed been in bed with his parishioner, found it hard to excuse this crass exploitation of the incident to discredit the priest and by extension his immediate superior, the archbishop.

Issues of religion became almost a daily part of my life. I had only been in Managua a few days when a group of religious leaders from the United States asked to see me. I had decided early on that I would see any American citizen who wanted to see me. I would listen to their views and give them the U.S. government's official position on the revolution and its trajectory. This first group, to be succeeded by dozens more in the weeks and months to come, was composed of Catholic nuns and priests, Protestant pastors, and concerned laypeople. Deeply suspicious of the Reagan administration, they suspected (correctly as it turned out) that it wished to overthrow the Sandinista regime. After I had laid out the U.S. concerns about the Sandinistas' efforts to export the revolution to El Salvador and their restrictions on democracy and free speech, a member of the delegation thanked me for my statement and answers to their questions and asked if we might all join hands in prayer. I had never prayed publicly in my office and wondered what to do. It seemed ungracious to say no, and so I stood up and joined hands with my visitors. There, in a circle in the ambassador's office, they prayed not for the overthrow of the Sandinistas but for an early end to the Reagan administration. Needless to say, I was taken aback and, happily, was never asked to pray again.

This group, like many that followed, came deeply convinced of the essentially good intentions of the Sandinistas and the malevolent intentions of the Reagan administration. Their moral fervor was intense. They understood that the United States was supporting counterrevolutionary forces, widely known as the Contras. As the Contra war gathered steam with the inevitable loss of young lives, the animosity of American church leaders to U.S. policy further intensified. Church groups all over America saw American policy as funding an unjust and unnecessary war. A leading example was Henri Nouwen, a leading Catholic intellectual and writer. In an article in the August 1983 *National Catholic Reporter* he observed: "Nicaragua is a deeply Christian country. It would be impossible to understand that without recognizing that its leaders have been deeply influenced by God's word and have found strength to resist injustice and the strength to forgive their enemies in their faith in Jesus Christ." To many in the U.S. government looking at the Sandinistas' repressive actions against the opposition and leading elements of the church, this was a naive and partial understanding of the situation.

It was not only the Roman Catholic Church that was divided. The Episcopal Church was equally ambiguous. Its Nicaraguan branch was an official part of the American church and was anxious to ordain local men to the priesthood. For that purpose, it had created a small seminary and brought professors from the United States to teach selected courses. One such course was on liberation theology, a subject popular with pro-Sandinista church officials. However, the small cohort of Nicaraguan candidates understood liberation to mean liberation from the Sandinistas. The visiting academics were completely confounded.

March 4, 1983, the day the pope came to Nicaragua, was in many ways a pivotal point in the evolution of the church's relations with the Sandinista government. Both sides eagerly awaited the Holy Father's arrival. The Sandinistas hoped that the pope would condemn the external, American-funded, organized violence directed against Nicaragua. The opposition was equally convinced that the pope would speak out against the Marxist orientation of the government and restrictions on religious education and speech. The day of the visit was declared a national holiday, and transportation services were made available to the Nicaraguan people so that they would have a chance to see the pope both in León, a large provincial city northwest of Managua, and at the vast open-air mass in the revolutionary heart of Managua.

Throughout that long and swelteringly hot day, the diplomatic corps was front and center for the major events. We were there to greet the pope at the airport, transported to the papal prayer service in León, Nicaragua's second city, and invited to the papal mass in the Plaza of the Revolution. On his arrival, the pope was greeted at Sandino International Airport by the ruling junta; the comandantes of the revolution; the entire government, including its two priests, Foreign Minister Miguel d'Escoto and Minister of Culture Ernesto Cardenal; the Nicaraguan bishops; and the full diplomatic corps. As customary with state visits, the pope reviewed a color guard and then solemnly greeted each of those in line to welcome him. There was a particular moment of anxiety as he approached the minister of culture. What would he say to Ernesto Cardenal, who was openly defying the Vatican's orders that priests not serve in any official government position? The pope did stop in front of Cardenal, and there was a brief exchange, inaudible to the rest of us farther down the receiving line. The pope appeared to wag his finger at Cardenal, but nothing more was known. At the papal mass later in the day I asked Cardenal what had happened. He said that the pope had urged him to regularize his situation. I asked, "What did you reply?" Cardenal smiled and said his only response was, "Sí, Holy Father." Many expressed skepticism about how sincerely expressed his "yes" was, since Cardenal continued in the government for many more months.

The pope's day was just beginning, and he was to have more to say before it was over. Much of his visit was out of the view of the press or the diplomatic corps as he met with the government junta and with the bishops of the Nicaraguan church. Two massive public events were on the program. The first, which followed shortly after his arrival, took place in León, where, at midday under a broiling sun, a large crowd had gathered. The scriptures were read, and prayers were offered for Nicaragua and even for those who had lost their lives in the now rapidly expanding internal civil war. The local bishop was the host, the crowd was polite and respectful, and the pope was at his most pastoral. No one could have anticipated what was to follow that afternoon in Managua.

The culmination of the pope's visit, as is customary on such occasions, was to be a large outdoor mass in Managua in the only vast open space available, the Plaza of the Revolution. There, some months before, the CIA had unsuccessfully tried to burn down the revolutionary billboards proclaiming Sandinista revolutionary fervor. The Sandinistas, while apprehensive about the pope's visit and fearful that he would attack their regime directly, went out of their way to ensure that the Nicaraguans had every opportunity to see the pope in person. Every bus in the country was mobilized, and citizens by the thousands were brought to Managua from every corner of the country. While no accurate estimates of the crowd were ever made, the best guess of experienced observers was that over half a million Nicaraguans assembled for this historic mass. The crowd was divided into distinct sections, each waving hundreds of flags: the blue-and-white flag of Nicaragua, the yellow-and-white flag of the Vatican, or the red-and-black flag of the revolution. These phalanxes of waving banners reminded me of a medieval festival, with knights from different clans jostling for places in front of the Holy Father. Facing the crowd was a series of large, raised platforms on which sat the bishops of Nicaragua, the Sandinista government, and the diplomatic corps. Daniel Ortega and the other members of the three-man junta sat closest to the altar. The diplomats were seated in a group with the rank-and-file members of the government.

The mass started uneventfully enough with the normal prayers and scriptural readings. It was only when the pope got up to give his homily that the situation began to get out of hand. In front of the pope and to his right was a large group of Sandinistas, with their red-and-black banners waving on high. As he began to speak, they began to chant: "We want a church on the side of the poor." The pope, visibly angered by this interruption, imperiously called out, "Silencio, silencio," but to no effect. While an elaborate amplification system had been set up to enable the pope's words to reach even the most distant of the worshipers, rather surprisingly it suddenly went off as the pope was warming up. Whether this was genuine mechanical failure or deliberate silencing of the pope, we will never know, but the partisan opposition knew for certain that it was sabotage. The pope soldiered on, unheard by the majority of those present. Angry cheering intensified from all sides. Many of us on the platform feared a massive riot that would lead to grievous harm or loss of life. Happily, the presence of the pope and a large number of security officers seemed to keep emotions in check, and the mass proceeded.

The consecration, the central point in the mass, passed relatively without incident, but as preparations for the distribution of Communion were under way, a group of women carrying photographs draped in black mourning crepe approached the altar. These were mothers of young men recently killed by the Contras operating in the northern mountains of Nicaragua. The women pushed their way to the front, seeking recognition from the pope and demanding to receive Communion. The priests who were preparing to fan out into the crowd to distribute the consecrated bread unceremoniously turned them away. Their rejection further angered the Sandinista wing of the crowd, and shouting again broke out, to the point that a decision was made to not even try to send priests out into the crowd with the Communion bread. Amid all this confusion, the final blessing was given, and the pope, under heavy security, was able to escape and be driven to the airport, where he departed shortly thereafter.

For the Sandinistas, the day was a disaster. The international media blamed them for the incidents at the mass, including the loss of amplification, and portrayed the event as a massive outpouring of opposition to the regime. That may be overstating the case, but the event provided the Contras and their allies ample ammunition to argue that the Sandinistas were viscerally anti-Catholic and would do anything, even disrupt the pope, to advance their agenda. The Sandinistas were never able to escape this image. Their hopes, unrealistic perhaps, that this would be a day of reconciliation were dashed. The gulf within Nicaraguan society only deepened. The Catholic Church hierarchy became increasingly hostile to the regime.

THE YANKEE ENEMY OF MANKIND

One of the most daunting dilemmas for an American ambassador in revolutionary Nicaragua was what to do about the constant barrage of hostile and inflammatory rhetoric focused on the past and present wickedness of the United States. The symbol of that rhetoric was the Sandinista hymn, sung with evident gusto at every official event. It contained the following lines: "The sons of Sandino never sell themselves and never surrender, they fight against the Yankee, enemy of humanity." The question that we faced on an almost daily basis was whether to stand with all others present when the hymn was sung or whether to walk out knowing that the offending lines were soon to be intoned. This was a problem that I never fully resolved. I did not impose a policy on my staff, and I allowed my colleagues to sit, stand, or absent themselves as they saw fit. In my own case, I usually stood, since the hymn was often accompanied by the national anthem. The ritualistic intoning of the enmity between Uncle Sam and humanity seemed to have little bearing on the actual state of our relations.

However, the first question that American diplomats had to answer after their arrival was whether the government to which they were accredited regarded them as that same Yankee enemy. At the personal level there seemed to be little animosity toward Americans. Nicaragua had been deeply impacted by American culture. American missionaries had been there for a century. American products were popular, as was American music. Every Nicaraguan seemed to have a relative in Miami or elsewhere in the United States. One of the nine comandantes of the revolution, Luis Carrión Cruz, had even been educated at Phillips Exeter Academy in New Hampshire. As a result, most members of the embassy staff did business on a reasonably cordial basis with all levels of Nicaraguan society, including members of the Sandinista government. At the highest levels, I was always received with personal courtesy, even when my interlocutor was strongly, even harshly, critical of official policy.

Even after the triumph of the revolution, the United States retained an enormous attraction for Nicaraguans, including the comandantes themselves. As I recall, in the Christmas season of 1982 Daniel Ortega expressed an interest in taking his family to Disney World for the holidays. Alone among the countries of Central America, Nicaragua made baseball its national sport. On the first weekend after my arrival I was invited to the Nicaraguan World Series between the Nicaraguan army team and the Frente Sur, a team from the southern part of the country. It was assumed that, as a *yanqui*, I would be on the side of the Frente Sur, since that was also the name of the military arm of the anti-Sandinista rebels operating out of Costa Rica. I was watched attentively by my military hosts to see whether I would limit my cheering to hits and runs scored by the Frente Sur team. I did my best to maintain a steady neutrality throughout.

Occasionally the rhetoric reached an entirely unacceptable boiling point of animosity. For me, that moment came on July 19, 1982, during the ceremonies commemorating the third anniversary of the triumph of the revolution. Present were the entire government hierarchy of ministers, as well as the nine comandantes of the revolution and a crowd of well over one hundred thousand. The government convoked the members of the diplomatic corps to the official celebrations, which were to be held that year in Masaya, a city some thirty miles south of Managua where the revolution had some of its bloodiest encounters with the Somoza regime. The day was hot, as it always is in July, and we were seated in the blazing sun. The event lasted several hours, the highlight being an impassioned address by Daniel Ortega, then, as he was to remain until the end of Sandinista rule in 1990, the leading member of the ruling junta. The crowd was fired up with revolutionary rhetoric and the reading of the Sandinista martyrology. One could not help but be moved by the fervor with which the huge crowd replied "¡Presente!" as each name was read, beginning with one of Ortega's own brothers, Carlos. For a moment the crowd knew that they still lived.

Ortega's speech was characteristically strident. After praising the achievements of the revolution, he launched into a bitter attack on U.S. policy, ending with the accusation that President Reagan had blood on his hands when it came to Nicaragua. At that point, I decided that enough was enough and got up from my seat in the diplomatic corps section. International photographers captured the event, and pictures of me in a white guayabera shirt and a rather dorky sun hat leaving the ceremony were widely published. The gesture was received positively by my colleagues in Washington, who still saw me as the staunch anti-Sandinista they thought they had sent to Managua.

As my tour advanced, the Sandinistas decided that I was a worthy target for revolutionary humor. Virtually every week in the Sandinista humor magazine, the *Semana Cómica*, there would be cartoons of me in some compromising antirevolutionary activity, often involving the CIA or the political opposition. The press often mocked my lack of influence.

A thick skin was a requirement of the job. I could have become a recluse, avoiding all but the most essential encounters with Sandinista officials and limiting my exposure to events involving visiting official dignitaries from the United States. However, I believed that an ambassador's job was to engage with the society in which he was serving. That engagement required going to events, social, theatrical, cultural, and sporting. It meant a willingness to engage in debate even when, as often, the odds were stacked against me. It was easy for the Sandinistas to trivialize and caricature my approach to my public role in Managua. There were certainly risks, and many of my colleagues felt that I went too far, sacrificing the dignity of my office for public visibility. I must admit to a degree of personal vanity in my approach. I enjoyed the visibility and publicity that went with it. I believe that I defused some of the hostility the United States continued to receive, although I surely did not fundamentally change the views of the comandantes and their most loyal followers.

For all the ritual revolutionary anti-Americanism, the Sandinistas were concerned not to let it get out of hand. After the U.S. invasion of Grenada, Comandante Borge, the interior minister, called me in to assure me that Americans would never be treated as hostages, as they had been in Grenada. If ever we decided to leave Nicaragua, we would be free to do so. In fact, Borge assured me that he had already designated a fleet of buses to take us safely to the airport. These assurances were widely publicized in the Sandinista press.

Borge was one of my most frequent contacts. I met with him alone to discuss our relations and often with visiting congressional delegations. He was always personally cordial and to everyone's surprise, including mine, came to our Fourth of July celebration in 1983, accompanied by Rafael Córdova Rivas, a member of the three-man junta, and the feisty vice minister of foreign affairs, Nora Astorga. Borge joined me in a toast to improved U.S.-Nicaraguan relations. This gesture amazed the guests and others who heard about it, particularly as he went out of his way to express positive hopes for the future of U.S.-Nicaraguan relations. The previous year no revolutionary comandante had attended our reception, although Foreign Minister d'Escoto and junta member Córdova Rivas did. On good days, the Sandinistas wanted to be friends with us, and on others we were little more than those enemies of mankind celebrated in the Sandinista hymn. I saw it as my job to keep open these positive channels to the extent possible, even though I could not control or greatly influence the policy process in Washington.

VISITORS GALORE

Hardly a day went by that I did not receive visitors, singly or in groups, large or small. International journalists were constantly seeking appointments to get my take on the situation. Groups of priests, pastors, and nuns arrived on a weekly basis. Indeed, a regular Thursday protest occurred outside the gates of the embassy in which a motley crowd of secular and religious protestors let my staff and me know how much they opposed the policies of the Reagan administration.

A seemingly endless stream of official visitors and congressional delegations, or CODELs, as they were officially known, composed of representatives and senators, sought to update themselves on the reality of the revolution and Sandinista policies in the region.

Most of the many groups that came to Managua wanted to know why we could not or would not support the social agenda of the regime, its emphasis on literacy, its provision of health services, and its mobilization of the poor and marginalized into local defense forces. While acknowledging these achievements, I pointed to the signs, already evident, of authoritarian abuse of power and pressure on the democratic parties, the free press, and the private sector. These themes were to form the basis of my meetings with dozens of groups in the months and years to come.

I established a policy, which my staff thought slightly crazy, of seeing any American individual or group that wished to see me. The visitors ranged from peace groups to reporters from the major American newspapers and TV channels, from passionate peace activists to skeptical conservative anti-Communists. I briefed seemingly endless CODELs, church groups, student activists, and journalists. For me, it was a crash course in nuance. All sides wanted me to confirm their interpretation of events and to provide grist for their mill. They all came armed with facts justifying or criticizing American policy. I was caught in the middle.

As my tour progressed, the tone of many of these meetings became increasingly hostile. A group of Hollywood activists accused me of being a war criminal. One young man told me that when there were Nuremberg trials in the future, I would be one of the guilty. At another large meeting, held on the outskirts of the city because the group was too large to be accommodated in my office or in an embassy meeting room, the eminent Protestant divine and pastor of the Riverside Church, William Sloane Coffin, accused me of being the power behind the secret bombing of Cambodia. This accusation resulted in a hissing and drawing in of breath by the audience. On that occasion I was able to defend myself. I told Dr. Coffin that I had

had no connection with the wars in Southeast Asia. To his credit, he admitted he had confused me with another ambassador. Nonetheless, the damage was done. The audience knew they had seen the sinister figure they had come to confront.

All these groups had great difficulty in assessing the situation in anything approaching a balanced way. The Witnesses for Peace, for one, traveled against our best advice to the northern border of Nicaragua to hold candlelight vigils to protest U.S. support for the Contras and their attacks into Sandinista-held territory. For my staff, who faced similar criticisms from Americans they met during their daily routines or who accompanied me on my encounters, this relentless hostility imposed an enormous emotional strain. They hated to see their government vilified and, I believe, did not like to see their ambassador personally scorned, even if they shared some of the criticisms of the visiting delegations. I shared this emotional strain as a particular target of hostility, especially for those delegations that had come to protest U.S. policy.

CODELs were less emotionally charged. Their visits followed a typical pattern. They usually came for a little over a day and stayed either at the residence, if the delegation was small, or, if large, at the Sheraton Hotel in the earthquake-shattered center of the city. They would hold meetings with opposition political figures, the editor of *La Prensa*, the archbishop, and the leaders of the private sector business group COSEP. They invariably met with senior Sandinista figures, almost always with Foreign Minister d'Escoto or one of his deputies, Victor Tinoco or Nora Astorga. They always wanted to meet Daniel Ortega or another senior comandante. In these various meetings they heard wildly conflicting accounts of the situation. They were encouraged by the opposition to step up pressure on the Sandinistas and told by the Sandinistas of the wickedness of the Contra effort to overthrow the regime.

At the middle and end of 1983 and in early 1984, the pace of visits picked up and kept the embassy extremely busy. In August, we had visits from Representative Ed Markey (D-MA) and Senators William

Cohen (R-ME) and Gary Hart (D-CO). In December, we had separate visits led by Senators Jeremiah Denton (R-AL) and Daniel Moynihan (D-NY) and early in 1984 from Representatives Edward Boland (D-MA), Sean Casten (D-IL), and Stephen Solarz (D-NY). Most delegations were bipartisan and accompanied by several staff members, either personal or from committee staffs. Delegations tended to leave as confused and ambivalent as they arrived. Invariably, I would offer a lunch, a dinner, or a reception in their honor at which I tried to bring together representatives of both sides and those local figures who still tried to maintain a dispassionate view of the situation. Democrats on these CODELs left reinforced in their skepticism about the administration's covert and overt programs to destabilize the regime but also concerned about the growing human rights abuses. Republicans favored greater pressure on the regime and tended to accept the view that the Sandinistas were dangerous Marxists who sought to promote revolution throughout the region.

Even though their perspectives differed profoundly, most visitors came away hoping to see the various multilateral and regional negotiating efforts succeed. Congressional delegations wanted to see democracy prevail throughout the region and an end to the violence in Central America. Some believed the Sandinistas' protestations of innocence in the export of revolution to El Salvador. Others were deeply skeptical of the honesty and integrity of the Sandinistas. Whatever their conclusions, most visitors would acknowledge that the situation was complex and that Sandinista policies were ambiguous. Very few of the groups that came had much of an understanding of the historical background to the revolution and the century-long history of American intervention in Nicaragua. Pro-Sandinista groups simplistically assumed that anything would be better than the decades-long Somoza rule. Righting the wrongs of American support for the Somozas and past American interventions seemed to justify virtually anything the Sandinistas did. Others, remembering the experience of Southeast Asia, assumed that the domino effect was real and that if the Sandinistas were not stopped, however good their stated intentions, Marxism would inexorably advance northward from Nicaragua through El Salvador, Guatemala, and Mexico, ending up on the very doorstep of the United States. It was easy to find facts and arguments that fitted one's incoming views. Very few opinions were changed.

Perhaps the most controversial visit was that of Lieutenant General William Odom, the army chief of staff for intelligence. In January 1983 he visited Central America to take stock of the situation for himself. He asked embassies to arrange meetings with appropriate local officials in each of his stops. Without asking for any further guidance, I went ahead and sought a meeting with senior Sandinista army officials and offered a dinner in General Odom's honor, to which I invited the chief of staff of the Sandinista army, Joaquín Cuadra. Odom received a formal and detailed briefing on the Contra war in Somoza's old bunker, where we clustered around the large map table with Nicaragua laid out on a grand scale. It was here that President Somoza had planned his response to the growing Sandinista insurgency in 1978 and 1979.

Cuadra came to dinner with several senior colleagues and engaged in a remarkably open exchange of views about the strategic situation in the region. Odom, who had previously been military attaché in Moscow, was impressed with the openness of his Nicaraguan colleagues, remarking to me afterward that this kind of briefing and open discussion would have been impossible in the Soviet Union. The visit, which was intended to be a private one, became a major news story when a local journalist spotted Odom and filed a story about secret negotiations between the United States and Nicaragua led by General Odom. Washington was caught entirely wrong-footed. When questioned the day after Odom's departure, the Pentagon spokesman said it was a private visit for Odom to meet his old friend and colleague Ambassador Quainton. We had in fact worked together when I was the department's counterterrorism head and Odom worked the counterterrorism account on the National Security Council staff. The State Department spokesman confusingly said it was a routine official visit. Because of the difference in stories, the press was convinced there was more to the visit than met the eye. There was not.

The visit had been cleared with State and Defense at a very low level, so the principals were caught completely off guard by Odom's personal initiative.

The Sandinistas were officially unaware of a fact-finding visit by the CIA's deputy director for operations, Clair George, and his Latin American Division chief. Both traveled under aliases, but the Sandinistas undoubtedly learned of the visit when, to his astonishment, the Latin America chief immediately recognized my wife as a fellow graduate of Beverly Hills High School, where they had been valedictorian and salutatorian of their class. For a moment, which presumably Sandinista microphones picked up, aliases were forgotten as the two greeted each other for the first time in almost forty years.

My own role for official, nonofficial, and congressional visitors was to present as balanced a picture of the situation as I could and to ensure that the visitors heard firsthand from Nicaraguans themselves about the problems they were facing. As I did with the later Kissinger Commission, I tried to be balanced, not concealing the arbitrary aspects of Sandinista rule but also not demonizing the regime. Looking back with the perspective of over a quarter century, I probably came across to some of my visitors as somewhat naive, to others, as too hard-nosed. I had become convinced that the basic social objectives of the revolution were positive. Education and literacy had improved. Healthcare was reaching a broader cross section of the population. Self-government had been pushed down to the local barrio level. While I admired the efforts of the opposition to stand up for basic human rights, including freedom of the press, I was aware of the social and economic gap that separated the rich in Nicaragua from the vast majority of the citizenry.

I did not find the Nicaraguan upper middle class particularly admirable. They were hospitable, charming, and intensely pro-American. I could sympathize with their sense of loss and outrage, but I did not find them terribly sophisticated in their understanding of their country's problems. The old order still looked to them better than the new. I could not entirely join them in that view. The Sandinistas sensed my sympathy and tried to take advantage of it. The opposition sensed my skepticism and worked hard to convince me of the need for a more vigorous set of American policies. When my recall was finally announced, both sides were gracious in wishing me well and thanking me for my efforts either to promote democracy or to mitigate the harsher side of American policies. A number of articles in the Sandinista press expressed regret at my going, saying I had fallen in love with the revolution. Perhaps they were right. Certainly, Republican officials in Washington and the opposition leaders in Managua thought so.

15
Diplomacy and Regime Change

In my previous tour in Central Africa, the intelligence community did not play a very large part in my work. Most of what the CIA station did was against third-country targets and did not involve my active participation or approval. Nicaragua was something else again. There the CIA was to play an ever-more-important role as the years went by, culminating in the eventual defeat of the Sandinista regime in the 1990 elections. When I arrived in Managua on what was to be the first day of the "secret war," I was almost completely unprepared for the darker side of my mission.

Before setting out for Managua, I had been briefed by the head of the Latin American Division at the CIA, Duane "Dewey" Claridge. When I first met him, he had just returned from Mexico from a meeting with Eden Pastora, known as Comandante Zero. Pastora had been an enthusiastic supporter of Nicaragua's revolution in its early days but had turned against the nine comandantes when it became clear that he was not to be included in their inner circle. Claridge was most enthusiastic about the prospect of working with him against the Sandinistas, assuming Pastora would be able to turn his charismatic and heroic image as a revolutionary to good effect in recruiting Nicaraguans to oppose the revolution. They were kindred spirits, with a boyish enthusiasm for covert operations.

In my meeting with Claridge, he briefed me about the work of the Managua CIA station and its efforts to carry out the presidential "finding" on Nicaragua, which authorized limited operations against the Sandinistas. As it was portrayed to me both in the department and at the agency, these operations were to harass the Sandinistas with the goal of persuading them to abandon their support for the leftist guerrillas in El Salvador and to live up to their democratic promises. It quickly became clear to me that while these goals were often and repeatedly stated by official government spokesmen, the real intention was not policy change but regime change.

I must confess that I did not think this effort to bring about regime change was likely to succeed. Over the next two and a half years, as I watched the escalation of agency-supported operations against the Sandinistas, that view did not change. While I was under the long-standing government policy not to confirm or deny intelligence operations, the hand of the CIA in the more egregious events could not easily be denied. Indeed, many of the land and naval operations, often using Zodiac boats, were obviously mounted out of Honduras. The international press quickly focused on the Contra training camps in Honduras, which benefited from American trainers, weapons, and logistical support for the "harassment" operations. The Contra effort was entirely outside of my purview and fell more directly under the watchful but sympathetic eye of my counterpart in Tegucigalpa, John Negroponte.

My relationship to all these operations was tenuous. I was sometimes informed of activities that were planned inside Nicaragua; but when it came to the blowing up of the offshore oil pipeline or the mining of Nicaragua's ports, I would learn of them only when they hit the press, always accompanied by official U.S. denial of any U.S. involvement. My observation of these covert operations left me somewhat less than an enthusiastic admirer. They were often of limited success and, in my view, had counterproductive results in strengthening Sandinista resolve and undermining international support for our policies. A few examples may suffice to make the point.

I happily welcomed two senior members of the Senate Intelligence Oversight Committee who had decided to tour Central America: Gary Hart, then an active candidate for the Democratic presidential nomination, and William Cohen, the committee's chairman. The Sandinistas were equally anxious to explain to them the damage that covert operations against their regime were doing. Neither side could have imagined what happened. On the morning of the senators' scheduled arrival, shortly after they had taken off from Tegucigalpa, their last stop before Managua, we learned that a small plane had dropped bombs on Sandino International Airport and crashed. We had no further details but were assured by the Sandinista authorities that the airport was still open, and it was safe for the senators to come ahead as planned. My senior colleagues and I, after much discussion, agreed that they should. I then went to the airport to greet them. After they landed safely, a senior Sandinista military officer welcomed them. He took them into the arrival hall, now unfortunately the site of the crashed plane, which had flipped over and landed in the VIP lounge. Its five-hundred-pound bombs had been pushed out of the plane as it flew over the airport. With a certain glee, the Sandinistas observed that this plane had come from Costa Rica, where it had been fueled and armed under a CIA training program. Had the senators arrived on time, they would have been victims of the attack. The embassy had not been informed of this activity and so was unable to warn the senators of the possible danger they faced. They were not impressed by this covert program, which had put their lives at risk.

In-country operations occasionally failed as well. One morning I opened my copy of *Barricada*, the pro-Sandinista daily, to find on the front cover a picture of an embassy officer sitting on a park bench taking documents from a Sandinista official. The Sandinista government responded in outrage and immediately declared the offending officer persona non grata and added, for good measure, the political counselor and the chief of station. I was not pleased at our performance or the Sandinistas' response. The officers being expelled were much admired by their colleagues and were the backbone of our reporting capability. Their departure from Sandino International Airport was an emotional one. The U.S. government immediately retaliated by expelling some twenty-nine Nicaraguan officials in the United States and closing Nicaragua's consulates. In the case of the consulate in Houston, FBI agents entered the building and, contrary to normal diplomatic practice, examined the consulate's files; the resulting publicity further heightened Sandinista outrage.

This was not the first time that alleged CIA operations had been exposed. Several months before, a small group of Nicaraguans were caught attempting to burn down the revolutionary billboards in the Plaza of the Revolution. I had been informed about this operation, which I was told would deal a psychological blow to the revolution. I was skeptical but was assured it had the highest-level support in Washington and could be done with little likelihood of exposure. When, after two failures, the perpetrators were arrested on their third attempt, my skepticism was confirmed. The only result was another black eye for the United States and the reinforcement of the Sandinistas' sense of revolutionary righteousness.

Among the external attacks two stand out: the blowing up of the pipeline connecting the offshore oil terminal with the Esso refinery and the mining of the Port of Corinto. The mining occurred shortly before my departure and led to a case being brought against the United States in the International Court of Justice (a case we eventually lost). In the pipeline case, I learned from the local Esso (now Exxon) representative that the operation had severed the underwater pipeline, cutting off the supply of crude oil to the local refinery. But the damage would be relatively easy to repair, he said, by divers inserting a new section of pipe into the damaged space.

Shortly after this attack, I was summoned to Washington for consultations. When National Security Advisor William Clark asked me about the attack, I told him that it had been successful but would affect refinery production for only about a week. He reacted strongly, turning on me to ask if I had done anything to expedite the repair process. I assured him that I had not involved myself in any way. He fumed that the CIA had informed him that the operation would impact Nicaragua's capacity to import crude for up to six months. I was not reassured either by his apparent lack of confidence in me or by the overestimation of the likely effect of covert operations on the regime's economy. In fact, these events strengthened the

Sandinistas' resolve and were useful handles with which to beat on the United States and to justify the ever-stricter controls imposed on the population as necessary for national defense.

Events constantly put me in the impossible position of having to deny U.S. involvement or, at a minimum, refusing to comment on it. No one in the embassy was under any illusions about what was going on, but we were frustrated at our inability to anticipate when and where the next incident would take place. In some cases, I was given an advance warning of an operation but rarely any of the details. I confess to not having been particularly courageous. I regarded many of the schemes of which I was informed as hare-brained or likely to be counterproductive. I realized they had originated in the fertile brain of Duane Claridge, who had the direct support of CIA director Casey and of the president himself. While I privately expressed skepticism to my colleagues and to the station chief, I did not make my negative views of these operations a matter of public or official record. I assumed, erroneously, that their obvious counterproductive impact would in due course be seen by Washington and lead to a change of strategy. I was wrong. The reaction to each failure was to increase the pressure for ever-more-dramatic attacks on the regime and for greater support to the Contra operation.

The Sandinistas, for their part, used these covert operations to ratchet up their propaganda attacks on the United States. Every visiting delegation had its attention drawn to these "illegal" activities. Even groups that came to Managua skeptical about the Sandinistas' commitment to democracy and human rights were put on the defensive as Sandinista officials described American covert operations. We explained that the impact of these attacks was in itself minimal, but they did underscore Sandinista vulnerabilities and eroded their capacity to govern. The Contra attacks from the North, which we essentially funded and equipped, forced the regime to take more draconian internal security measures and to ratchet up the draft of young men. The resulting steady erosion of popular support culminated in the electoral defeat of Daniel Ortega and the Frente Sandinista in

1990. The Sandinistas looked for ways to mobilize South American friends and Central American neighbors behind a variety of peace initiatives and used these American-sponsored "acts of aggression" as a rallying point for nationalistic forces in the region. While this approach had a certain resonance, it did not bring an end to the conflict in which we were increasingly embroiled.

In retrospect, I have often asked myself what, if anything, I might have done to slow down the CIA's juggernaut. So many of the operations of which I was informed turned out to be fiascos, and those of which I was ignorant, such as the bombing of Sandino International Airport and the mining of the ports, were self-evidently counter-productive. I knew that they had been authorized at the highest levels of the U.S. government and enjoyed the active support of the director of Central Intelligence himself. I rationalized my silence with the thought that by protesting the futility and possible illegality of these operations, both great and small, I would be on a fool's errand. It would have marked me out even more clearly in the eyes of the White House as soft on Communism and unprepared to fight for American values. I was not prepared to put my career at risk. Pusillanimity is not a great virtue, and my silence is not something of which I am proud. I fell short. Ironically, after my return to Washington in the summer of 1984, I was honored for my creative dissent with the Christian Herter Award.

THE SEARCH FOR PEACE

The search for a negotiated settlement in Central America became a central issue throughout my time in Nicaragua. Six months before my arrival in August 1981, Assistant Secretary of State for Latin America Thomas Enders had visited Managua and presented the Sandinistas with a comprehensive offer of peace if they would agree to end their export of revolution to El Salvador and uphold their original commitment to democracy, a mixed economy, and a nonaligned foreign policy. The Sandinistas saw the second part of this proposal as a case of the United States moving the goal posts, adding new conditions.

In October, Secretary Enders testified before the Senate Foreign Relations Committee that they had rejected his proposals as "sterile."

Within weeks of my arrival, I was tasked to present a revised version of the Enders proposals (State 92351, April 8, 1982). Known as the eight-point plan, it was an effort to lay out the parameters for a serious dialogue between our two governments. The central point I was asked to make was, "There can be no improvement in our relations until the arms flow, training, and other support activities for the Salvadoran guerillas cease." The Farabundo Martí National Liberation Front (FMLN) control center operating in Nicaragua must also close down. Unspecified activities aimed at destabilizing Honduras and Costa Rica would also have to cease.

While we were obsessed with Nicaragua's destabilizing activities in the region, the Sandinistas worried about activities of Nicaraguan exiles in the United States that appeared to be in violation of American law. Reports of military-style training in Florida and elsewhere had made the news. In my presentation of our eight-point plan, all I could say was that we could make a declaration supporting the implementation of applicable American laws and regulations. We also indicated that we would be willing to make a joint statement committing both countries to the principle of nonintervention in each other's internal affairs. For the rulers in Managua, this was quite thin gruel.

In this proposal we also expressed concern at the growing numbers of Cuban and Soviet advisors in Managua and the transfer of "offensive" weapons from those countries to the Sandinistas. With this in mind, we proposed a prohibition on the importation to the region of heavy offensive weaponry and agreed to maintain military forces at levels "commensurate with their security needs." In addition, we proposed that the number of foreign military and security advisors be reduced to "reasonable low levels" in each of the countries of the region.

On a more positive note, we expressed willingness to consider the Sandinista proposal for joint border patrols along the Honduran border but suggested that this was something the Organization of

American States might take up. (Needless to say, it never did.) I said we would be willing to exchange artists, musicians, and sports groups, to open a binational center, and to reestablish a Peace Corps presence. Finally, we took note of a recent Sandinista statement committing the revolution once again to political pluralism, a mixed economy, and a nonaligned foreign policy. These points were repeatedly rehashed over the next several years but never received a coherent or positive Sandinista response. Many of these ideas were included in the Contadora initiative, organized by the foreign ministers of Mexico, Colombia, Panama, and Venezuela.

On their face, these proposals seemed reasonable and were presented to Congress in Washington as such. In fact, the devil was in the details. We sought to push the Russian and Cuban military out of Central America. The Sandinistas wanted to push us out. We were never willing to accept this implied parity. Central America was our backyard, and we asserted a privileged right to provide military support to all of the countries of the region that requested it. The Russians and Cubans were interlopers with no legitimate claim to be in the region militarily at all.

Even as we maintained our core objective of ending the export of revolution to El Salvador, we wanted to use our leverage to dictate the nature of Nicaragua as an open political and economic society. While the Sandinistas occasionally showed some flexibility on these points, including a willingness to stop their shipment of arms across the Gulf of Fonseca, they remained deeply suspicious of American motives and concluded that our proposals were little more than a demand that they surrender the revolution to the policies and priorities of the United States. This was something that these proud and tenacious young revolutionaries were not willing to do.

TELLING TRUTH TO POWER

For a neophyte ambassador in a strange land, the greatest challenge is how to report on the complexities of the situation with which he or she is faced. In Managua, I had a talented staff, several of whom had previous Latin American experience. Before my arrival, many of them had already established a wide circle of contacts in Managua and around the country. Those who had been there the longest when I arrived were bitterly disillusioned. They had hoped for a more open and democratic revolution and were unhappy at the human rights abuses they saw. Those who came at about the same time as I tended to be more open and willing to accept at least some of the *logros*, the achievements, of the revolution. Those who came much later tended to find the expected Marxist totalitarian regime that Washington insisted was in the making. The acting AID director came with an ideological agenda, believing that our policy should take a strong anti-Communist position. That was also the position of the CIA station chief. The political, economic, and public affairs sections were much more nuanced.

What was the story that needed to be told? For the neoconservatives in Washington, Marxist ideologues in Havana and Moscow had already written the script. The challenge for the White House was to tease out the facts that confirmed the diagnosis that Nicaragua was on a steady and defined path toward a Marxist-Leninist totalitarian state. The consequences of that diagnosis were profound. Jeane Kirkpatrick, a close advisor of President Reagan and a distinguished scholar at Georgetown University, had written about the difference between totalitarian and authoritarian systems. She had argued that you could not negotiate with Communists. They would not change their stripes under external pressure. Ultimately, she argued, they would have to be overthrown. A senior Foreign Service Officer with extensive experience in Moscow who accompanied special envoy Richard Stone to Managua in 1984 said he could "smell" Soviet-style Communism as soon as he stepped off the plane.

The alternative narrative was that the Sandinistas were, to be sure, Marxists but not doctrinaire Communists. They wished to avoid the excesses of the Cuban revolution, as Interior Minister Tomás Borge once told me, and create a unique, distinctively Nicaraguan political structure with a mixed economy, limited political pluralism, and a nonaligned foreign policy—always under the guidance and direction of the FSLN, the people's vanguard party. They claimed that they had a more nuanced view of revolution and did not want to copy all things Cuban or Soviet. They insisted that they were open to negotiation and modification of some of their behaviors and approaches.

Wherever one's analysis began, it was always possible to find facts that would confirm one's point of view and that would seem to discredit the alternative view. The problem for the embassy was that the White House had accepted the first set of assumptions, and the State Department, by tradition and inclination, tended to buy into the second, more nuanced view. The result was an environment of competing policy approaches, one leading to negotiation and limited accommodation and the other to regime change. Whatever the embassy reported would be grist for one or other of those ideological mills. The Sandinistas' systematic human rights abuses confirmed the first interpretation. Other facts seemed to suggest the viability of the second view. The Sandinistas tried and ultimately failed to get a negotiated regional settlement and permitted the church and the private sector to have some independent influence. We were all too aware of this fundamental debate in Washington and of the reality that our reports would be reinforcing or weakening one school of thought or the other. Events never spoke for themselves; they were always being interpreted through one policy vision or the other. Hence, getting the facts right and the story straight had real-world consequences and often imposed a moral dilemma for the embassy's reporting officers.

For all these differences among us, I was extremely gratified by the extent to which the staff supported me even when they did not agree with my assessments. Many thought I was much too publicly visible and much too sympathetic to the regime. On the other hand, the public affairs section welcomed my effort to use public diplomacy to get the administration's message across. I felt that being visible was a vital part of my job. I appeared on television and radio whenever I could. On those occasions I was always able to present the administration's criticism of Sandinista policies, particularly their support for the revolutionaries in El Salvador and the restrictions on political and press freedoms. The questions were often hostile, but I was never prevented from answering them as fully as I chose, while the media remained free to caricature me. I was mercilessly satirized on the radio, notably on a daily satirical show called *El Tren de las Seis* (The six o'clock train) and in various pro-Sandinista publications and magazines such as the *Semana Cómica* (Comic weekly). For the Sandinista satirists I was always Mister Cuentón, the storyteller or liar.

In this climate my challenge was how to manage reporting by officers with widely different views of the situation. One of the great dilemmas in this period was how to get the facts about what was actually going on, as partisans on one side or the other skewed the information. I took the position that I would not try to censor any reporting critical of the regime or seek to promote a particularly sympathetic view of it. The only criterion was that the information be reliably sourced and credible. That was not enough for Washington.

During my second year in Managua, I was invited to Washington for consultations. I met with a number of senior officials, including National Security Advisor William Clark. At the president's morning briefing, he presented me as "our ambassador from the trenches in Nicaragua." I was able to give a short synopsis of the situation, much like the one that I later gave the Kissinger Commission, modestly optimistic about the possibility of a negotiated outcome.

Following that meeting, Clark suggested that I see Faith Ryan Whittlesey, special assistant to the president and chief of the Outreach Working Group on Central America. Located in the White House, the group had been created to provide convincing evidence of the Communist menace in Central America. In her office, only a few yards from the president's, she greeted me cordially and told me that my reporting was read with interest in the White House. I expressed suitable appreciation, acknowledging that most ambassadors' reports were not read in the White House at all. However, she went on to say, I was reporting too much good news. She urged me on my return to Managua to report more bad news. I demurred, saying we would report all the news, whether good or bad. She reminded me that I was the president's representative and that I had an obligation to help him succeed in Central America. For that to happen, she insisted, the administration needed ammunition—in short, more bad news.

This conversation was symptomatic of the skepticism with which embassy reporting was regarded in the White House. An example of that lack of confidence was reflected in an article in the *New York Times* in May 1983 alleging that the embassy was covering up Sandinista anti-Semitism. A report prepared by B'nai B'rith alleged that the Sandinistas had systematically persecuted Jews in Nicaragua, driving them into exile. The article asserted that the government had seized and desecrated the one synagogue in Managua to make it into a revolutionary center, with pictures of Gaddafi and other heroes of the revolution on the walls. The B'nai B'rith report was sourced to Jewish exiles in Miami, who described their experiences at the hands of the Sandinistas at the outset of the revolution.

We were completely stunned by this report, which suggested that the embassy was covering up the facts. To the best of our collective knowledge, anti-Semitism was a nonissue. We certainly had never reported on it or discussed it. This story appeared in the *New York Times* coincidentally with the visit to Managua of human rights activists from the United States. In their honor, I gave a reception to which I invited both the Sandinista human rights commission and the anti-Sandinista human rights commission. I said to my staff that they should circulate and find out what the human rights activists thought about this story, because we had never seen any previous allegations of this kind. Not surprisingly, the pro-Sandinistas said there was no truth to this allegation. What was more surprising is that even the anti-Sandinistas said there was no truth to it. Nicaraguans, everyone agreed, had never shown any anti-Semitism. Both sides agreed that the vast majority of Jews had fled for personal reasons, mainly because of their relations with the Somoza family. I then asked the political officer to do a more in-depth report. He visited the synagogue and talked to people there. It had been made into a childcare center, with no pictures of Gaddafi. He found that there were not enough Jews in the city to hold a service and that the synagogue had therefore been closed. He interviewed some of the remaining Jews, who said they had not been harassed because of their faith. However, everybody agreed that the Sandinistas were anti-Zionist and pro-Palestinian; there was no question about that. So I put all this into a report, which, I regret to say, did not convince B'nai B'rith. They saw my report as further evidence of the embassy's cover-up and continued to criticize us for trying to protect the Sandinistas.

Eliot Abrams, then assistant secretary of state for human rights, decided to come down to find out the facts for himself. He demanded to meet with members of the Jewish community. I invited to breakfast Jaime Levy, a businessman and importer and one of the very few Jews remaining in Nicaragua. After enjoying a frugal breakfast of fruit, Secretary Abrams asked Levy about the persecution of the Jews in Nicaragua. Levy denied there had been any. Abrams pressed on, saying Levy could speak freely even though the ambassador was present. He said that he knew that almost all the Jews had been forced to leave the country. Levy acknowledged that most had left, in his view because they had been associated with the Somoza regime. He continued, "Look, you don't understand. I import Maidenform bras from Guatemala. I hold them off the market for six months and make a lot of money. Nobody here is harassing me."

I think Abrams assumed that I had set him up with a caricature Jew and that, as alleged by B'nai B'rith, the embassy was not telling the story honestly. Like many in Washington, Abrams did not accept the embassy's argument that anti-Zionism did not equate to anti-Semitism. To be sure, there was a PLO office in Managua. The Sandinistas had broken off relations with the State of Israel, and the Sandinista press frequently criticized, often in strident terms, Israeli policies in the Middle East; but there was no evidence or history that we could find of bigotry or animosity toward Jews as individuals. As this incident made clear, there was no right answer. Most Jews had left Nicaragua. The synagogue was closed. The Sandinistas were anti-Zionists.

In order to ensure that we were telling the whole truth, the embassy maintained very close contacts with the opposition. I met regularly with Pedro Joaquín Chamorro, the editor of the only opposition newspaper, *La Prensa*. We assiduously covered the repeated closing of the paper, its difficulties in obtaining newsprint, and its regular censorship by the government. Similarly, I worked closely with Enrique Bolaños, the president of the business alliance, COSEP. He was a prominent cotton farmer who became president of Nicaragua in the post-Sandinista period. I visited his farms and at one point actually tried picking cotton. The cattle farmers, the coffee producers, the banana growers all had organizations and kept me regularly informed of their travails. They all had stories to tell of harassment, confiscation, and intimidation. I spoke at their conventions and meetings and made a conscious effort to be seen to be supporting the private sector and the free press.

The business class was extremely hospitable to me and my colleagues, inviting us to their beach houses or summer cottages on Lake Managua or at the beach. They hoped that I would accept their critical analysis of the regime without question. But these efforts to maintain contact and our vigorous support for a small aid program to the private sector were never enough. They were aware of my efforts to promote a dialogue and negotiations with the Sandinistas and my attendance at Sandinista-sponsored events. They regarded these efforts as misguided, even when they occasionally led to a reduction of Sandinista pressure. They shared the White House view that regime change was the only viable outcome for their country, and they sensed my resistance to that view.

How one understood the facts and conclusions and what one drew from them played into the underlying debate about the true nature of the Sandinista regime. It was clear to Washington that I tended to take a less dramatic view of Sandinista policies than many would have liked. My personal reporting continued to be optimistic about the possibility of a negotiated outcome. At the same time, much of the embassy's detailed reporting on Sandinista policies and actions seemed to contradict my analysis. At the end of the day, the pessimistic view prevailed. The embassy had provided much of the material to justify it.

THE KISSINGER COMMISSION VISITS MANAGUA

If there had been a steady stream of visitors over the preceding eighteen months since my arrival, nothing was as dramatic or eventful as the eight-hour visit of Dr. Henry Kissinger and the National Bipartisan Commission on Central America. That visit, on October 15, 1983, not only impacted the administration's policy toward the region but also changed the course of my career, although I did not know it at the time. The commission, created by executive order on July 19, 1983, presented its report to the president some six months later, on January 10, 1984, by which time Deputy Secretary Kenneth Dam had informed me that I was being replaced in Nicaragua, although the search for a replacement had not been completed. The Kissinger Commission was my undoing.

The commission had been created with an explicit mandate "to study the nature of U.S. interests in the Central American region and threats posed to those interests," with a view to building a national consensus on a comprehensive policy for the region. The context was the Cold War and the perception that the Soviet Union, operating through its surrogates Cuba and Nicaragua, was seeking to impose totalitarian Marxist-Leninist regimes throughout Central America, historically our own backyard. Although the commission explicitly stayed away from the controversial issues surrounding the funding and arming of the Contras, the Nicaraguan exiles operating out of Honduras with covert support from the United States, it was clear that the commission saw its mission as one of devising a political and economic strategy to thwart the ambitions of our global adversary. Early in the process of formulating the commission's work plan, Kissinger had decided that it would have to visit the region. After extensive consultations in Washington he decided that the period from October 9 to 15 would be appropriate for visits to each of the six Central American capitals. Managua was to be the sixth and final stop on the itinerary.

When I informed the Sandinistas of the commission's prospective visit, they seemed eager to welcome its members. They saw it as an opportunity to justify the actions of the revolution and to explore any possible basis for a reduction in tensions and an enduring understanding between our two countries. They indicated that they would put no obstacles in the way of the commission's meeting with the political opposition, the business community, and the church, although they wanted to ensure that they had adequate time to present their side of the story. As a sign of their goodwill they offered to host a lunch in honor of the commission.

I traveled to Washington in the third week in September for consultations with the State Department and to brief Kissinger on the Managua portion of his visit to Central America. Kissinger received me in the ground-floor offices of the department, where the commission was housed. I shared with him what I understood to be the Sandinistas' hope for a productive set of meetings, their offer of a luncheon in the commission's honor, and the plans that we were making to ensure that the commission met with a cross section of Nicaraguan leaders. Kissinger seemed broadly satisfied with the arrangements the embassy was making but stressed that the visit was a working one and that he and his fellow commissioners did not want any ceremonial events, including a formal lunch in their honor. Kissinger insisted that what they wanted was a working lunch—sandwiches and soft drinks would be fine.

On my return to Managua, I conveyed Kissinger's views to the Foreign Ministry, which expressed disappointment at the refused hospitality but otherwise put no obstacles in the way of the program we were developing. That program was to begin by my briefing the commission, followed by meetings with the opposition and Archbishop Obando y Bravo, a working lunch and intelligence briefing by the Sandinistas, followed by meetings with Sandinista organizations, Foreign Minister d'Escoto, and, finally, Daniel Ortega. These plans were approved in Washington, and the embassy went ahead working out the logistical arrangements on that basis.

The commission arrived by special U.S. military aircraft on the morning of October 15. Less than half the commission and its senior counselors (a bipartisan group of senators and representatives) made the trip, but those who did were an influential and highly engaged group. They included Chairman Kissinger; Lane Kirkland of the AFL-CIO; Henry Cisneros, mayor of San Antonio; John Silber, president of Boston University; Carlos Diaz Alejandro of Yale University; Senator Pete Domenici (R-NM); and Representatives Jack Kemp (R-NY) and Michael Barnes (D-MD). They were accompanied by an array of advisors, including, most notably, Lieutenant Colonel Oliver North of subsequent Iran-Contra fame. It was a motley crew, clearly exhausted after a week on the road and anxious to get back to the United States.

My staff escorted the group to the Casa Grande, the old ambassadorial residence overlooking Managua. My predecessor had abandoned it as a symbol of a changed postrevolutionary attitude, since it was from the Casa Grande that my predecessors had exercised their proconsular relationship with the Somoza family. The house, a large white colonial structure, had been one of two houses dominating the city, the other being that of President Anastasio Somoza, the former dictator. Symbolically at least, the American ambassador had been seen as the coequal political figure in Nicaraguan politics. Larry Pezzullo, my predecessor, thought this symbolism did not comport with the new reality and had moved his residence to a smaller, though elegant house in an upper-class suburb of Managua.

The morning's meetings were held in the dining room of the Casa Grande at a long ceremonial dining room table that had seen virtually no use over the previous three years. The commissioners sat on one side, and those who were to brief them sat facing them across the table. As arranged, I was to open the morning with my personal assessment of the situation, followed by a series of presentations from the leaders of the opposition and the business community and then anti-Sandinista journalists, political parties, and trade unions. This opening phase would last some two hours before the commission moved on to its meeting with the archbishop of Managua, Miguel Obando y Bravo.

After the usual words of welcome on my part, I launched into my assessment. I had, by this point, been in Nicaragua for eighteen months and had met virtually every Nicaraguan of importance both within and outside the revolution. I had concluded that while the Sandinistas were bent on consolidating their power and had little sympathy for their opponents, they were not embarked on an enterprise designed to copy the Cuban model. They were all too aware of the costs to Cuba two decades earlier of its estrangement from the United States and had no desire to burn all their bridges with us. While they were committed to revolutionary solidarity with their neighbors, particularly the FMLN in El Salvador, their primary concern was their own survival and that of the revolution to which they were committed. To that end, they were willing to tolerate opposition and permit the private sector to continue to function, if under considerable restraints from the government. I concluded that it would be difficult, though not impossible, to negotiate an understanding with the Sandinistas to end the export of the revolution in Central America in return for our acceptance of the flawed, though still pluralistic, system that then existed under Sandinista authority. If ending the export of the revolution—in other words, the flow of arms to the FMLN in El Salvador—was our principal goal, this could be achieved, but not if the price was "regime change." Thirty-five years later, I continue to believe that this was true.

As time was short, there were few questions, but one sticks in my memory, that of Dr. John Silber. Silber was clearly skeptical of what I had said. He fixed me with his rather formidable stare and demanded to know whether my assessment was that of the White House. I said that it was my best estimate of what could be achieved based on my extensive contacts and conversations in Nicaragua. He persevered and demanded to know whether President Reagan would agree with me. I again demurred, but it was clear from the expressions on the faces of at least some of the members that they had just heard from an ambassador who was out of step with the administration. I believe that my fate was sealed from that moment, and if not from that moment, at least after the commission had heard from the opposition, led by Enrique Bolaños, who became president of Nicaragua in the post-Sandinista period.

Bolaños, a feisty and articulate cotton farmer and a graduate in industrial engineering from St. Louis University, was then the president of COSEP, the umbrella organization for Nicaragua's private sector. Accompanied by several of the leading businessmen and agriculturalists in Nicaragua and other members of the opposition, he described with eloquence and passion the harassment that the private sector had faced over the three years since the Sandinistas had taken power. He noted the expropriation of lands and businesses belonging to the Somoza family and to those alleged to have ties to the former regime. He explained that even those who were never in the Somoza camp risked expropriation if they criticized the Sandinistas. He described the Sandinista commitment to a mixed economy as a sham and insisted that Nicaragua was on a path that would eventually and inevitably lead to an economy on the Cuban model. He outlined the problems faced by the Catholic Church, the democratic political parties, the free trade unions, and the press, meaning the one remaining independent paper, *La Prensa*. It was an impressive catalog that called into question virtually all of the Sandinistas' stated goals of a democratic political system based on a mixed economy.

Bolaños, however, was not one to rely only on words to convince his audience. He knew that a picture was worth a thousand words. And so to emphasize the points he had made, he produced a series of first-day postal covers commemorating the centenary of the death of Karl Marx, described thereon as the world's greatest thinker. If proof were needed of the Sandinistas' Marxist-Leninist orientation, he said, these stamps could leave no dispassionate observer in doubt.

The commissioners were clearly impressed, as was the administration to which they reported on their return to Washington. Eighteen months later, in a briefing at the White House, President Reagan cited these same stamps as evidence of the Marxist orientation of the regime. I must confess to having been taken aback by this adroit piece of show-and-tell and was not quick-witted enough to point out that these stamps were among many the Sandinista regime issued and that in the previous year they had produced an extensive George Washington series. But the damage had been done.

The speakers who followed from the political parties, democratic trade unions, and *La Prensa* only confirmed what Bolaños had said. Their unanimous conclusion was that reconciliation or negotiation with the Sandinistas was not possible. The Sandinistas, they insisted, had one goal: the creation of a totalitarian Marxist state. Bolaños and others appealed to the commission to convey this reality to the American people and to take every appropriate measure to prevent this goal from being achieved. The commission expressed its satisfaction at the frankness and openness of the presentation without pressing Bolaños or other members of the opposition on what it might take to force the Sandinistas back from the totalitarian brink.

A small group of commission members led by Kissinger then traveled to see Archbishop Miguel Obando y Bravo. Obando was a charismatic figure known for his humble origins and identification with the poor. He had originally sided with the Sandinistas and opposed the Somoza regime, but he subsequently became deeply disenchanted with what he had seen and with the efforts the Sandinistas had made to mobilize Catholics into the revolution and denigrate those who remained outside. (Ironically, almost two decades later, Obando, then a cardinal, was reconciled with Daniel Ortega and presided at his wedding.) Although Obando was cautious in his comments, he left Kissinger in no doubt about his profound skepticism toward the ultimate intentions of the Sandinistas.

Notwithstanding my efforts to inject some degree of balance into the morning's discussions, there is no doubt that the overall impression the commission received was an exceedingly negative one, confirming what they had already heard in the other capitals of Central America. The message was clear: the Sandinistas were Marxist-Leninists under the tutelage of the Cubans. Not only were they bent on putting an end to the freedoms Nicaraguans enjoyed, but they also sought to export their revolution throughout the region. Though plenty of evidence supported this position, it seemed to me then, as it does now over a quarter of a century later, overly simplistic.

THE COMMISSION AND THE SANDINISTAS

By the end of the morning, the stage was set for the second phase of the visit: meetings designed to present to the commission the Sandinista side of the case. But the die had been cast. Commission members had little doubt about the likely veracity of what they were about to be told. Marxist-Leninists, as they knew too well, could not be trusted to tell the truth. If the morning had been characterized by goodwill and a predisposition to listen, the afternoon was a dialogue of the deaf. The commissioners did not know that they were to move from one disastrous meeting to another. Ironically, notwithstanding the Sandinistas' desire to tell their story in the most compelling way possible, the impressions of the morning were to be repeatedly confirmed. Having left the meeting with the archbishop, the commission moved to the palatial former Somoza country club, where the afternoon's sessions were to be held. As I, at Kissinger's insistence, had requested, the Sandinistas organized a working lunch of sandwiches and soft drinks. Although no slight was intended, since the Sandinistas thought they were following American desires, several of the commission members complained at the quality of the lunch and the implied disrespect for the commission.

Immediately following lunch, the head of Sandinista military intelligence, Guerrilla Comandante Julio Ramos, briefed the commission on the military situation in the country, particularly in the Northeast, where anti-Sandinista (Contra) activity was most active. Using a large wall-size map, the comandante described infiltration routes from Honduras, the size and nature of Contra units, and the areas where fighting had taken place. It was a comprehensive and extremely professional briefing, so professional, in fact, that Oliver North, the National Security Council's advisor to the commission, took members of the commission aside to tell them that the briefing was clear confirmation of what they had heard that morning, namely, that the Sandinistas were in the clutches of the Cubans. North argued that the Sandinistas could not have provided such a detailed and accurate briefing on their own. The briefing, he asserted, showed the extent of their technical capability to monitor Contra operations, a capability that could only have come from Cuban and Eastern Bloc sources. I tried to point out that the Sandinistas were known to have infiltrated the Contra ranks and would have had up-to-date information about the Contra operations from their own sources, but the commission accepted North's judgment almost without question.

What followed was a mirror image of the morning's session at the Casa Grande. The Sandinistas produced representatives of small political parties allied with their movement and pro-Sandinista trade union leaders and businessmen. All asserted that they were free and independent, shared the social objectives of the revolution, and were not Marxist-Leninists. Nonetheless, they made a rather poor impression. The repetitiveness of their assertions sounded hollow. Unlike in the morning, none of those whom the Sandinistas produced spoke English, and as a result their message had none of the force or coherence of Bolaños's presentation. They were clearly very small fish in the revolutionary pond.

Fatigue was setting in. It had been a long day and a long week. Henry Cisneros was ill, and the others were exhausted. But two final meetings lay ahead: Father Miguel d'Escoto Brockman, the foreign minister, and Comandante Daniel Ortega, the chairman of the ruling junta and a leading member of the nine-man Sandinista Directorate. The meeting with d'Escoto took place in a conference room on a lower floor of the country club. The minister, flanked by senior aides, sat on one side of the table, the commission and staff sat on the other. D'Escoto, never a favorite of American officials, who regarded him as devious and meretricious, was at his most combative. A plump bespectacled Maryknoll priest who had grown up in Los Angeles, d'Escoto addressed the commissioners in English. He lectured them about the errors of past and current U.S. policy in Nicaragua and denounced the various forms of pressure being brought to bear on the revolution, including economic sanctions, political pressure, and, most notably, the Contra military effort. The minister showed little flexibility and was combative in his defense of Sandinista policies.

The commissioners were not amused. As soon as the minister stopped speaking, Senator Pete Domenici asked to speak. He reminded the minister, whom he insisted on calling derisively "Father," of a meeting that had taken place several years before in Washington. Domenici had taken d'Escoto to lunch in the Senate dining room, and the minister had assured him that the revolution was committed to democracy, a mixed economy, and a free society. Domenici, his words filled with contempt for the minister, said that he had now seen the reality of Nicaragua and knew that everything the minister had told him then was a lie. He would not believe anything the minister said.

D'Escoto was quick to respond and was equally acerbic. He reminded the senator that he and others in the U.S. government had expressed their repeated concern about democracy in Nicaragua. That concern was nothing more than hypocrisy, given American policies throughout the Somoza period. As far as he was concerned, he would never believe anything the senator had to say either. The meeting then broke up, with no further discussion but with the commission in a very sour and hostile mood.

The final meeting of the day, and indeed of the weeklong trip, was scheduled immediately after. In a sense, it was to be the culmination of the trip, an encounter with the leader of the Sandinista revolution, Comandante Daniel Ortega. We went upstairs in the country club to an anteroom outside the large and rather elegant ballroom where Ortega and his government were to meet the commission. As we waited, Kissinger turned to me and asked, "What do we do now?" Taking this as a logistical rather than a substantive question, I described how the meeting would be organized. Ortega would be seated at the end of the room with his government, including Foreign Minster d'Escoto to his left. The commission would go in, shake hands with Ortega, and take their seats on his right. After an exchange of pleasantries, the commissioners would then be free to ask any questions they wished.

Kissinger seemed unhappy and inquired incredulously, "Do you mean I have to shake hands with the son-of-a-bitch?" I ventured that it would be customary to do so, but I did not pursue the question further, as we were then immediately summoned into the ballroom. To this day I do not know whether the handshake took place, as I was at the rear of the group. However, what is certain is that as soon as Kissinger and his colleagues sat down and donned their headphones for simultaneous translation, he turned to Ortega and brusquely and imperiously demanded, "Comandante, what do you have to say?"

Ortega, dressed in revolutionary military uniform, seemed some-what taken aback at this curt beginning to the meeting, which had been billed to both sides as a dialogue about the difficult state of U.S.-Nicaraguan relations. However, undaunted by this inauspicious beginning, Ortega launched into his remarks. He began by saying that, in his view, the United States had only an episodic interest in Latin America, which was driven by crises. When the Cuban revolution took place, the United States had responded with the Alliance for Progress. After the revolution in the Dominican Republic, it had appointed the Rockefeller Commission. Now that there was revolution in Nicaragua, he said, "We have you." However, he added, if the United States had truly cared about democracy in Nicaragua over the past thirty years, "you wouldn't have us. But here we are." It was, perhaps, his finest moment.

Ortega then launched into a forty-minute monologue. In it, he recapitulated in excruciating detail the history of U.S. relations with

Nicaragua over the past century, beginning with William Walker, the great *filibustero* who in the 1850s had made himself briefly president of the country in the hope that Nicaragua would become a slave state in the Union. Ortega recounted the various interventions by U.S. Marines in the first half of the twentieth century, U.S. support for the various Somoza regimes, and now the United States' hostile polices toward the revolution. Covering much of the same ground as d'Escoto before him, Ortega spared his listeners no sin of commission or omission committed by the U.S. government. The commissioners became increasingly angry at this tirade and one by one detached their earphones and ceased to listen to Ortega's screed. Only Kissinger listened to the end. When Ortega finally stopped speaking, Kissinger turned to him and said, "Comandante, I did not like either the tone or substance of your remarks. If there is to be any further communication between us, it will be in writing."

With that, Kissinger and the rest of the delegation got up and walked out into an adjacent room, where the press was waiting to question him about the meeting. Kissinger was suitably circumspect about the encounter with Ortega, and little of the anger and frustration of the commissioners came through. The delegation then headed to the airport to board the military airplane to take them straight back to the United States. The farewells were correct, but I could see that the day in Managua had only confirmed the opinions that each member had brought with him. The dialogue that I had hoped would take place had not. Both sides emerged angry and resentful, and relations with the Sandinistas continued their downward trend. What lay ahead was an intensification of the secret war and a more aggressive effort to bring about regime change.

The pro-Sandinista *El Nuevo Diario* carried a cartoon the day after the commission's departure showing me being flattened by a cart drawn by Kissinger and containing all of the anti-Sandinista groups with which the commission had met. I am seen rather desperately crying out in broken Spanish, "No confundir. Yo ser el embajador" (Don't be confused. I am the ambassador). The paper understood the situation: the commission had little respect for the American ambassador. They did not know then that Washington would conclude that a new American ambassador for Managua was needed to oversee the administration's policies.

THE END OF THE STORY

In early December, less than six weeks after the Kissinger Commission's departure, I received a phone call from Deputy Secretary Kenneth Dam informing me that the president had decided to make a change of ambassadors in Nicaragua. I was not entirely surprised, given the commission's skeptical reception of my ideas. Dam assured me that another job would be found for me, but nothing specific was suggested. Word of my imminent replacement quickly leaked in Washington, with the explanation that the normal two-year tour for ambassadors would soon be up. Few were fooled by this explanation, since the normal tour was three years, and the local and international press began to speculate that my removal was connected to the Kissinger Commission's visit and dissatisfaction in the White House with my overly soft line toward the Sandinistas. The Sandinistas speculated that I had fallen in love with the revolution.

Although I had clearly lost the confidence of the White House, I was kept in place for almost six months while the search for a successor went on, until our ambassador in Hungary, Harry Bergold, agreed to take the job. Work went on in a normal fashion. We reported on plans for the elections scheduled for later in 1984 and the ongoing reaction to Contra attacks in the North. We managed congressional and other delegations and worked with senior department officials seeking to influence the Contadora process and other peace initiatives, for which we had little stomach. I participated in the Central American Chiefs of Mission Conference in San Salvador, attended by Secretary of State George Shultz. In due course, Shultz arranged for me to be sent to Kuwait, where a vacancy had suddenly opened up when the Kuwaitis refused to grant agrément to Brandon Grove, the former U.S. consul general in Jerusalem.

The Sandinistas handled my departure with due regard to protocol. I was offered a farewell reception, at which Daniel Ortega presented me with a gift, a small folk art painting, which hangs in our living room to this day. On the day of my departure the *Semana Cómica* published a cover cartoon entitled "El Regreso" (the return) in which President Reagan is shown spanking me over his knee with a briefcase while Henry Kissinger and Jeane Kirkpatrick look on admiringly. For all that, in retrospect the Sandinistas regarded me with a certain affection, given the increasingly hard line of my successors, and told visiting journalists that I had had my face shaved at a local barbershop, willingly putting my neck at the mercy of a Sandinista razor.

At the State Department, colleagues expressed regret that I had been forced out, although there were some in the Office of Central American Affairs who thought that I had taken too much of an accommodationist view. Subsequently, I was nominated for and received the American Foreign Affairs Association's Christian Herter Award for what was described as constructive dissent.

In retrospect, it is not clear to me whether I did constructively or effectively dissent from the administration's regime-change policy. I struggled publicly to explain the administration's policies and to convey its concerns about Sandinista foreign policy—its support for the FMLN in El Salvador, its military and economic relationships with Cuba and the Soviet Union, and its enthusiastic endorsement of the policies of the nonaligned movement. I shared many of the administration's criticisms of Sandinista domestic policies—censorship of *La Prensa*, restrictions on the democratic political parties, harassment of the church, and pressure on those parts of the private sector that opposed the revolution. I reported on the situation as honestly as I could, covering both the good and the bad news stories as they arose. I encouraged the staff to do the same.

My principal concern was to explain the complexities of the situation. I was, and am, congenitally incapable of seeing in ambiguous situations glasses that are half empty. I remained convinced that if we desired a constructive solution that would end the Sandinistas' interference in El Salvador but leave them in power, we could have had it. I was not successful in persuading Washington of the correctness of that view. The Sandinista regime was not going to be our ideal of a democratic pluralistic government, but at the end of the day Nicaragua was a small country with little ability to influence fundamental U.S. interests. The Sandinistas did not want to be mere pawns of the Soviet Union or of Cuba. As Comandante Tomás Borge once told me, they would never be a lifeless, colorless copy of Bulgaria. In Washington, however, ideology triumphed over reality: dominos were about to fall if we did not change the regime. And I was powerless to alter that view.

In a sense, the Sandinistas understood me too well. A Catholic, much influenced by the liberation theology of the day, I could and did sympathize with the social goals of the revolution. I had little admiration for the conservative traditional ruling class of businessmen and large landholders. I admired the success of the literacy campaign and the efforts to provide basic medical care across the spectrum of Nicaraguan society. I saw virtue in the grassroots system of social organization the Sandinistas favored. I thought the limited area of pluralism allowed could be expanded. As it turned out, pluralism did expand, as the Sandinistas allowed themselves to be voted out of power eight years after I left. Daniel Ortega was no democrat, as we saw with his return to power three decades later. He was also not, at that time, a brutal autocrat but rather a self-serving, lightly principled politician who seized the main chance whenever he could to advance his own and his family's interests.

Forty years later, Nicaragua, with its revolution passed into history, is by no means the most desperate of Central American countries. Gang violence is almost nonexistent. Tourists flock to its beaches and tropical riverine beauties. The private sector thrives. Until the protest demonstrations of April 2018 outraged the hierarchy, Ortega had made his peace with the church. Signs of emotional anti-Yankee suspicions remain. The government has aligned itself with radical regimes elsewhere in the hemisphere, such as those in Venezuela,

Bolivia, and Ecuador. It has become once again an illiberal democracy, partially free. It remains poor, but it is no longer a threat to vital American interests. Reluctantly, until April 2018, we had learned to live with it. Eighty-five years after Sandino's murder with U.S. complicity, Daniel Ortega could still claim that the revolutionary vision lived, if only as a pale shadow of its former self. Yet even that assertion was challenged when riots and disturbances protesting Ortega's policies and autocratic rule erupted in the spring and summer of 2018.

As I reflect on my time in Nicaragua, I believe I consistently and honestly stood up for my views. At times I enjoyed being the butt of Sandinista humor, even when it demeaned me as ambassador and representative of the United States. This constant attention was not healthy. Not only was I thrust into a political role as the agent of regime change for which I was unprepared and unsympathetic, but I was even less prepared for my role's high visibility. I found it exhilarating to be always in the news, my every word parsed for some indication of a change in Washington's views. That visibility was also corrupting. I became absorbed in this public dimension of my position, at times to the consternation and chagrin of my embassy colleagues. In this respect, I was not a particularly good role model for the team of officers I led. They would have preferred more dignity and less frivolity, more earnest steadfastness and less public involvement with and seeming tolerance for the revolution. By 1984 it was time for a change.

1. Author in Sherborne School uniform, 1951. Author photo.

2. (*below*) Author in Moscow during 1957 Youth Festival, August 1957. Author photo.

3. Author in front of Smolny Institute, Leningrad, August 1957. Author photo.

4. Author (*below, bottom left*) at the 1957 Moscow Youth Festival. The caption under this AP wirephoto reads: "American Anthony Quainton, 23, dark-headed youth looking out of photo at lower left, is surrounded by Muscovites as he tells them, in Russian, about the United Nations report on the Hungarian revolt." *New York Times*, August 13, 1957.

5. Washington DC, 1961, President John F. Kennedy greets members of the Foreign Service in the Rose Garden. Quainton is the very young-looking officer immediately to the president's right who seems to be looking off into the middle distance. White House photo.

6. (*above*) Kathmandu, Nepal, 1975, arrival of King Birendra at the royal command performance of *The Crucible*. Quainton is seen shaking the queen's hand, while the play's co-director, David Handforth of the British Council, is next in line. Government of Nepal photo.

7. (*opposite top*) Bangui, Central African Republic, 1976, conversing with President Jean-Bédel Bokassa after the presentation of credentials. CAR government photo.

8. (*opposite below*) Comandante Tomás Borge at the 1982 Fourth of July reception in Managua, toasting with Susan and Tony Quainton. USIS Embassy photo.

9. Cartoon in Managua's *Semana Cómica* on the author's departure from Nicaragua, May 1984. *Semana Cómica*.

10. Kuwait, 1984, presentation of credentials to Emir Sheikh Jaber al-Ahmad al-Sabah. Government of Kuwait photo.

11. Lima, Peru, 1991, conversation with President Alberto Fujimori. Government of Peru photo.

16
Desert Sands

When my appointment to Kuwait was confirmed, Susan and I plunged into a crash course of Arabic, with less than two months before we were to go to Kuwait. We thus made only limited progress in that extremely challenging language. I made the usual rounds of agency briefings, which were absolutely essential, as Kuwait was a blank slate for me. I had never served in the Arab world and knew little of the internal political dynamics of this small, oil-rich sheikhdom in the Arabian Gulf. I did my best to catch up, but the department could only manage three weeks of Arabic, not enough to give Susan or me any serious claim to be area specialists. We greatly benefited from our knowledge of the Arabic script, in which we had become fluent when we studied Urdu many years before. I went through the usual round of briefings and, for the second time, attended the Ambassadorial Seminar, or "charm school," as it came to be known.

A shadow over the assignment was the fact that in the previous September Embassy Kuwait had been the target of a major terrorist attack. A truck loaded with explosives succeeded in entering the compound, destroying the administrative building and Marine House, badly damaging the chancery building itself, and killing several local employees. This bombing, following closely on two bombings in Beirut, raised the level of fear and anxiety among the embassy's personnel. The ambassador's residence had been converted to administrative use and included the medical unit. Security became an obsessive concern.

I arrived in this tense atmosphere. The bombings had so traumatized many embassy families that they would not come to the Chancery compound, where there was a tennis court, swimming pool, and snack bar. Even though overall security had dramatically improved, there was an evident divide within the official community. Those who had been at post at the time of the bombing remained highly nervous and fearful. They believed that those of us who came later would never understand what they had gone through. We, on the other hand, tended to be less anxious and assumed that another attack was unlikely. We thought the enhanced security measures, including a new substantial perimeter wall, would be sufficient to protect us.

The regional context further aggravated the sense of insecurity. The Iran-Iraq War was raging to Kuwait's north and east. The Kuwaitis supported the Iraqis throughout. When the Iranians launched their offensive on the Faw Peninsula in February and March 1986, the exchange of cannon fire could be clearly heard in Kuwait City. When the Iranians mined Kuwait's ports, the war seemed closer and closer.

The Kuwaitis, gravely concerned about the security of their oil exports, turned to the United States for protection. Defense Minister Sheikh Salem al-Sabah, a former ambassador to Washington, approached me with a request that we permit Kuwaiti tankers to be registered in the United States, fly the American flag, and receive the protection of American naval forces in the Gulf. Not surprisingly, the U.S. Navy was extremely unenthusiastic about the prospect of taking on any substantial new responsibilities in the midst of a war zone. Only when the defense minister told me, with a twinkle in his eye, that if we were not able to help, the Soviet ambassador had indicated that the Soviet Union might be willing to step in, did U.S. policy change. Washington policy makers turned on a dime. Keeping the Soviets out of the Gulf was a far more important strategic objective than the logistical difficulties of protecting a handful of Kuwaiti tankers. I spent much time in this period working out the final agreement, which ended in the summer of 1987 with my raising the first American flag on a Kuwaiti tanker.

Oil was the all-consuming subject for Kuwaitis. Not only were they concerned to maintain the flow out through the Gulf, but they also wanted to maintain prices at a level that would continue to build their sovereign wealth fund. To support those goals, Kuwait was an active member of the Organization of the Petroleum Exporting Countries (OPEC). The Reagan administration looked with considerable distrust on OPEC's price-fixing policies, which violated the administration's cherished open market and free trade policies. Consequently, in 1986 I was instructed to see the oil minister, Sheikh Ali Khalifa, to urge the Kuwaitis at an upcoming OPEC meeting to vote against firm price targets and instead allow the market to operate normally.

Sheikh Ali received me cordially enough. He was a recent graduate of Claremont College in California and spoke perfect English. I made my pitch, to which he listened attentively. His response was unexpected. "Mr. Ambassador," he began, "you don't know what you are talking about." I was no oil expert, but I thought I had made the administration's case clearly. Sheikh Ali then gave me an introductory course in oil economics. If Kuwait agreed to the American suggestion, oil prices would fall to approximately eight dollars a barrel. Kuwait, he noted, produced oil at two dollars a barrel and would still make money. In the Texas oil patch, however, production costs were closer to fifteen dollars a barrel, so the American oil industry would go out of business. Surely, he suggested, that was not the goal of American policy. What the Americans and the Arabs wanted was a price of roughly twenty dollars a barrel, which would ensure profits for all. I had no plausible answer but reiterated our faith in a free oil market.

In the event, the Saudis dramatically increased their production, and OPEC could not agree on a price. As predicted, the market price for Dubai light fell precipitously to the predicted levels below ten dollars a barrel. We quickly abandoned our insistence on a free market and accepted OPEC price-fixing at levels satisfactory to our own oil industry.

My lack of Arabic was a constant obstacle in my work. I often visited the principal Kuwaiti families' *diwaniyas*, a kind of family or clan open house on a given day or evening each week and on major feast days such as Eid. I was always warmly received and, whenever possible, placed next to an English-speaking member of the family. While the gesture of reaching out to these leading families seemed much appreciated, I rarely learned much, as I could not join in the general conversation that animated these evenings. I was told that sensitive political matters were often discussed.

The Kuwaiti winter, though short, is delightful: cool nights, moderate days, and wildflowers everywhere in the desert. Kuwaiti families take this time to set up camps in the desert surrounding the capital. These are small tent cities often ten to fifteen miles from the city. One winter a leading family invited me to join them for a traditional evening. They suggested that I not arrive until after midnight, as the party did not get going until then. Upon arrival I was shown into a large tent where some twenty men, all in white *dishdashas*, sat around the edge of the tent on Oriental carpets and against highly embroidered cushions. All seemed to be drinking Black Label scotch, while in the background a small musical band played traditional instruments. The atmosphere was quite relaxed. At about one a.m. provocatively clad dancing girls emerged with whom guests were expected to dance. I politely, if nervously, complied and joined the general activity. Somewhere between two and three a.m. another group of dancers appeared, this time, transvestites. Again, guests were asked to dance. I was understandably squeamish, but my Kuwaiti hosts eventually persuaded me to participate, to their great amusement. The dancing was, in fact, quite harmless, but it testified to the ambiguous male sexuality in a society often seen by outsiders as conservative and straitlaced.

Although the embassy had two qualified Arabists, both with tested levels of professional proficiency, neither could do professional-level interpreting or translating. I was forced to deal almost exclusively with those Kuwaitis who spoke English. At one point in the debate about the reflagging of the Kuwaiti tankers, I found myself in an awkward position. The department had sent me a top-secret telegram instructing me to convey the official U.S. government position to the ruler, Sheikh Jaber al-Sabah. The emir did not speak or read English, so I was faced with the challenge of putting the démarche into Arabic. None of the American officers was capable of doing that. After a lively debate in the country team I decided that we would have to entrust the translation to a Syrian working in the consular section whose translation skills were well known to the political section. I then solemnly cut the top-secret designation off the top and bottom of each page of the instruction and ordered that it be given to this uncleared local employee for translation. The text came back, my staff said it looked satisfactory, and I duly presented it to the emir. No doubt the substance of my démarche made its way to some Arab intelligence agency, but the job was done, and with the emir's authorization, the reflagging went forward.

◆ ◆ ◆

One of the idiosyncrasies of life in Kuwait revolved around the use and consumption of alcohol. Alcohol was served in private homes. When guests included Kuwaiti officials, the senior official set the tone. If he ordered orange juice, his comrades followed suit. If he opted for scotch, many would do the same.

The basic problem was where to get alcoholic beverages, since none were on sale in the country. There were two solutions to this problem: judicious smuggling and home production. A typical briefcase could hold three bottles of Black Label scotch, enough for several receptions. That was often the solution for diplomats, since their baggage was never opened on arrival at the Kuwait airport. For Kuwaitis, there was a flourishing black market based on spirits illegally smuggled in by truck from Iraq. Diplomats and other expatriates in general stayed away from the black market. The alternative was home production of beer and wine. The British community and many expatriate contractors were into beer making.

Home production was also a possibility for wine lovers. Colleagues quickly introduced us to the art of oenology. On Fridays we would go off to the local supermarket and buy reusable one-liter bottles of Austrian grape juice, which had the advantage of not being pasteurized and not containing any preservative. (Kuwait reportedly had the highest per capita consumption of grape juice in the Middle East.) We would then solemnly empty the juice into a plastic garbage can and add sugar, yeast, and water. Within days the grape juice would ferment. We would then decant it into other containers to eliminate sediment, add tea bags to provide clarity, and, after two or three such exercises, rebottle what had now become wine. It was usually drinkable within about six weeks. One would serve homemade wine with a certain pride, identifying the best vintages by month. At a dinner party one might, for example, assure the guests that the wine they were drinking was a very fine February. Early on in our stay we managed to make a dozen bottles of white wine from grapes we collected in the back of the residence garden. I cannot honestly say the quality was up to what could be made from Austrian juice, but at least it was homegrown Kuwaiti wine.

For hard drinkers, the problem was more complicated. Some expatriates attempted distillation, but the equipment needed was complicated and the risk of discovery high. Discovery would lead to expulsion from the country and the end to a lucrative contracting career. However, there was another solution: industrial carpet cleaner. Carpet cleaner, as imported into Kuwait, was 100 percent unadulterated methanol, which, when diluted with water and orange juice and the addition of gin or whiskey extract, became a potent and popular tipple, particularly in certain quarters of the British community. The resulting headache was annoying, but at least one did not go blind.

Unlike Saudi Arabia, its neighbor to the south, Kuwait was a religiously tolerant country. There were a small Anglican church in the port city of Ahmedi, an old American Protestant missionary compound in the center of Kuwait City, and a substantial Catholic cathedral. Expatriates were free to worship. Leading members of the royal family had been born in the American missionary hospital and retained affection for the missionaries, often going to greet them on Christmas. Several American Roman Catholic priests whom we had known at earlier posts transited Kuwait from time to time, and we would ask them to celebrate mass in the residence for any embassy personnel who wished to attend. They were happy to do so, although the more orthodox staff members were scandalized when the priests celebrated mass without proper vestments and had to make do with store-bought bread and locally brewed wine.

Kuwait, unlike its neighbors, had the distinction of being technically a democracy. There were regular elections for the National Assembly. Outsiders often criticized the Kuwaiti political process as being a fake or controlled democracy because of the very small size of the electorate. The electorate was, to be sure, small, less than 120,000 in a country of 1.7 million inhabitants. However, over a million of Kuwait's residents were foreigners and not eligible to vote. Among Kuwaitis, over half were women and half were under eighteen and did not have the right to vote. Eligible Kuwaiti males did engage in lively political debates and active campaigning. Candidates would provide camel roasts for voters and other incentives to gain their support. The system was not a Western democracy, but there was real choice.

Although criticism of the ruler was forbidden and effective authority rested in the hands of the emir, there was a free press, free debate in the assembly, and a sense of openness that did not exist at the time in the other Gulf emirates or in nearby Saudi Arabia.

The embassy maintained an active commercial and cultural program. On the twenty-fifth anniversary of U.S.-Kuwaiti relations, the commercial counselor sponsored a trade fair in a local hotel at which dozens of American companies presented their products, which included cigarettes. Kuwaiti men, like most Arabs of that generation, were avid chain smokers. In the interest of promoting sales, Marlboro representatives persuaded me to mount their mechanical bull with a ten-gallon hat upon my head. This mechanical contraption could be made to twist, turn, and buck at accelerating speeds. Desperately clutching the pommel, I rode the bull for some thirty seconds until I was unceremoniously thrown to the ground, to the cheers and applause of the Kuwaiti businessmen in attendance. The cigarette importers were delighted.

Later in our tour, the Buffalo Bill Wild West Show came to town, presenting a "typical" American rodeo experience. This was a private commercial endeavor, but it was one that both the public affairs officer and the commercial counselor urged me to support. Once again, the organizers outfitted me in a ten-gallon hat. They persuaded Susan and me to board a stagecoach imported for the occasion and drive into the stadium. The show featured a selection of rodeo events, including bareback riding. Unfortunately, the riders were scantily clad young ladies. The Kuwaiti authorities closed the show after the first public performance on the grounds that it was offensive to public morals.

Susan was active on the local music scene, playing in the White House Orchestra. The White House in question was an apartment building where many expatriates, particularly Japanese contractors, lived. The orchestra's conductor, Mr. Toyoma, lived there and christened the orchestra. With the American ambassador's wife playing the bass and the orchestra's markedly American name, many assumed that it had some official sanction. This assumption may have contributed to the good attendance at its concerts.

USIA was constantly sending artists our way. The most controversial turned out to be a group of graffiti painters from the Bronx, who did a tour of the Gulf under U.S. auspices. We arranged for them to give a demonstration of their art on the inside of the newly constructed security wall. They were highly skilled artists, but the Kuwaitis whom we invited to see them perform were horrified at the thought that we might be encouraging graffiti painting on the marble walls of Kuwaiti residences and official buildings.

As in other posts, the ambassador's residence was the venue for innumerable events, official receptions, and cultural presentations. We hosted a steady stream of official visitors, including Walter Cronkite and Senators John Warner and Arlen Specter. Senator Specter insisted on playing squash, and since I was the only squash player in the embassy, I offered to play against this vastly fitter opponent, who defeated me decisively. The combatant commander of Central Command came regularly. Toward the end of my stay, General George Crist arrived with his political advisor, Nathaniel Howell. To my consternation, during a dinner for the country team that Susan and I gave for General Crist, he offhandedly announced that his political advisor was present to "measure the drapes." Startled, I inferred that Nat Howell would soon be living in the house. In this way I learned of my imminent transfer. I expressed to George Vest, the department's director general, my displeasure at the embarrassment and discourtesy shown on this occasion. His apologies notwithstanding, the damage had been done.

There were lighthearted moments in Kuwait, despite the background of general tension created by past terrorist attacks and the ongoing Iran-Iraq War. We had a successful amateur dramatic night in the garden of the residence, in which Susan and the political counselor played a scene from Neil Simon's *Plaza Suite*. I was also active on the local amateur dramatic scene, as I had been in other countries. I enjoyed taking roles in *The Odd Couple*, *The Seven-Year Itch*, and *The Real Inspector Hound*.

A great deal of socializing and reciprocal entertaining went on among members of the mission, much of it lighthearted. On one free Saturday afternoon during a community-wide pet show, the DCM organized a banana-eating contest between his monkey, Anastasia, and the Marine Security Guards. The monkey and three marines sat on the wall of the DCM's residence. Each was given a banana and instructed to eat it as quickly as possible. The crowd of embassy colleagues cheered. Anastasia, whose technique of sucking all the fruit from the skin without peeling, won hands down.

On the local side, Kuwait's leading families were most generous and open. But getting inside their culture was not easy for those who did not speak the language or have previous Middle Eastern experience. Keeping up with Kuwaiti wealth was also a challenge. Kuwaiti social events tended to be extravagant, with dozens of dishes being offered. Embassies could not compete, although Kuwaitis seemed happy to accept invitations to more modest official events.

Representation was an important part of my work. We hosted the standard national day party not on July 4 but on February 21, Presidents' Day. Traditionally we reached out to a wide cross section of the Kuwaiti business elite, who always seemed to enjoy coming to our events. In 1984 the twenty-fifth anniversary of U.S.-Kuwaiti relations presented a rare representational opportunity. As a result, instead of a national day reception we put together a special event in September to commemorate the anniversary. In the large Hilton Hotel ballroom we set up elaborate and tastefully decorated food stands representing the different regional foods of the United States— Californian, Texan, and others. The event was well attended. For the occasion we had special commemorative bone china plates prepared, which we distributed to select Kuwaitis.

For all the extravagance of that event, the embassy's representation funds were quite limited; about half of the annual allocation went for these major receptions, to which several hundred Kuwaitis had traditionally been invited. In 1987 the department, in its zeal for cost-cutting, urged embassies to scale back the national day reception. I took the advice seriously and decided to limit our effort to a *vin d'honneur*. We sent invitations to other heads of mission and the secretary general of the Foreign Ministry, but we did not invite the business community. We saved a great deal of money, but private Kuwaitis were not impressed. I received several telegrams the next day from prominent Kuwaiti families, sending us best wishes for our national day and expressing regret that their invitation, which they had always received in the past, must have been lost in the mail.

Overall, Kuwait was a fascinating and difficult post. The work was challenging and, in the context of the Iran-Iraq War and America's long-term interests in the Gulf, important. Of all our many endeavors in this period I was most proud to have been associated with the reflagging of Kuwait's tanker fleet. When the opportunity presented itself in the summer of 1987 to move back to the State Department, I was not entirely displeased. I welcomed the opportunity to work in the newly established Office of the Inspector General.

17
Rooting Out Corruption and Incompetence

Of all the jobs in the Foreign Service to which I might have aspired, deputy inspector general was not one of them. I had had some experience with embassy inspections during the previous thirty years of my career, none of them totally positive. I often perceived inspectors as obnoxious busybodies who sought out minute flaws in the system and then did little to improve them. Thus it was with some surprise that I received a telegram from the State Department in the summer of 1987 asking me to go to Vienna to meet with the recently appointed first statutory inspector general (IG), Sherman Funk, an experienced government official. I was coming to the end of my tour as ambassador to Kuwait, and the department indicated that I might become the new inspector general's deputy.

Historically, the department had appointed a senior Foreign Service Officer to be inspector general. But Senator Jesse Helms, who had a deep suspicion of the Foreign Service, believed the existing system only put foxes in the henhouse, and the department was not serious about rooting out mismanagement, inefficiency, and fraud. So in creating a statutory Office of the Inspector General (OIG) at State, he explicitly precluded any Foreign Service Officer from holding that post. Looked at from within the Foreign Service, the new office was assumed to have a hostile agenda toward the department and the Foreign Service and to be little more than Senator Helms's tool for undermining the department and emasculating the Foreign Service. We were proven wrong.

It was with some trepidation that I set off to meet Sherman Funk. Vienna was the perfect place for Sherman to be introduced to the Foreign Service and for me to be introduced to him. Its highly cultured atmosphere, its understated but vigorous independence, and its love of tradition made Vienna a place where diplomats felt at home.

Sherman was at home in Vienna, and so was I. Over several meals enhanced with lots of wine, Sherman and I discussed the culture of the Foreign Service, my perceptions of structural and organizational problems in the State Department, and the role of diplomats in a rapidly changing world. We hit it off immediately, and Sherman offered me the job.

The exact nature of the job was not clear either to me or, as it turned out, to Sherman. Under what circumstances could I act in his absence? Which elements of the Office of the Inspector General would I supervise? I had no background in either audits or investigations, both areas dear to Sherman and central to his understanding of the IG's role. Yet I could not just spin my managerial wheels supervising the ongoing embassy inspection process. It took time for us to work out an understanding on these points. Sherman eventually decided that I would supervise both the inspection and audit divisions. He oversaw the investigation branch. While we were extremely compatible intellectually, to the degree that a Harvard man can be compatible with a Princetonian, Sherman was not altogether sure whether my loyalties to the Foreign Service would trump his expectations of a tough, honest, and critical inspection and audit environment.

To the surprise of my most suspicious colleagues, Sherman proved to be an almost ideal choice for inspector general. He demanded absolute loyalty and rigor from his subordinates in their work and brooked no compromise when it came to presenting findings of inefficiency or wrongdoing. He was an articulate and convincing exponent of the OIG point of view, made more credible by the fact that he had strong congressional backing for all that he did. He quickly gained the confidence of Secretary James Baker and, over time, the respect of the Foreign Service.

Sherman was a man of extraordinarily broad culture and experience. He had served bravely in the Second World War: his crippled arm was there for all to see. He had had a broad liberal education and interests far beyond the promotion of government managerial efficiency. He talked on equal terms with senior Foreign Service Officers who shared that same culture. They in turn quickly came to realize that he was not out to destroy the traditional career service but rather to improve and strengthen it. Both sides went through a learning process that ended in mutual respect, if not always in substantive agreement.

I, too, had to gain his confidence, and over time I did. He entrusted me with difficult investigations of the behavior of several ambassadors and had me lead an inspection of the Bureau of Intelligence and Research, one of the department's most sensitive. Not all of his recommendations were implemented; not all of his staff's conclusions went unchallenged; he was not always right. But he always ferociously defended his staff and the integrity of their work. He was proud of us, and we were proud of him.

Sherman never pulled his punches. While he showed himself to be sensitive to the traditions of the Foreign Service and the State Department, he was equally tenacious in his commitment to seeing both improved. He was a man of integrity, generosity, and intelligence with a marvelous sense of humor and a recognition of his own foibles. All these qualities he put to good use as he assembled his new team of auditors, inspectors, and investigators. It was a pleasure, indeed an honor, to have been his first deputy. Not a conventional boss, he was one who commanded the respect, loyalty, and affection of all who served on his team.

In addition to supervising both inspection and audit staffs, I often had to take on special missions, as when, to gain firsthand inspection experience, I headed a team that inspected the Bureau of Intelligence and Research. We identified many management problems and a lack of leadership in the bureau. We did, I think, modestly improve the working of that critical bureau. In addition, I traveled on several occasions to investigate problems involving chiefs of mission. In one case, a politically appointed ambassador had been accused of abusing his position by personally consuming food and drink charged to official residence expenses and by arranging for his brother to get embassy contracts. His staff had turned against him and reported every misstep to Washington. He was eventually recalled from his post. In another case I had to examine the use of embassy funds originally earmarked for employee housing for the construction of a squash court. Embassy staff alleged that the ambassador had made illegal use of appropriated funds to indulge his own personal love of squash, a sport in which he was reported to be extremely proficient. We found no official wrongdoing, but I learned how damaging to an ambassador a resentful staff could be.

Sherman Funk exacted high standards and expected Foreign Service personnel to adhere strictly to the rules. Profiteering with government funds was something he particularly abhorred. I found myself caught in the crosshairs of his scrutiny when a complaint came in about our ambassador to Nicaragua, who was allegedly profiteering on the black market, cashing dollars obtained at the tourist rate and claiming reimbursement at the less advantageous official rate. This had become standard practice in Managua for many years, and I discovered to my consternation that I had done exactly what the ambassador was accused of doing. In my case, and I think in the case under investigation, there was no question of conscious impropriety. This was how the budget and fiscal section of the embassy had set things up. However, it was clear the ambassadors were profiting from this system, and I quickly reimbursed the government for any overpayment I had received several years before.

It was a rewarding two years. I learned a great deal about the cumbersome but effective audit process. I saw the overall strength of the performance of our ambassadors and embassies overseas, but I also witnessed a remarkable amount of carelessness and failure to follow instructions exactly and carefully. Omnipresent ethical issues demonstrated how poorly many of our chiefs of mission managed the perks of their office and how they mishandled the team-building side of their responsibilities. We were assiduous in following up on our recommendations, but many remained unresolved without penalty to the embassy concerned many months after the inspection had concluded. The OIG made an important difference in improving the department's operations. But there were limits to how far the OIG could move a large and venerable institution proud of its traditions and modus operandi.

18
Andean Adventure

After two years as Sherman Funk's deputy, I was offered the chance to go to Peru as chief of mission. I jumped at the opportunity, which made considerable sense, given my experience in Nicaragua and my work on counterterrorism a decade before. It was an exciting time in Lima. I would be going to a Peru that was facing a prolonged economic and security crisis. The Maoist Shining Path (Sendero Luminoso) was making increasingly violent attacks on basic infrastructure. The policies of President Alan García had brought about economic chaos. Inflation was running at over 6,000 percent per annum. Elections were about to take place, which Washington was convinced would change Peru for the better.

For all that, I had no previous exposure to Peru's millennial culture and history. I knew little of Lima. My extensive predeparture briefings did not entirely prepare me either for the complexity of Peruvian politics or for the dirty, rundown capital city and its surprisingly demoralized population, fearful of each new Shining Path attack. Although Lima had a rich colonial past, its republican present reflected little of that glory. Gloomy half the year from the mists produced by the Humboldt Current and dilapidated from lack of expenditure on infrastructure, it was by no means the glamorous center of Latin American culture to which I had imagined going.

For the United States in 1989, Peru's significance arose from its role as the principal producer of coca, the base product for the cocaine that was decimating America's cities. Peru was a central focus in the administration's Andean drug war. In addition, Peru's approaching elections might significantly alter the country's drug policy. Greater cooperation with the United States might be on the horizon. It seemed certain that the great Peruvian novelist Mario Vargas Llosa would win the presidency. In all my briefings at State and at the CIA, his victory was assumed. Senior department officials urged me to get to know the Vargas Llosa team as soon as possible after my arrival.

For a while I feared that my arrival might be held up, given the complex and lengthy process of senatorial confirmation. To my pleasant surprise, Secretary of State James Baker, anxious to get me to Lima well before the elections, asked Senate Foreign Relations Committee chairman Jesse Helms to expedite my confirmation. As a result, no hearings were held, and my name was expeditiously voted out of committee and onto the Senate floor. I was confirmed in early December 1989 and set out with Susan for my post almost at once. But first, President George H. W. Bush most hospitably received the entire family in the Oval Office for the usual photo opportunity and took some fifteen minutes to chat with us. Mrs. Bush invited Susan to tea in the private quarters of the White House with several other ambassadorial wives. The graciousness of the Bushes had a positive impact on both of us.

We quickly settled into what is one of the most beautiful Spanish-style colonial residences in the Americas. The rundown embassy was less prepossessing, and security measures had made it ugly. Its position opposite a park in the center of Lima made it vulnerable to Shining Path terrorists, who could, and did, launch rockets at it.

Lima's social and political elite quickly lionize American ambassadors, and I was no exception. Susan and I found ourselves the guests of honor at a series of dinners at which we were introduced to members of the Vargas Llosa team. Many of their wives were not shy about indicating which ministerial posts their husbands would hold in the next government. I felt I was off to a good start.

Shortly after my arrival on December 11, I presented my credentials to President Alan García in the great gilded ceremonial hall of the presidential palace. I was quite nervous, not having been in Latin America for several years, and my Spanish was quite rusty. After I read my formal statement and presented my appointment letter, García invited me to sit with him for a cup of coffee and a private informal conversation. I was pleased at this opportunity to discuss our official agenda with the president but spoiled the pleasure when, in my nervousness, I spilled my small cup of strong black coffee across my lap. With characteristic charm, President García reached out and patted my arm. "No te preocupes" (Don't worry), he assured me.

Although García had bankrupted the country and enriched himself in the process, we were able to do business with his administration. In the remaining six months of his mandate, our programs carried on normally, even as we prepared for the arrival of the next president. The several occasions on which I met with García were always cordial and substantive. This reflected the fact that other elements in the embassy had developed close working relations on drugs and terrorism with many levels of the García government. This was particularly true with Interior Minister Augustín Mantilla and several of the armed services chiefs.

I worked to maintain those relationships. In fact, my first call after presenting my credentials to García was on Minister Mantilla on December 12. Several days later I went to the Huallaga Valley with the president and representatives of the press and diplomatic corps to take part in the ceremonial inauguration of our counternarcotic base at Santa Lucía. Cooperation at all levels seemed to be going well. The Lima press gave the event substantial coverage.

The darker side of the government's antidrug and antiterrorist operations was the repeated abuse of human rights, including numerous disappearances, apparently the result of police or army operations. In late March, I took up the issue with the Foreign Ministry and left a long and detailed list of cases we were following, requesting that the government urgently investigate them. This message was not just mine to carry; all levels of the embassy were engaged in making the same points to their contacts in the police and army. Little did we know at that point that human rights issues would become even more salient with the next administration.

Although we continued to do business with the García government, the first six months of my tour were otherwise consumed with preparations for the next government and consequently with detailed analysis of the electoral process. We maintained close touch with Fredemo, the party supporting Vargas Llosa. We studied each weekly poll as it came out to determine how substantial the Vargas Llosa win would be.

However, in the first three months of 1990 a strange phenomenon appeared on the political horizon: an unknown political hopeful, Alberto Fujimori, the rector of the Agricultural University at La Molina. In January and February, Vargas Llosa was clearly well ahead in all the polls. By March the little-known academic, a candidate for both the Senate and the presidency, was beginning to attract attention. Traveling the country from one end to the other, often in the distinctive dress of the Andean peasant, Fujimori slowly gained in popularity. Although popularly referred to as *el chino*—a sobriquet Peruvians give to anyone of East Asian extraction, whether Chinese or not—he strongly identified with ordinary Peruvians. He won over great swaths of the electorate with his two campaign slogans, "Un presidente como tú" (A president like you) and "Honestidad, trabajo, y tecnología" (Honesty, work, and technology), three qualities for which Peruvians were not well known. Between March and April his standing rose by a percentage point each day from nearly zero at the beginning of the campaign. To the astonishment of most observers, including those of us in the embassy who were following the elections, in the first round in April, Fujimori came in a close second to Vargas Llosa. In the run-off required under the Peruvian Constitution, it quickly became clear that Vargas Llosa would lose when all the smaller parties not associated with Fredemo announced that they would support Fujimori.

The Roman Catholic Church entered the fray at the last minute in the hope of saving the Vargas Llosa candidacy. The archbishop of Lima, Vargas Alzamora, known affectionately in the press as "Piolin" (Tweety Bird) because of his small stature, openly tried to influence the outcome by suggesting that Fujimori was in the clutches of evangelicals. (Fujimori's second vice presidential candidate, Carlos García, was a little-known evangelical pastor.) To motivate the faithful, the archbishop ordered that Lima's most holy religious symbol, the painting called *The Lord of the Miracles*, be taken in procession from the Church of the Nazarenas, where it was normally kept, through the streets of Lima as an indication of the church's concerns. Normally, the painting only left the Nazarenas church once a year, in October. Never before had it been used for political purposes. This effort had no discernible impact on the campaign, but after the election relations between Fujimori and the church remained extremely tense. While occasionally attending mass, Fujimori refused to have anything to do with the archbishop or other church authorities.

When the results of the first round came in, Vargas Llosa privately indicated that he intended to withdraw rather than face the humiliation of an electoral defeat in the second round. Washington instructed me to persuade him to remain in the race, if only for the sake of democracy in Peru. I visited him in his unpretentious home in Barranco, the trendy artists' quarter of Lima, and made my presentation. Though he made no commitment, he did not withdraw.

The embassy then began to scramble to brief Washington about the likely next president of Peru. No one in the embassy had ever met him. One USAID officer who had worked with him on an agricultural project prepared for us a rather scathing memorandum, portraying Fujimori as a crafty and manipulative university rector. Having seen Vargas Llosa and in order to maintain the embassy's official neutrality in the elections, I sought an appointment with Fujimori. He received me in his extremely modest home, which was almost completely bare of ornaments beyond several bottles of sake and a few Japanese dolls. I found Fujimori surrounded by huge piles of paper, which he had evidently been studying. He welcomed me cordially and offered me tea, which his wife, Susana Higuchi, served in typical Japanese style on her knees at a low table. We had a cordial conversation. I laid out the principal elements of American policy with respect to drugs and terrorism. He listened attentively, clearly unaware of the details of our programs. It seemed an auspicious beginning to our relationship.

In due course, Fujimori won the second round. He had run on a platform explicitly rejecting Washington consensus policies of fiscal austerity and economic reform, a program to which Vargas Llosa had been committed. However, Fujimori recognized that national fiscal policy had to be addressed. In the interim between the second round of the elections and his installation on July 28, he traveled to Washington and New York, where he met with leading figures at the World Bank, the IMF, and the United Nations. He returned a new man, convinced of the need for a dramatic "shock" to break the back of Peru's inflation.

Indeed, shortly after his inauguration he put in place a dramatic series of measures, cutting subsidies for petroleum and other basic goods and reducing government expenditures. The impact was immediate, with inflation falling to double digits within weeks. Throughout much of this period of economic transition Fujimori's finance minister, Carlos Boloña, was in direct touch with the U.S. Treasury's deputy secretary. As neither the State Department nor I was in this loop, I only learned what was going on when Minister Boloña would call and bring me up to date on the state of the reform discussions.

Washington sent Secretary of Education Lauro Cavazos to represent President Bush at Fujimori's installation on July 28, 1990. Cavazos was a relatively low-level head of delegation, given the fact that five Latin American heads of state were in attendance. His designation seemed to indicate to the Peruvian establishment that we did not have great hopes for this obscure, inexperienced Japanese Peruvian president. Cavazos was a gracious guest but certainly not a political heavyweight in the Bush administration. He stayed with us during the inauguration festivities and in appreciation for our efforts in organizing his visit gave us an engraved school bell, which we still display among our Foreign Service mementos.

Our relations with Fujimori steadily improved over the ensuing twenty-two months until his infamous *autogolpe*, or self-coup, of April 5, 1992. He had won the presidency, but his party, Cambio 90, did not command a majority in the National Assembly. He eventually solved this problem by dismissing the assembly in its entirety. This antidemocratic action seriously damaged our relations.

In the summer of 1990, Vice President Dan Quayle made an official visit to Peru and had productive discussions with Fujimori. And in September 1991 Fujimori and his wife, Susana, made an official working visit to Washington, where he met with President Bush and other senior officials. He also managed to include a visit to Disney World in Florida, for which I was his escort officer. Susan was the Washington escort for Mrs. Fujimori, a civil engineer for whom the State Department had arranged visits relating to engineering projects. Mrs. Fujimori, however, expressed disappointment that her day had not included anything "spiritual." Unlike her husband, she was a devout Catholic and had wanted to see the important churches in Washington. Susan, although mortified that we had overlooked something so important, ultimately arranged for her to attend mass at St. Matthew's Cathedral.

These official visits reflected a steadily improving relationship focused on our common participation in the drug war in the Andes. We increased our aid as Peru improved its participation in counter-drug efforts. However, our failure to come up with what the Peruvians considered adequate alternative development projects constantly intruded into the discussions and impeded a swifter and deeper Peruvian engagement. At the San Antonio drug summit in late February 1992, President Fujimori thwarted a clear statement on eradication, arguing that greater resources for alternative development were needed if he were to agree to our objectives. He criticized the U.S. Congress for holding up aid out of concern for human rights abuses in Peru's struggle against the Shining Path.

The embassy's substantive agenda focused on drugs, with a large Drug Enforcement Administration (DEA) presence and a dynamic narcotics unit. We pushed continually for a more aggressive program to destroy coca labs and eradicate coca plants. Because of strong political and emotional opposition in Peru, we were not at that time able to use herbicides. Manual eradication was limited by pressure on the government from the farmers themselves, particularly in the Huallaga Valley, where most of the coca was produced. Fujimori, abetted by his close personal advisor, internationally famous economist Hernando de Soto, consistently took the position that without a convincing and viable program of alternative development, he was unwilling to deprive a substantial number of peasants of their livelihood.

Destroying labs was another matter, and he permitted the drug police and the military to work closely with us on this project. We already had several c-130 planes and a base at Santa Lucía in the Huallaga Valley, constructed during the García administration for antidrug operations. Our Narcotics Assistance Unit used these planes to deploy DEA agents to Santa Lucía in support of Peruvian narcotics police operations in the valley. Under both the García and Fujimori regimes, I traveled frequently to Santa Lucía and tried to maintain close relations with the senior Peruvian police and military officials involved. I was thereby able to keep a close eye on all the counterdrug programs. In August 1991 I was invited to visit Uchiza, another major town in the drug-producing area, with the president and Hernando de Soto. My inclusion was designed to make sure I understood Fujimori's message to the drug-producing farmers: that they were not "criminals" and that he would not take away their livelihood without a viable alternative being put into place. The search for alternatives was already on the agenda of our USAID mission, but no projects had yet been activated.

◆ ◆ ◆

If the war on drugs was our priority, we quickly became embroiled in difficult discussions about human rights, a subject that had been on our agenda with the García administration. In August I sent a long cable to the department (Lima 11976) outlining a human rights strategy in an effort to meet Washington's concerns. Fujimori's inaugural address had suggested that his administration was committed to improving human rights. I noted that our demands would have to be presented in ways that did not affront Fujimori's pride:

"Exposing Fujimori to charges of kowtowing to Yankee intrusiveness, or demanding human rights performance from the military without dedicating our own assistance funding to that purpose would invite a decided rebuff." I made clear that "lots of good old-fashioned diplomacy" would be needed and that we would be able to get a human rights revaluation only if it became a "genuine" Peruvian priority.

Unfortunately, we were not able to effectively link our assistance to our human rights agenda and never provided sufficient incentives to change abusive police and military behavior. At the same time as we were coming up with proposals about human rights, we became aware of the sinister influence of Fujimori's lawyer, Vladimiro Montesinos, who as deputy director of the intelligence services became Fujimori's closest advisor on all matters relating to drugs, terrorism, and human rights—the very issues of greatest concern to the United States.

Tensions with the Fujimori government arose in November 1991 when a group of masked armed men assaulted an apartment in the working-class area of Barrios Altos, killing fifteen adults and an eight-year-old child. The attack, we subsequently learned, was carried out by the Grupo Colina, a secret paramilitary group of military officers tasked with finding and executing suspected Shining Path members. Unfortunately, in the Barrios Altos incident, the Colina Group chose the wrong target and in so doing brought new focus on the entire Fujimori human rights program. The embassy reported extensively on the incident, its background, and its perpetrators. Washington tasked me to raise the issue with Fujimori (State 404511, December 11, 1991), demanding that he investigate the issue fully. That was the message that I took to Fujimori and to other senior members of his administration as well (Lima 17520, December 13, 1991). We became increasingly convinced of the government's involvement. However, the active investigation of the case was terminated after the *autogolpe* of the following spring, after which Fujimori granted blanket amnesty to all past perpetrators of human rights abuses in the war against the Shining Path. Subsequent investigation after Fujimori's overthrow demonstrated that both Montesinos and Fujimori had probably authorized the attack. Indeed, the incident became the basis for the trial against Fujimori after he had been extradited from Chile in 2003 and for which he was sentenced to twenty-five years in jail.

Our cooperation was dramatically slowed by Fujimori's announcement on April 5, 1992, that he had dissolved the National Assembly. This *autogolpe* immediately led to the suspension of a substantial amount of humanitarian aid and a distinct cooling in every aspect of our bilateral relationship. The *autogolpe* took place while Assistant Secretary for Latin American Affairs Bernard Aronson was in Lima. Indeed, he first heard about the coup sitting in the living room of our family quarters at the residence. He was outraged and saw it as a personal affront. He had been scheduled to see Fujimori the following day to present what we thought was a generous package of American aid. Aronson could not understand why Fujimori had acted when he did. That meeting, of course, did not take place, although Secretary Aronson was able to express our surprise and concern to the foreign minister by phone the next day.

Given the importance of the overall relationship, however, the department showed considerable resiliency. Aronson returned to Peru less than a month later for a two-and-a-half-hour meeting with Fujimori. As I reported at that time (Lima 6530, May 4, 1992), Fujimori assured his American interlocutors that he wanted a "real democracy," with respect for civil liberties and human rights. He stressed that he would not be bound by the "failed formalities of the discredited political elites."

Aronson accepted the need for reform but repeatedly returned to the theme that these reforms must be transparent and lead to a "constitutional process." Without such a process, Peru would not be able to benefit from any international financial assistance. Fujimori would not be able to retain the substantial U.S. financial and programmatic support for his reforms and the struggle against narcotics trafficking, which had been the basis of our past relationship. The meeting with Aronson was long and productive. Both sides deployed carrot-and-stick diplomacy. Benefits were stressed, and costs were made clear on both sides. In due course, Fujimori moved to create a constituent assembly that returned Peru to a democratic constitutional order. Joint counternarcotic programs were expanded, and the provision of U.S. aid resumed.

In August I put together a comprehensive democracy-promotion strategy (Lima 10872), naming the AID mission director as the coordinator of our efforts. He chaired a task force that included USAID, the Military Assistance Group, USIS, and the political and narcotics sections of the embassy. We put particular emphasis on USIS resources such as the International Visitors Grant Program, visits by American speakers, and teleconferences focused on democracy. The AID mission constructed an Administration of Justice program. Department of Defense resources went to developing a training program and to strengthening the Peruvian military justice system. The Combatant Commander Initiative Fund provided $400,000 to support these two initiatives. Unfortunately, USAID's congressionally imposed prohibition on working with the police made it impossible to develop a new accusatorial justice system, which we believed Peru needed. It was a comprehensive effort involving many agencies, but its total impact was limited. I urged Washington to work with other democratic countries to get supplemental resources for this effort.

Other serious problems in our relationship had emerged shortly after the *autogolpe*. On April 26, 1992, counternarcotics cooperation between our two governments came to a halt after the Peruvian Air Force shot at an American C-130 that had been carrying out a counternarcotic photographic surveillance mission over the Huallaga Valley. The incident represented a complete breakdown of procedures. The embassy had established a classified channel to the Peruvian Defense Ministry to alert it of any drug surveillance flights over Peruvian territory. The Defense Ministry in turn was expected to inform local Peruvian Air Force units that these missions were authorized. In this case, the Defense Ministry had been informed of the impending flight, but the word had not been passed down the line. As a result, when the c-130 entered Peruvian airspace it was immediately challenged by the Peruvian Air Force, which apparently assumed that it was a hostile drug trafficker's plane. Fighters were sent up to intercept it. They asked it to identify itself but got no response. They tried to persuade the plane to follow them to a safe landing place, but the plane instead turned westward to the Pacific with the intention of returning to its home base in Panama. Failing to get a response, the Peruvians then opened fire on the plane, killing one crew member and wounding another. At that point the American pilot decided to follow Peruvian instructions to land at a base in Talara in northern Peru. The Peruvians immediately informed me, and using the defense attaché's aircraft, I flew to Talara, where the Peruvian defense minister and the commander in chief of the air force joined me.

It was clear to all that a terrible mistake had been made, but it was not clear who was responsible. Since the plane carried clear USAF tail markings, we felt that the Peruvians should have seen that they were shooting at a friendly aircraft. They in turn argued that the suspicious refusal of the pilot to acknowledge radio and other visual signals indicated some sinister purpose. We learned only later that the pilot had been following instructions to maintain radio silence in intelligence-gathering operations, developed for use along the North Korean coast. While neither side admitted responsibility, both sides agreed to improve coordination procedures. I worked to ensure that the crew were treated properly, and in due course they and the plane were allowed to depart to Panama. The Peruvian government eventually paid a cash indemnity to the U.S. government, although they never admitted that they had been at fault.

All military antidrug operations were under the jurisdiction of the U.S. Southern Command (SOUTHCOM) in Panama. The combatant commander, then referred to as the CINC, was General George Joulwan, who had a fine sense of how to treat diplomats. He held regular annual conferences with ambassadors from the Andean countries. He wined and dined us and provided detailed briefings of his command's programs and priorities. He invited the commander of the

Peruvian army, Jorge Zegara, and his wife to make a special visit to his headquarters, which resulted in even greater cooperation. General Joulwan did not try to impose his will but lobbied strongly with me and with the Peruvians for a larger U.S. military presence. This eventually led to the establishment of a small radar unit in Tarapoto, which in subsequent years came in for criticism when misidentification of a small aircraft led to the shooting down of a missionary plane with the loss of all aboard. But for now there were relatively few frictions between the embassy and SOUTHCOM. Joulwan ordered his senior officers to wear badges proclaiming, "One Team One Fight," emphasizing that cooperation was the cornerstone of his approach. He insisted that his representative on the country team, the Military Assistance Advisory Group (MAAG) chief, keep me fully informed of all SOUTHCOM's plans and programs. In that spirit we worked together collaboratively.

◆ ◆ ◆

With the breakdown of the constitutional order, the focus of our relations shifted away from the drug war to efforts to bring about a restoration of democratic institutions and practices. Fujimori was by temperament an authoritarian figure, but he saw the advantages of having a pliant assembly that would endorse his policies and pass the laws he sought for reforming state institutions. Unfortunately, in the first eighteen months of his term he faced relentless opposition from Fredemo and other non–Cambio 90 members, making the assembly anything but pliant. The *autogolpe* with one stroke did away with the legislative branch of government. While there was press outrage at this "murder" of democracy, Fujimori moved swiftly to call a constitutional convention to put in place a new national assembly.

In the subsequent weeks and months, my successor and I both pushed for full restoration of democracy and were particularly active in trying to influence the government over the shape of the constituent congress elections scheduled for November 1992. These were to result in a congress that would draft a new constitution, under which presidential and legislative elections would be held. In a meeting with Prime Minister Oscar de la Puente a few days before my departure in September (Lima 12011), I emphasized that the forthcoming elections needed not only to be free and fair but also to be perceived as such. I urged the government to revise the electoral law to permit greater participation by smaller parties and to make clear that the new congress could revisit decisions taken since the *autogolpe*.

I found little flexibility in the prime minister's position. He clearly shared the president's view that the government was moving with determination to create a new Peru and that there would be no going back to the situation prior to April 5. The fact that the way elections were handled would affect assistance levels did not seem to impress the prime minister. Elections were duly held and judged to be basically free. In the end we came to terms with the "new" democracy in Peru and returned our focus to our principal objective: fighting the drug war.

One consequence of Peru's central place in the production of narcotics was that young Americans were often arrested there for the possession or sale of cocaine. I tried to visit those imprisoned to assure myself of their well-being and to offer them the opportunity of returning to the United States to serve the remainder of their sentences in American prisons. This exchange was made possible under an existing agreement with the Peruvian government.

Visiting prisoners in the vast and infamous Lurigancho prison with its many cellblocks was a bizarre experience. Prisoners, not prison authorities, were in charge of the cellblocks. One such block was filled with women members of the Shining Path, who proudly decorated their building with Shining Path slogans and banners. The men I visited were in a separate building. I went accompanied by the embassy's security officer and a consular officer. We were escorted to the appropriate cellblock by prison guards and then handed over to the prisoner in charge of that building. After we were admitted, the prisoner in charge locked the external door behind us. To the horror of the security officer, we were now incarcerated by and with the very felons we had come to assist. The men serving their time had their own cells, many of which were decorated more like a college dorm room than a prison cell. Since they had money, they could get almost anything they wanted: cigarettes, alcohol, and women. They quickly rejected our offer of transfer to the United States, pointing out the relative comfort of their current situation and claiming that if they returned home, they would be subject to violence and rape in an American prison, something they did not have to fear in Lurigancho. Nothing I could say persuaded them.

◆ ◆ ◆

I traveled widely and often in the country, using the defense attaché's aircraft for security reasons, as well as for convenience. Over three years, I managed to visit all but one of Peru's administrative departments. On each trip I tried to meet with local civilian and military officials. Some of these visits posed considerable challenges for my security staff, particularly a visit to Ayacucho in December 1991. Ayacucho was the heart of Sendero country. In fact, it was from the University of Huamanga in Ayacucho that Abimael Guzmán launched the Shining Path. When I descended on this small Andean administrative center, a team of submachine gun–toting American and Peruvian security officers accompanied me as I made the rounds. I called on the local bishop, Juan Cipriani, and the military commander, Fernández Dávila. Cipriani, a conservative Opus Dei bishop, was a strong supporter of the firm (and controversial) policies adopted by the military to deal with the Shining Path. He later went on to become cardinal archbishop of Lima. Both he and Fernández Dávila defended the human rights record of the military and contrasted it with the brutal outrages committed by the Shining Path.

The issue of human rights was a constant preoccupation of the embassy. Though well aware of the atrocities committed by the Shining Path as it terrorized villagers throughout the Andes, we were equally concerned about the military's response. We were in constant touch with the human rights *coordinadora*, which brought together

Peru's human rights activists. They were well informed and regularly reported to the embassy about the excesses of the army and the police. I was instructed on several occasions to approach the president and express our concern about Barrios Altos and other incidents. Fujimori always expressed ignorance about them and offered to investigate. Those investigations never took place.

In general, I worked assiduously to cultivate a relationship with the leaders of the Peruvian armed forces. I became a good friend of the army's senior leadership and had a regular tennis game in 1991 with the commander in chief of the army, Pedro Villanueva. He had the distinction of being only the second to become the commander in chief after having graduated with the Sword of Honor as the top cadet at the Peruvian Military Academy. The other was General Juan Velasco Alvarado, who had carried out a military coup in 1978 and ruled as a dictator for half a decade thereafter. I developed close personal relations with the head of the air force, Arnaldo Velarde, as well as Jorge Zegara, a subsequent army commander in chief with whom I traveled to Panama at the invitation of the Southern Command. He confided to me during that trip how the army skimmed off 10 percent of all defense contracts in order to supplement the salaries of senior officers. He frankly pointed out that he earned only $250 a month as commander in chief. Other lower-ranking officers earned less. How, he asked rhetorically, were they to survive into retirement if they did not have some mechanism to supplement their earnings while on active duty?

On the political front, one of my closest contacts was Máximo San Roman, Fujimori's first vice president, whom the opposition briefly tried to make president after the *autogolpe*. Max was a remarkable figure. An engineer and self-made businessman, he had developed a bread oven for use in the Andean communities from which he himself had come by laboriously retroengineering ovens from the catalogs of foreign producers. I also tried to stay in touch with former presidents of Peru Morales Bermudez, Belaúnde, and García, although my efforts in the last case did not turn out well.

In the spring of 1992, I decided to make the rounds of the heads of all the leading parties in Peru. After meeting with the Acción Popular's titular head, former president Fernando Belaúnde, and the Popular Christian Party leader Luis Bedoya, I decided to call on Peru's most recent president, Alan García, head of the American Popular Revolutionary Alliance (APRA). When I informed DCM Charles Brayshaw of my proposed visit, he advised strongly against my going to see such a controversial politician, who had ruined the Peruvian economy and strained relations with the United States. I rejected his advice, saying I was going to see all political leaders whose parties were legal and who were not themselves in jail.

Having ignored what turned out to be good advice, I duly arranged to meet García at APRA headquarters in the Casa del Pueblo, the People's House, where APRA offered classes and ran a dispensary and a food bank. Greeting me was Augustín Mantilla, García's interior minister, a shady character with a reputation of being unscrupulous and corrupt. Under my predecessor, the embassy had had a close working relationship with him on issues relating to drugs and terrorism. He took me to García's office, where to my surprise and consternation I saw on the table crossed flags, one of Peru and the other of North Korea. Normally one would expect to see one's own country flag displayed, but García's inattentive staff had failed to make the switch. García was at his most affable, and we had an open and frank conversation. When I asked him what he considered the greatest success of his period as president, he confidently replied, the regionalization of the country's institutions. And his greatest regret? He smiled and said that APRA for the first time in its history had supported a candidate (Alberto Fujimori) who did not belong to the party or support its goals. APRA would never do that again.

My visit made the evening news, as García's staff had arranged to film my arrival and meeting. The next morning, an angry foreign minister, Augusto Blacker-Miller, phoned and berated me for meeting with a crook who had ruined Peru. He said he was astonished that the American ambassador would be so disrespectful. I made the usual demurral that I would meet with all legal political parties as part of my job and regretted that he felt so strongly about my meeting with García. But the damage was done, and my relations with the foreign minister remained strained. Happily, for our bilateral relations, he did not have President Fujimori's confidence and was soon replaced.

The most onerous aspect of the job was the security constraint on my activities. Lima was, to be sure, a dangerous place. The embassy was rocketed several times during my tour, the Marine House was bombed, and Shining Path operations against the electricity grid caused daily blackouts. I traveled in an armored car with an American bodyguard in the front. I also had two lead cars and a follow car, with heavily armed American and Peruvian agents. When we went to dinner at a Peruvian home, the security detail would insist on inspecting the host's premises to develop a plan for my protection and escape if necessary. Much of this security did not sit well with Peruvians and even less so with my diplomatic colleagues, who did not enjoy equivalent protection. On one occasion, my cortège ran the French ambassador off the road, to his great annoyance.

When our three grown children arrived from the United States for Christmas in 1989, their arrival at the embassy residence was an exciting one. Just after my security detail entered the residence compound with the family in my official car, a motorcyclist whizzed past the residence gate and raked it with a brief burst of machine gun fire. As we entered the front hall, the security officer ordered us all to lie on the floor until the danger was passed. We immediately complied. For our grown children, this was a more exciting beginning to their holiday than they had imagined, even though they knew about severe security problems in Lima.

I regret to say that I was not always a good role model for my staff. I chafed against these restrictions. On one occasion I managed to escape, after the protective detail had gone home, to see a leading member of the American private community sing in a local nightclub. The regional security officer (RSO) showed up in my office the next morning to rebuke me for my foolishness and to assure me that he would be available day or night if I wished to go out on the town.

The situation took a nasty turn for the worse halfway through my tour when the RSO informed me that the Shining Path was planning my assassination. He said that a reliable DEA source had overheard a conversation between two Shining Path sympathizers describing a plot to kill me. The embassy security apparatus went into overdrive. A special counterterrorism team came down from Washington. My travel was further reduced and my routes were modified to the point where on at least one occasion I was driven to the office in my wife's small car while the official car followed its usual route with a dummy ambassador in the rear seat. I expressed some skepticism about this threat, particularly when at a second meeting the DEA source described the nature of the attack, including the use of a garbage truck to take away any bodies after the attacks. I was frankly incredulous but, given the supposed reliability of the source, could do little more than grumble and accept the ever-more-restricted freedom of movement. A third meeting with the source led to the identification of the actual location where the terrorists were said to be organizing the operation. We contacted the Peruvian counterterrorism police, who dutifully assaulted this residence only to find two quite harmless elderly Peruvians watching television. At that point, the DEA decided to polygraph its source and, not surprisingly, learned that he was a fabricator.

As I had at earlier posts, I continued to be an active member of Lions International and to seek opportunities to participate in amateur theatricals. I joined the Lima Host Lions Club, the original Peruvian club, and made many friends in the business community as a result. At one of the annual Lions district conventions in Chiclayo, I marched in the Lions parade with fellow club members. Once again, my security detail was unenthusiastic but agreed to march with me through the streets of this important provincial town.

My security team was even less enthusiastic when the local British theater group offered me the chance to play one of the two lead roles in Neil Simon's *The Odd Couple*. From security's point of view, my participation went against all the standard security rules: never do the same thing at the same time at the same place. Naturally, the curtain went up at the same time on each of the four weekend performances at the small British Council theater. Most of the embassy staff were unwilling to attend any of the performances, assuming, I suppose, that a terrorist attack against me was likely.

The issue of my security surfaced rather more dramatically in February 1992, when a substantial car bomb was detonated outside the residence, doing considerable damage and killing several of the Peruvian guards. By chance, Susan and I were not in the residence at the time. I was engaged in a tennis match against a member of the Peruvian Foreign Ministry in the annual diplomatic tennis tournament. We were immediately evacuated to the Hilton Hotel, where we spent several nights before I insisted that we return to the residence, notwithstanding that most of its windows had been blown out. With substantially increased security around the residence perimeter, the RSO agreed to our return. The department suggested that I take some leave and get out of the country for a while. We had long-standing plans to visit Chile and Argentina. At the last minute we had to postpone the trip because of the forthcoming visit of the assistant secretary for Latin America. We did successfully get away later in the month and had a splendid trip to Santiago, Puerto Montt, Bariloche, Buenos Aires, and down to Ushuaia in Tierra del Fuego. Susan was able to satisfy a long-standing desire to sail across the Straits of Magellan, which we did on a cargo ferry. We retuned though Mendoza in the north and then by bus across the Andes to Santiago.

A recently enacted law required the State Department to set up an Accountability Review Board to investigate the car bomb incident, since there had been both loss of life and damage exceeding $500,000. The board was to determine whether there had been any failure on the part of the embassy to adopt appropriate security measures. A retired former ambassador chaired the board, which included a former CIA director of operations. They arrived in Peru in May and began by interviewing me. The central question that seemed to interest them was whether the attack had been directed at me personally or at the residence as a symbol of American power and presence. Shortly after the bombing and after my departure on leave in South America, the country team had reviewed the incident and concluded that it was probably a symbolic attack, since the time of the bombing in late afternoon was not one when I was likely to be at home. This was a judgment with which I concurred. I feared the department would have been inclined to withdraw me from post if they thought it was a real assassination attempt.

The board had an alternative view to contend with. After I had been formally sworn to tell the truth, the chairman of the board pushed a document across the table for me to read, which stated quite clearly that the attack was an assassination attempt. It had been drafted by the station chief and sent to Washington through his channels. I had not seen it, nor had he discussed it with me. I was naturally taken aback and could only refer back to the earlier country team assessment, with which I understood the station chief had concurred. In the end the board found no security failing on the part of the embassy, recognizing that it was virtually impossible to provide total security to a building that stood close up against one of Lima's busiest thoroughfares. The board reached no conclusion about the question of assassination.

As far back as the summer of 1991, when the security situation was gravely deteriorating, I had suggested to the department that it might be a good idea to reduce the size of the embassy staff. I told Washington that I would be willing to undertake such an exercise, similar to Operation Topsy in Brazil some years before, but only if Washington would help me fight the agency battles that would inevitably ensue. The under secretary for management gave me the green light. I then asked the DCM to send a memorandum to all agency and unit heads asking them to come up with a one-paragraph description of what each of their American employees did. Considerable pushback came from the intelligence community, but in the end everyone complied.

I then looked over this list and made arbitrary decisions about which positions should be retained and which should not.

My focus was on positions that clearly supported the core mission strategy in the areas of drugs, terrorism, democracy, and human rights. I decided, for example, that NAMRID, a naval research team looking at malaria in Peru, did not meet critical mission needs. I also suggested eliminating the air attaché's aircraft, which had generously been flying me around Peru and providing rest and recuperation flights to Panama for defense attaché personnel. All other agencies took some hits, including the embassy's political and economic sections and the CIA station. Everyone complained bitterly that I was weakening their ability to carry out essential mission objectives. As a result of my review I identified some sixty-five positions that could be eliminated out of a total of two hundred. Most of the positions I slated were to become vacant with the departure of the incumbent. No one was happy with the outcome, and the actual immediate drawdown was quite limited. In any case, within six months after my departure, my successor overturned all the decisions. The embassy complement returned to prereview levels. Twenty years later, there were over four hundred Americans serving in Lima. So much for efforts to right-size the embassy.

In those days embassies often operated as skilled travel agents for the seemingly endless flow of high-level visitors. Lima was no exception. We had numerous visits from high-level officials, especially the assistant secretary of state for Latin America. But we also had congressional visits, including one by the chairman of the House Ways and Means Committee, Charles Rangel. Congressman Dan Burton was a rather special and difficult visitor. Although the department had informed me that he was on a private visit and did not need embassy help, his staff made it quite clear that he expected to stay at the ambassador's residence, going so far as to threaten to cut the State Department appropriation if he was not invited to stay there. I, of course, immediately offered my hospitality, though not with very good grace. All of these visitors wanted to see high-level Peruvians, particularly President Fujimori. Because of the positive overall state of our relations, before the *autogolpe*, this was usually possible.

Over a long career, I never had a presidential visit or a visit by the secretary of state, though in Lima we did host Vice President Dan Quayle in 1991. I did not know Quayle well, but during the transition he had interviewed me to be his national security advisor. As he had just come off the Senate Armed Services Committee, his principal interests were disarmament and the military. These were areas in which I had no experience and where I could be of no help to him. Although our conversation was friendly, it did not lead to my joining his staff. In Lima he comported himself with both charm and skill. The Secret Service had agreed to let him stay at the residence, but only if we put steel plates on all of the windows of the guest bedroom. We complied, and VPOTUS, as the official messages referred to him, slept soundly and safely in our home. After breakfast on the morning after his arrival, Quayle and his small team of advisors met with the country team in the residence library for a briefing on the day's program. Quayle began by asking what he could do to advance U.S. interests in Peru. We gave him a shopping list of items relating to the drug war and human rights. He listened attentively, and when he finally met with President Fujimori later in the day, he went over our talking points accurately and forcefully.

He was also a gracious guest. At a reception in his honor for embassy staff, he apologized for having arrived on our wedding anniversary and was lavish in his praise of the embassy and the work it was doing. The only difficulty with his visit was helping him get in touch with a small evangelical Christian NGO, Project Nehemiah, which had its base in the Midwest and was working in one of the poorest districts of Lima. Luckily, with her network of contacts, Susan was able to find the site and accompany him to it. He left pleased with the personal and official results of his visit.

In the summer of 1992, the security situation reached its nadir when the Shining Path blew up a large upper-middle-class apartment house in an exclusive neighborhood of Lima. Embassy staff and families were under "authorized departure" and could return to the United States if they so chose. With the end of my tour in sight, I endeavored to assess the pluses and minuses of the first two years of Fujimori's rule. I concluded that the glass of our relations had moved from being at least half full to now being half empty. Agreements we had hoped to sign had been pushed back. Democracy had come under severe challenge. But I was not without hope. My concluding paragraph summed up my views at the time:

> Whichever way we look at Peru, we will have to remember a few basic facts about this complex and benighted country. Nothing will happen as rapidly as we hope. Fujimori will continue to rely on his own talent, improvising when necessary, using brilliant gestures and exploiting surprise. He has consistent long-term goals but tortuous and often inconsistent tactics for achieving them. His unwillingness to accept the connection between enforcement and alternative development in a counternarcotic strategy will continue to lead him to positions contrary to our interests and, although he cannot yet see it, his own. Suspicion of the United States and its policies is deeply rooted, and we will face continued public and press criticism of our seriousness, of our staying power, and of our resource commitment. Nonetheless, Peru is heading in a direction which is consistent with our long-term interests. We have every reason to help this government arrive at a democratic, market-oriented, peaceful, and uncorrupt Peru. That is our challenge in the months and years ahead.

My time in Lima ended on a most positive note. The usual round of farewell events often culminated in the gift of an engraved silver plate. (Since their value significantly surpassed the allowable gift threshold, I had to buy them back from the U.S. government if I wanted to keep them.) The Peruvians generously decorated me with the Order of the Sun.

The highlight of my tour took place only a few days before we left during a dinner we were hosting in honor of the departing USAID director, Craig Buck. The guests included a number of Peruvian ministers. In the middle of dinner, the butler discreetly called me away to take a call. It was the chief of station with the news that the Peruvian counterterrorism police had captured Abimael Guzmán, "Presidente Gonzalo," the head and founder of the Shining Path. He asked me not to tell my guests, as President Fujimori had not yet been informed. A second call half an hour later gave me the green light at the precise moment I was about to give my toast to the AID director. I began with the words "On this historic occasion," which guests assumed was simply a flowery way of honoring Craig Buck's achievements. When I continued—"the moment when Abimael Guzmán has been captured"—the ministers, unwilling to believe such an astounding announcement, immediately got on their cell phones to confirm the news that it was indeed true. Guzmán's capture brought an end to a long period of devastating violence against the Peruvian state. To be sure, some isolated terrorist attacks continued, and another smaller terrorist organization, the Túpac Amaru Revolutionary Movement, remained active, but the battle against Sendero had been won. Life in Lima gradually returned to normal.

Before departing Lima, I drafted a valedictory telegram to the department entitled "The New Peru—Present at the Creation" (Lima 12528, September 19, 1992). In this long message, I pointed to President Fujimori's relentless and single-minded determination to create a new Peru encompassing not just radical structural economic reform but also reform of the legislative and judicial branches of government. Fujimori, the son of Japanese immigrants, had shown himself to be more in touch with the mass of his countrymen than the traditional elites had been. He was determined to tear down much of the old Peru that these elites represented. However, I said, "Too much seems to depend on a single individual who was skeptical of almost all institutions and did not trust his colleagues." Fujimori believed he had a messianic solution to Peru's historic problems. I could not imagine that Fujimori would remain in power until the end of the decade, but I did assume he had at least two and half years in which to create popularly based institutions and channels for the people to express their beliefs and aspirations. I left Peru convinced that a fundamental change was coming and that in many ways a "revolution" was under way. I was less certain that the results would be benign, particularly if the process remained "exclusively the property of one man."

I noted that the United States shared much of the Fujimori vision of a new market-oriented, democratic, and peaceful Peru, for which the foundations had been laid. That building, I added, was not yet "fully designed and certainly not built." With a somewhat exaggerated optimism, I concluded that the "prospects for the future are better than ever before." Peru was a country rich in human and natural resources. A new Peru was "a-forming." I counted myself lucky to have been present at its creation.

History proved my concerns to be well founded. Fujimori did change Peru profoundly, but his autocratic style, systematic abuse of power, and secretive modus operandi eventually brought him down. Many of the achievements of his ten years in power remained, particularly in the areas of economic and social policy. A new Peru, with all its faults, did emerge to become one of Latin America's success stories in the two decades after Fujimori's departure from power.

19
Final Washington Years

After almost three years in Peru, the State Department recalled me to Washington to take over as assistant secretary of state for Diplomatic Security (DS). I was not a security expert, but my counterterrorism background had given me considerable familiarity with the issues the DS had to confront. I was one of only two Foreign Service Officers in the bureau. The DS had only become a full-fledged bureau in 1986, an expansion from the Office of Security the department created after the Second World War. Like me, the first two assistant secretaries were Foreign Service Officers, although both were experienced administrative specialists directly supervising security officers in the field. Notwithstanding my ambassadorial tours, I had had little direct exposure to the day-to-day work of the regional security officers (RSOs). They assumed that I, like so many other ambassadors to whom they had been exposed, had a dislike of security and a congenital suspicion of their work and the restrictions that security programs imposed on the normal functioning of diplomacy. I never fully overcame that suspicion or the perception that Foreign Service Officers regarded their DS colleagues with a certain disdain and sense of superiority.

One of the greatest challenges in managing this large and diverse bureau was its hierarchy of personnel systems and values. I, an FSO, was perched atop the bureau. Under me were the diplomatic security officers, the core of the bureau, who were proud of their law enforcement and diplomatic skills. They had all been trained at the Federal Law Enforcement Training Center (FLETC) in Atlanta and saw themselves as professional law enforcement officers, the equal of their colleagues in the Secret Service, FBI, or DEA. They were also proud to be diplomats. They came under the same 1980 Foreign Service Act as their Foreign Service Officer colleagues. They enjoyed the same rank-in-person and were subject to the same up-or-out system. They typically began their careers at one of the dozen field offices around the continental United States and in Puerto Rico, conducting investigations into passport fraud and overseeing background investigations of State Department employees. They would move on to positions overseas as regional security officers and immediately become part of the ambassador's country team.

The diplomatic security officers formed the Diplomatic Security Service, which was recognized as an autonomous law enforcement service. The bureau's principal deputy assistant secretary served as the head of the service. He asserted an autonomous and protective role, and I often had difficulty in having my views prevail when they ran counter to the traditional practices and prerogatives of the service. My first deputy assistant secretary, Clark Ditmer, whom I inherited from my predecessor Sheldon Krys, worked actively to undermine my authority. When Mark Mulvey replaced him, I had a much more cooperative relationship with him, although there were times when our approaches clashed. This was particularly true when budgetary mandates forced me to impose draconian cuts on DS programs and personnel.

The bureau included several other categories of employees: the security engineers, the couriers, and the Civil Service administrative personnel. Just as the RSOs assumed that I, an FSO, looked down on them, they in turn looked down on the engineers, who in turn looked down on the couriers. All looked down on the low-level secretarial and administrative staff, who were almost entirely minority Civil Service employees. I fought against this culture of disdain but with little success.

In the early 1990s one of the principal legacy issues from the Cold War was the question of homosexuality and security. Throughout much of that period, gay people could not get security clearances because of the assumption that their "secret orientation" would make them susceptible to coercion and blackmail by foreign intelligence services. Although this was no longer true in the early 1990s, when homosexuality was increasingly openly declared, deep suspicion remained. One of my first meetings as the newly appointed assistant secretary was with representatives of GLIFAA (Gays and Lesbians in Foreign Affairs Agencies). I wrongly assumed that they were coming to complain about continued restrictions on the hiring of gay people. In fact, they had come to ask that DS agents doing background investigations in the field stop asking openly proclaimed gays: "Does your mother know?" I had no idea whether we were asking the question, but I undertook to have the policy changed. To my surprise, I found that we were, indeed, still asking the question. There was a certain grumbling when I ordered this line of questioning stopped, as the investigators continued to believe that if individuals were concealing their sexual identity from anyone, even their mothers, they might be susceptible to blackmail.

To overcome the institutional suspicion of my role, I traveled to every domestic DS field office, as well as to all our critical threat posts abroad to demonstrate my support for the officers and their mission. However, I had to face the difficult reality that the Clinton administration was cutting agency budgets to achieve an overall balancing of the federal budget. The DS budget for 1994 had to be reduced by about 10 percent, an unimaginable cut considering the extraordinary expansion of diplomatic security in the post-9/11 period. We limited hiring, cut guard forces overseas, and adhered faithfully to the priorities identified by management. In making budgetary decisions, we relied on the interagency threat assessment group, which prioritized posts abroad in terms of the threat levels they faced. Even though this was an inexact science, we had to categorize posts as critical, high, medium, or low for terrorism, crime, civil disorder, and technical vulnerability. Embassies often pushed back against being classified as critical threat posts in any category, since that almost always ended in the imposition of at-post travel restrictions and limitations on family assignment.

In my travels to the critical threat posts, I repeatedly observed the inconsistent implementation of security policies and the morale issues that posts faced when families were evacuated for security reasons. In Algeria, families had been evacuated, but the American school had been left open for nonofficial members of the American community. With the school in the backyard of the DCM's residence, he was distressed every day to hear the happy voices of American children at play when his own had been sent back to the United States. In Zaire, a family member decided to ignore department policy and returned to post even though an across-the-board evacuation order for family members had been put in place. Contrary to embassy policy, she was allowed to live in embassy housing and use the commissary, and her presence had an extremely negative effect on morale. In several other posts, one or more officers got around a family evacuation order when some wives found employment in the mission and hence, as employees, were exempt from the evacuation requirements. Those who were unemployed were sent home and could not rejoin their spouses.

I made one visit to the Soviet Union, about which I had been knowledgeable thirty years earlier. This time I went not as a Soviet expert but to examine security issues at our consulate general in Leningrad and our embassy in Moscow. Washington was concerned about the repainting of the facade of the Leningrad consulate. The Soviets had undertaken a campaign to brighten up the city by repainting the facades of its principal buildings. The local Soviet administration announced that it would paint our consulate. It put up scaffolding and did the work. Unfortunately, from Washington's perspective, the consulate people did not seem to have exercised much, if any, security oversight. This was a worry, given the Soviets' known proclivity for installing listening devices in walls whenever and wherever they could. I delivered a strong message to the consul general about the need to step up security awareness. A subsequent review to look for listening devices was inconclusive, as it was impossible to thoroughly check the exterior wall.

Moscow was a more serious matter. There, security awareness was extremely high, and staff were constantly reminded of the risks. However, when it came to building an annex to the embassy, the department entrusted the construction to Russian workers. On-site security inspections later discovered that the structure had been compromised, and all but the bottom few floors would have to be torn down to be completely rebuilt by an entirely American construction team. The purpose of my visit was to be fully briefed on this and other security problems facing the embassy so that I could answer the questions of higher authorities in Washington.

One of my efforts to comply with budgetary strictures ran into political opposition. My staff suggested that one way to save money would be to discontinue the special security detail we were providing the Saudi ambassador, Prince Bandar bin Sultan. He was the only ambassador in Washington receiving full-time personal protection. (The only other foreign mission with a DS presence was the Turkish ambassador's residence, where the DS maintained a fixed guard post.) For reasons unknown to me and to my colleagues, the department had agreed to provide, on an exceptional basis, a two-officer detail to protect Prince Bandar, even though he had his own substantial and highly qualified private detail provided by the British firm Control Risks. My staff told me that previous efforts to cut this program had failed because of the prince's access to the White House. I approached Secretary Warren Christopher and asked for his go-ahead to terminate the detail, which cost several hundred thousand dollars a year. I warned him of possible political opposition from the White House. However, he agreed to the idea and said he would take care of any White House objections. With that encouragement I went ahead and informed the ambassador of my intention to withdraw the diplomatic security detail in thirty days. It was not to be. Within forty-eight hours, the king of Saudi Arabia called the president asking why some idiot in the State Department was putting his ambassador to Washington's life at risk by withdrawing protection. Prince Bandar provided me with a sheaf of intelligence reports designed to prove that he was at risk. In fact, they referred to terrorist threats in the Middle East and showed no specific risk to the ambassador. Nonetheless, I was ordered to stand down, and the protection continued.

The White House also intruded into diplomatic security business in the middle of my tenure by ordering us to provide protection to the Haitian prime minister, Robert Malval, in Haiti. The Diplomatic Security Service had never undertaken the job of protecting a foreign dignitary in his own country, although it routinely protected senior foreign visitors inside the United States and American ambassadors abroad. Providing around-the-clock protection in a foreign country was no easy task. It required a substantial deployment of special agent resources and armored vehicles. Many other problems arose while trying to protect someone from a very different culture. Malval's view of security was that we should carry out his every personal wish, whether or not it related to security. I visited Haiti to see the program firsthand and was impressed by the professionalism of our officers. The prime minister expressed suitable gratitude, but I left with the strong sense that this was not a role that the DS should play.

My efforts to be a successful part of the diplomatic security team were doomed toward the end of my tenure. Under budgetary pressures and the reinventing-government efforts of Vice President Al Gore, I went to Under Secretary for Management Dick Moose with an out-of-the-box idea: transfer the diplomatic security law enforcement function—investigating passport fraud—to the FBI. I argued that law enforcement was intrinsically alien to a foreign ministry, that it consumed a lot of resources, and that in fact it led to very few prosecutions. Local prosecutors did not want to spend time on passport fraud cases that, if successfully prosecuted, would lead to short or suspended sentences. I argued that the return on our budgeted resources was relatively low. Moose, himself a rather unorthodox outsider in the department, liked the idea and proposed that we explore it quietly with the Justice Department. He and I called on Deputy Attorney General Jamie Gorelick and proposed the idea of transferring the investigative responsibilities for passport fraud to the FBI. She listened patiently and said she would discuss the idea with her FBI colleagues, but she made no commitment, as quickly became apparent, since passport fraud was a low priority for the FBI. Within hours the proposal leaked back to my colleagues in the DS. They were outraged that I was about to give up one of their most cherished programs. In internal communications I became known as "Black Dragon," the sinister Foreign Service figure seeking to destroy the Diplomatic Security Service.

For all that, the work in the DS was fascinating and challenging. We struggled with the problems of how to fix the Moscow embassy construction project that the Soviets had successfully compromised, and we set in motion the rebuilding required. We also worked to develop a sensible system of triage to determine where and how embassies should be upgraded. This effort was in response to the Inman Commission, which had recommended after the 1983 bombings in Beirut that we build new and more secure embassies in the most dangerous regions of the world. We did not develop a perfect system, as the bombings in Nairobi and Dar es Salaam in August 1998 later demonstrated. We tried to make sure that our scarce resources went to the highest-threat posts.

Another kind of challenge occurred when senior officials were involved in serious security breaches. I remember one case of a senior official who by mistake left his briefcase filled with classified documents in the Chinese Embassy in New York. I was also the department's interface with ambassadors who came to me to discuss security programs at their posts. They invariably pushed back against the bureau's listing of their embassy in a high or critical threat category. In the field, the threats our embassies faced never seemed to them as grave as they did from Washington's perspective. As an FSO heading up the security service, I always felt caught in the middle.

I did take away from my three-plus years in Diplomatic Security an important personal lesson. On a visit to the Philippines, the senior RSO, Bob O'Hanlon, gave a dinner in my honor with the various DS entities represented at post. After dinner, he asked me to bring the "troops" up to date about what was going on in the DS. I launched into an explanation of what I had done, what I proposed to do, and so on. After about ten minutes, he interrupted my remarks, saying: "Mr. Ambassador, I have a piece of advice for you. Stop using the word 'I' and begin using the word 'we.'" This was the best advice I ever received, a little late perhaps, but one I tried to keep in mind in subsequent years.

DIRECTOR GENERAL

In the spring of 1995, I was asked to take the position of director general of the Foreign Service, one of the two top career positions in the service (the other being under secretary for political affairs). Although I had no background in personnel management, I quickly accepted. But six months were to elapse before I took up my new responsibilities. The reason: my clearance was held up. Assistant secretary–level appointments and above have their required screening done not by Diplomatic Security but by the FBI. Once again, I filled out all the required forms, assuming that there would be no problem. There I was wrong. Months dragged by without the clearance coming through. The under secretary was impatient, and the incumbent wanted to move on to her next post as ambassador to Australia. I asked the DS staff to check with the FBI, but all they could find out was the rather cryptic response that the FBI had one more source to check. In midsummer the answer came through. The under secretary called me and said that he had the FBI's report, in which they noted that I had been accused of being a cross-dresser but that they had been unable to confirm the allegation. I was non-plussed and acutely embarrassed. I told my boss that I had been an active participant in Scottish country dancing both in Washington and abroad, for which I wore a kilt, and that that might have been the source of this allegation. I thought of another possibility: my appearance and that of other officers in *The Stone Age Follies* in New Delhi, where in a lighthearted skit a group of us appeared in drag. I will never know what the basis of the accusation was and can only suspect that a disgruntled colleague had gratuitously thrown this idea over the transom in the hopes of embarrassing me and, perhaps, even keeping me from getting the director general's job. If that was so, it failed as a tactic. My nomination went forward, and I never heard any further reference to the issue.

As director general, I found myself once again on unfamiliar ground. I was not a personnel specialist. I had a basic understanding of the department's recruitment, promotion, and selection procedures but had had little exposure to the intricacies of the laws and regulations that governed the system. This was particularly true with respect to the Civil Service side of the equation, to which I had had no previous exposure.

Much of my time, energy, and focus was spent on the fallout from the department's two long-standing class action discrimination cases: the Palmer case on behalf of women, and the Thomas case on behalf of African Americans. In both cases the courts had found the department's procedures deficient and discriminatory. Proving that we had remedied the situation by changes in the examination and entry process, by careful guidance to promotion boards, and by evenhanded treatment of all grievance cases turned out to be insufficient. Unexplained discrepancies remained in promotions for minority groups. The courts kept our procedures under active review throughout my time of service.

A major responsibility was the care and handling of senior officers who either sought ambassadorial appointments or wanted to ensure that they would receive onward ambassadorial postings after their current one. They would come to see me about their future. The conversations could be difficult when I had to inform long-standing senior officers that the golden ring was not going to come their way or that there would in all probability not be an onward assignment from the post where they currently served.

The selection process for ambassadors was not transparent. The "D" committee, chaired by the deputy secretary, made the choices. I was the de facto secretary of the committee, on which the various undersecretaries sat. I presented candidates and made recommendations, but the final decision often did not go as I recommended. My task was to try to maintain the integrity of the system, making sure that the officers with the right experience, knowledge, and language capabilities got a fair review. However, many times the personal view of the secretary, the deputy secretary, or committee members prevailed. They often advanced candidacies of their special assistants, thereby undermining an orderly credential-driven process.

My colleagues assumed that my job was to defend the Foreign Service against predatory politicians and the ambitions of outsiders. In this I was not always successful. Former vice president Walter Mondale came to me after he was nominated to be ambassador to Japan, asking that I authorize the assignment of Professor Kent Calder, a brilliant Princeton economist, as his principal economic advisor. Calder had studied in Japan and spoke Japanese. He was a recognized expert. However, I balked. I told Mondale that this position was normally held by a senior Foreign Service Officer and noted that we had plenty of qualified senior economic officers who spoke Japanese and who could do the job. Mondale was insistent. If I continued to stand in the way of this appointment, he politely assured me, he would speak to the president, and it would then go through. Recognizing that I was up against an immovable object, I reluctantly agreed. Calder by all subsequent reports was an outstanding asset to the embassy and to Ambassador Mondale and to his successor, Ambassador Thomas Foley.

I am probably most remembered and criticized for my decision to allow a career civil servant to go to Lima as deputy chief of mission. There had been the occasional but rare presidential appointment of civil servants as ambassadors, but this was a watershed decision. One of the cherished traditions in the Foreign Service was that no matter who the ambassador was—political or career—the deputy would always come from the career service. Traditionally, ambassadors chose their own deputy. In this case, the ambassador had identified a candidate from the career Civil Service, Roberta Jacobson, the director of the Office of Regional Affairs in the Bureau of American Republic Affairs. She was a member of the Senior Executive Service, spoke excellent Spanish, and had a solid understanding of Latin America. When news of the possibility of her going to Peru became public, an immediate outcry arose from the American Foreign Service Association and many of my senior colleagues. All argued that no matter how talented Jacobson was, she should not be allowed to break a long-standing tradition. In the view of those who opposed this appointment, her going would be the beginning of a process of eliminating top Foreign Service jobs. Notwithstanding her lack of field experience, I believed that she was qualified for the position and that the ambassador's wishes should be honored, so I approved the assignment. She later became deputy assistant secretary, assistant secretary, and ambassador to Mexico.

My decision reflected what was then a deep tension between the Washington-based Civil Service and the worldwide-available Foreign Service. That tension continues to this day, as recent secretaries of state have allowed an expanded role for the Civil Service both in Washington and abroad. I am convinced that the approval of Jacobson's appointment was the right decision. However, it turned out to be the harbinger of more fundamental changes that weakened the career service in the twenty-first century.

In the summer of 1997 our deputy ambassador at the United Nations, Edward "Skip" Gnehm, came to see me. He, too, had served as ambassador to Kuwait, and I knew him well. We talked amiably about his plans. He told me he hoped to return to Washington after his tour in New York. Indeed, he was certain that he would be returning. I knew what senior-level positions might be available to him, and I asked if he was in fact coming to take my place. Somewhat embarrassed, he said that was the case and that Ambassador Madeleine Albright, his boss in New York and recently named secretary of state, had made the decision. He had assumed I had already been told. I immediately sought confirmation from Deputy Secretary Strobe Talbott, who confirmed Gnehm's assignment and assured me that something would be found for me. But that was not to be. After less than two years in the job, I found myself facing unexpected mandatory retirement.

I understood that the secretary had wanted to reward her deputy in New York, but I think her decision was influenced by my failure to carry out her wishes with respect to a senior member of her staff. Some months before, she had asked me to arrange the transfer of an officer with the Senior Executive Service (SES) on her staff. She believed that officer to be disloyal to her, passing inside information to Senator Jesse Helms. Although well disposed to act in this matter, I quickly discovered that existing personnel rules made the forced transfer of an SES officer difficult. It required a repeated finding of unsatisfactory performance and a willingness of some other agency or office to accept the officer. Neither of these requirements was easily met, and Ambassador Albright became increasingly frustrated with my inability to carry out her wishes. Try as I would, my efforts failed. My successor had equal difficulty in arranging for the officer to be moved, but by then Ambassador Albright had moved on, and a new set of problems was on the director general's plate.

I spent the last month of my career working on the Board of Examiners, interviewing and conducting oral examinations for Foreign Service candidates. This was an experience that I wished I had had earlier in my career, as it gave me many insights into the workings of the system and a greater appreciation for the extraordinary quality of the officers we were admitting to the service.

In those last weeks, I also gave a number of valedictory speeches and wrote several articles for the State Department magazine outlining my concerns for the Foreign Service. My basic theme then, as it was to become in my subsequent teaching of diplomatic practice at American University, was the need for the Foreign Service to adapt to the changing technologies and agendas that lay ahead in the twenty-first century. The Foreign Service, it seemed to me, was stuck in a nineteenth-century mold with twentieth-century technologies inadequate to deal with the emerging issues of globalization. While much has been done to modernize the service, many of these concerns remain valid thirty years later. The increasing politicization of the department over these years has further weakened the role of the career service in the making and implementation of our foreign policy.

In retrospect, I realize that I paid too little attention to the need to diversify the service. We had successfully survived the Palmer and Thomas discrimination suits and assumed that we had solved the basic problem of discrimination against women and officers of color. Subsequent events were to prove that we had profoundly underestimated the depth of the problem. We continued to see the service as a special group of men and women generalists uniquely capable of grappling with all the world's problems. We did not see the structural discrimination that continued to exist as white officers all too easily prospered within the elite expectations of the system.

And so, a thirty-eight-year career came to an end. I had served eight presidents and twelve secretaries of state. I had enjoyed a long and successful run and loved the challenges of a variety of jobs. For more than twenty years, I had been in leadership positions both at home and abroad. I became more adept at the management and representational aspects of diplomacy. But I was not always an effective leader or role model. I chafed under the increasing security requirements of the job. I found that my penchant for what I thought were humorous and clever off-the-cuff remarks had often offended minorities and women and did not sit well with my colleagues. In all, I was proud to have been a part of history in several crucial places and to have been of service to my country. I did not know what lay ahead.

PART 3
Putting Experience to Use

20
Challenges in the Nonprofit World

The end of my Foreign Service career had come unexpectedly fast. I had assumed, incorrectly as it turned out, that after my tour as director general I would be offered another overseas post. That had been the pattern with my predecessors, and I expected that it would be the case for me. I had not seriously considered retirement. The Foreign Service had been the framework for my life for almost forty years, and I expected and wanted it to go on forever. I had made no plans for retirement; I had no desire to build a harpsichord, or learn to play the cello, or retire to Arizona to play golf. I was at a loss.

Luckily for me, the Una Chapman Cox Foundation was looking for a new executive director. The current executive director, Ambassador Alfred L. "Roy" Atherton, was preparing to retire, and I was approached about taking his place. I accepted the position and held it for about a year. A wealthy Texan, Una Chapman Cox, had established the foundation in the early 1980s. A young officer of the U.S. consulate, which looks after American citizens abroad, had come to her rescue when Indian authorities detained her during a cruise stop in Bombay. She was so impressed by his dedication and his efforts to get her out of detention and back on her cruise ship that she created a foundation devoted to supporting the professionalism of the Foreign Service. After her death, a hardheaded, single-minded lawyer from Corpus Christi, Texas, Harvie Branscombe Jr., ran the foundation's board. He had been Mrs. Cox's personal lawyer and guarded the foundation's assets with ferocious zeal, carefully scrutinizing the work of the executive director. Although irascible, he was not unreasonable. He insisted that any project proposed be carefully vetted and meet Mrs. Cox's basic desire that it contribute to a professional U.S. Foreign Service. While I enjoyed the continued association with the Foreign Service that this position offered, I never felt I had the complete confidence of Mr. Branscombe, who was somewhat suspicious of the elitist attitudes of senior Foreign Service Officers.

I moved on from the Cox Foundation in late 1998 to work on a part-time basis for the American Academy of Diplomacy, managing the Hushang Ansary Forums. That year I had been elected to the academy, an organization of retired senior Foreign Service Officers whose purpose was to promote diplomacy as a profession. Its president asked me to manage a substantial grant from the former Iranian diplomat and businessman Hushang Ansary. My job was to organize forums on current foreign policy issues, to find appropriate speakers and venues, and to administer the expenditure of grant funds. In all, I arranged over half a dozen forums on widely varied topics. The leaders of the academy were concerned that I not get into controversial subjects that might offend Mr. Ansary's known conservative views. Somehow, I managed to do this, although the academy's efforts to persuade Ambassador Ansary to renew his grant were not successful at that time.

Since my jobs at the Cox Foundation and the Academy of Diplomacy were only part-time, I continued to look for a full-time executive position in the nonprofit world. I busily hawked my résumé to various international organizations and domestic think tanks, with no success and usually with no acknowledgment. However, in late 1998, I received a call from Malcolm "Mac" Lovell, the president and CEO of the National Policy Association (NPA), asking if I would be interested in applying for his position. I knew nothing of NPA but accepted his invitation to meet in his office on the corner of 16th and P Streets Northwest, now the home of the Church of Scientology. Mac Lovell and his large black Labrador presided. The dog, kept on a leash tied to Mac's desk, would lunge forward at visitors, barking loudly. Fortunately, his leash had been arranged so that he could only get within six inches of a visitor's knees.

Mac sketched out for me the work of NPA, founded in 1934 as a think tank designed to bring together business and labor leaders to discuss questions of national policy. Since I was evidently not a national policy expert, he explained that NPA also ran two international committees: the British North America Committee (BNAC), involving the United Kingdom, Canada, and the United States; and the North America Committee (NAC), with members from Canada, Mexico, and the United States. Their focus on transatlantic and North American issues interested me, and I expressed a willingness to be considered for the position. In the ensuing weeks, several members of the NPA board interviewed me, including Richard Shmeelk, chairman of CAI Associates and a former NPA board chairman, and Moeen Qureshi, former prime minister of Pakistan, senior official in the World Bank and the International Finance Corporation, and the incumbent chairman of the NPA board. As the interviews went well, they offered me the job. They seemed pleased at getting a senior ambassador to head the organization, and I was enthusiastic about the opportunity to move into broad areas of policy debate. The other leading candidate for the job was NPA's senior vice president, Jim Auerbach. He had been with the organization for many years and was an acknowledged labor expert. His contacts in the labor movement were wide and deep. He was unhappy that the job went to an outsider with no labor experience, and our relationship remained fraught throughout my time at NPA.

My initial enthusiasm was entirely premature. In accepting the job, I took at face value what my colleagues had told me about the success and impact of the policy committees for which NPA was responsible. In addition to the two international committees, there were also a Food and Agriculture Committee and a Committee on New American Realities. Each had an exciting agenda and seemed to be functioning well. However, Mac Lovell had warned me that the BNAC had complained about NPA's logistical support of their meetings. He suggested that I talk with the committee's leadership at a meeting scheduled for later in the fall. When I met with the top BNAC executives, I discovered that they had already decided to separate from NPA and seek administrative support elsewhere. My assurances of improved support were of no avail, and one-quarter of NPA business disappeared within weeks of my arrival.

Another shock was the state of NPA's finances. I confess to having done no due diligence. I accepted assurances that all was well. To my consternation, I learned shortly after my arrival that NPA had been running a deficit of over six figures and that there had been a steady downturn in contributions from both business and labor in recent years. Raising money would have to be my first and continuing priority. However, I had had no experience in fundraising and found it uncongenial work. I concentrated on reducing the hemorrhaging of funds from our principal donors, but the tide was running against me. Both business and labor saw a decreasing value in the kind of dialogues we were offering. I had two wonderful financial vice presidents, but neither could come up with successful strategies for raising revenue. We became increasingly dependent on our annual Gold Medal dinner, held at the Pierre Hotel in New York to honor distinguished figures in the corporate or trade union world. These dinners often netted over $250,000, but that was not enough to compensate for declines in the budget elsewhere.

By May 2003, NPA had essentially run out of money. I decided to ask the board either to put up money or to agree to the closure of the organization. The board, with very little discussion, agreed that we should close and authorized me to expend the remaining cash to give employees a generous severance package and pay such legal fees as might be necessary. This I did over the next three months. Longtime employees were dismayed, but I had no choice. Susan and I packed up the voluminous and historically valuable NPA archives, going back over six decades, and arranged to ship them to the Walter Reuther Library at Kent State University. The task of selling the office furniture remained with me. As no one wanted to buy it, we had to pay to have it taken away to a scrap heap. I arranged to sell at auction a few rather valuable Postimpressionist paintings that had been given to NPA in its heyday. The articles of incorporation were formally revoked on December 31, 2003, and my career as a nonprofit executive came to an end.

In hindsight, those five years at NPA were not by any means wasted. The three committees functioned well, meeting on average three times a year around the United States, Canada, and Mexico. We explored ways to deepen the North American relationships in trade and energy, the challenges of genetically modified foods, and the need for corporate responsibility. We engaged a wide cross section of academic, business, and labor leaders in our discussions. We produced a series of reports that highlighted and made recommendations about these issues. In addition, we engaged in several autonomous projects looking at the personnel problems of both the State Department and the U.S. Agency for International Development, which the personnel managers in both agencies found useful.

Overall, I learned a great deal from these five years. I became involved in policy issues of current relevance and importance. I enjoyed the managerial side of the job while recognizing that I had failed in an executive's fundamental responsibility: to ensure the viability of the organization he leads. In its day, NPA's vision of labor and business cooperation and dialogue was a bold one. Our society is the poorer for the loss of an institution dedicated to building bridges across these two vital sectors of our economy.

21
The Classroom and Beyond

Having had rather mixed success as a nonprofit executive, I once again found myself on the job market. Many of my peers, on their retirement from the Foreign Service, had accepted positions as adjunct or endowed professors at one of the many schools of international relations around the country. Washington has at least four such schools, with many former colleagues on their rolls. Perhaps, I thought, there was a place for me. I went to see the dean of the School of International Service (SIS) at American University, Louis Goodman, whom I had known through my time working on Latin America. He was a distinguished Latin Americanist and had done considerable work on the military in Peru. He graciously received me in his office, where we had a wide-ranging discussion of politics in Latin America. At the end of our meeting he asked me to send him my résumé. He would get back to me if anything turned up. I had been in the job-search business long enough to know that this was the standard polite way of telling a candidate that no job was available.

My skepticism was entirely unjustified. Several weeks later in mid-July, less than six weeks before the start of the next semester, Dean Goodman called to ask if I could begin teaching at the end of August. The school had an urgent need for someone who could take on one of the sections of a core course, Analysis of U.S. Foreign Policy. I expressed some dismay at the short time horizon and asked about the syllabus and textbook for the course. He assured me that would be no problem. He arranged for me to get the syllabus and textbook recommendation of another vastly more experienced professor. These arrived in due course, and I went off on a family holiday in the Mediterranean with a textbook in hand. I had not used or read a textbook in almost fifty years and found the one he sent me excruciatingly dull, if full of useful content. But it was too late to change what had already been ordered through the campus store.

Having accepted the challenge, I adapted the syllabus to my own expertise and, with some trepidation, set about teaching. Little did I know that this would be the start of a very happy sixteen-year third career. As the years went by, I gradually added courses to my quiver and was rewarded in 2008 with a regular term contract, obliging me to teach six courses a year but also entitling me to a real salary and associated benefits. I was now a full member of the faculty, although not a fully accepted member. My problem: I did not have a PhD degree. I could hardly claim my Oxford work as the equivalent, since I had actually failed to get my DPhil.

Early on in my time I was asked to consider teaching a graduate-level course on U.S. policy in Latin America. Several tenured faculty members objected, asserting that graduate students should not be taught by someone without a PhD. After further discussion, it was agreed that I could team-teach the course with someone appropriately credentialed. That seemed a reasonable compromise. I was paired with Dr. Margaret Sarles, an experienced USAID economist and Latin Americanist, and we successfully taught the course. My colleagues observed that the graduate students did not seem to be upset or harmed by my lack of a doctorate. From then on, I taught various graduate courses: U.S. Policy in the Middle East, Diplomatic Practice, and Public Diplomacy.

◆ ◆ ◆

One advantage my academic colleagues lacked was my network of contacts throughout the foreign affairs community in Washington. In both my graduate and undergraduate courses, I was able to use this network of friends and former colleagues to provide added background, context, and depth to the courses I was teaching. This was particularly important in the School of International Service, since many students had come to American University to profit from the human and other resources available in Washington. My own credentials as a former senior Foreign Service Officer boosted my stature among students and faculty alike.

Diplomatic Practice, which I taught at both the undergraduate and graduate levels, became my signature course. While the course relied heavily on my own experience serving on all inhabited continents and in a variety of functional assignments, its distinguishing feature was a series of scenarios based on the mythical country of Erehwon, created (with apologies to Samuel Butler) in my first year of teaching and enhanced with colorful details every year thereafter. Located in a remote and obscure region, Erehwon had many of the characteristics of the Central African Republic but was not, in fact, an African country, as my students tended to assume. The American embassy in the capital, Erehwemos, was under the leadership of a fictional junior ambassador, Henry Feckless, while the Erehwonese ambassador in Washington was the inexperienced soccer star Victor Ludorum. Feckless interacted more or less successfully with the Stanford-educated Erehwonese president, Dieudonné Nemo. The country suffered from almost every known problem in terms of economic development. It was landlocked, resource poor, and politically unstable. It lacked democratic institutions. As the semester advanced, it faced a major earthquake and then a terrorist-led insurrection by the jihadist Sheikh Bukra Inshallah. While the fantasy surrounding Erehwon at times went beyond my own professional knowledge, the country provided a useful framework for exploring a full range of political, economic, and administrative problems and for testing the students' ability to set resource priorities and manage crises.

About halfway through my sixteen years at American University, I began to teach in the University Honors program. Though substantially modified during the period of my association with it, the program offered its two hundred undergraduates a selection of special honors colloquia each semester. These were small classes designed to offer cross-disciplinary opportunities in ways that students taking the course would get appropriate credit in their respective schools, whether in the School of Public Affairs, the School of International

Service, or the College of Arts and Science. I plunged into this program with enthusiasm, offering a variety of classes, often far outside my narrow Foreign Service experience. In 2011 I developed a course, 9/11—Ten Years Later, bringing in some of the leading players in the events that followed 9/11, including our first administrator in Iraq, L. Paul Bremer, and former director of national intelligence John Negroponte. Although both were controversial, I thought it important that students hear their differing views. Both provided unique and important insights into the working of the U.S. government.

Given the growing focus on diversity across the university, another course I developed—Who Are We?—was designed to force the students to look hard at and question the national, ethnic, and racial markers of identity. The course might have also been entitled Whatever Happened to the Melting Pot?, given the assumption of the present generation that America is more a salad bowl than a melting pot. The salad bowl metaphor assumes the preservation of a range of diverse identities but does not presuppose the abandonment of one's original culture in order to become American. The classroom became a forum for students to explore their own identity and to compare it with that of others. It was a privilege for me to witness this very American salad bowl.

The invitation to Ambassadors Bremer and Negroponte was the source of some controversy. Some of my colleagues felt passionately that we should not invite onto campus men who had been architects of U.S. policy in Iraq, widely condemned on campus as immoral. Both turned out to be thoughtful and critical speakers. Bremer had, in fact, partly at my suggestion, already been offered an adjunct position to teach during the next semester. When news of the appointment became public, a group of professors in one of the SIS programs unanimously asked that the appointment be revoked, as in their eyes it would not be appropriate to hire someone who might be indicted as a war criminal for his actions in Iraq. In the event, Bremer never took up the appointment. The incident, however, was a dramatic reminder of the moral intensity of academic life.

Over these years the search for diversity and inclusion became the driving objective of the university's leaders, with considerable success. My classroom became increasingly diverse as the university recruited African American, Asian, and Hispanic students. Having a diverse student body did not, however, ensure an inclusive environment. Racist incidents continued to occur. That should not have been surprising, since the larger American society was facing the same challenges.

This diversity/inclusion agenda impinged on the teaching environment. How were we to make all students feel comfortable in class? What kind of trigger warnings of difficult and complex subjects, particularly relating to sexuality, should we provide? How were we to address the gender diversity of the classroom? Who could we call he, she, or they? How in fact were we to introduce ourselves? At one faculty seminar on diversity, the course leader said she had found it useful on the first day of a new course to introduce herself as "a cisgender person who preferred the pronoun she." At some level, I found these discussions difficult. I was an old, white, straight man, born into a world still at least partially patriarchal and imperial. Some students regarded that pedigree with suspicion. Erehwon, I hoped, would be a neutral venue where these issues could be managed, if not altogether pushed aside. I was generally successful.

My focus on identity issues was given more scope in a course I created and offered on four different occasions entitled Peru: Where Two Worlds Meet. Students got an opportunity to consider the history, culture, politics, and economics of contemporary Peru, with a particular focus on the substantial divergences in Peruvian society between the Indians of the Andes and the Spanish and mestizo populations of the coast. Students were asked what it meant to be Peruvian. They were offered the chance to visit Peru either during the break between the two semesters or during the spring break. These visits enabled me to put my extensive range of contacts in the government, embassy, and private sector to good use. The groups were always briefed by the Foreign Ministry, by the American ambassador or his deputy, and by Peru's leading economist and development thinker, Hernando de Soto. All the groups traveled to Cuzco for an extended visit to the Sacred Valley and Machu Picchu. On some of the trips the students got a taste of upper-class life either at a small private beach at La Honda some thirty miles to the south of Lima or at an Anglo-Peruvian ranch in Chincha farther south. There they had a chance to visit a colonial hacienda and enjoy a taste of Afro-Peruvian music, food, and culture.

After the university redesigned its honors program in 2016, it abandoned these colloquia. In their place, each school established its own honors program. SIS quickly moved in that direction, creating a program for juniors and seniors that required writing a senior thesis and taking two in-house seminars given by senior professors. I was lucky enough to be asked to participate in the program and so, for the first two years of the new program and my last two years teaching, I offered a course titled The Responsibility to Protect (R2P). In these seminars we looked at the genocides or mass killings of the twentieth and twenty-first centuries, beginning with the Armenian massacre of 1916 and ending with the contemporary killings in Libya and Syria. The central question we tried to answer was why the international community seemed singularly incapable of stopping this kind of mass violence. The consensus the 2005 Global Summit had reached that there was a responsibility to protect ethnic and other minorities facing systematic persecution and oppression had had little effect. The R2P course provided an opportunity to examine the limits of diplomacy when the international community at large or a major power such as the United States lacked the will or interest to become involved.

◆ ◆ ◆

Academia provided great flexibility in the scheduling of my life outside the classroom. During these years at American University I was able to pursue my long-standing interest in ecumenical and interfaith work. I joined the board of both the Washington Theological Consortium and the Interfaith Council of Metropolitan Washington.

Both organizations seek to overcome the deep suspicions that divide Christians among themselves and from the other great world religions. I was privileged to support their work from the perspective of a practicing Roman Catholic.

During my career I often found I could look to religious leaders for advice and information. Usually these were missionaries, both Catholic and Protestant. They often lived in remote and inaccessible corners of the country, as they did in the Central African Republic and Peru. They were also in the major cities of the Indian subcontinent, providing health care and education to the rich, as well as to the marginalized and poorest sectors of society. In the subcontinent they were not aggressively proselytizing. Indeed, that was often forbidden. They sought to set an example of their faith by the way they served others. Theirs was invariably a lifelong commitment. They rarely went home, being content to live among the people they were serving. The parochialism and competition for souls that often characterized their parent bodies were rarely evident on the ground. For a diplomat, they provided access to levels of society that might otherwise have been unobtainable. To outsiders, these missionaries have often been an object of derision, with allegations that they were simply buying souls with food and medicine, creating so-called rice Christians. This was a superficial judgment. We saw their selfless work firsthand. We benefited in our personal life from the generosity of many missionaries. They received us cordially in many out-of-the-way places. One of our children was born in a Seventh Day Adventist hospital in Karachi, another in the Catholic Medical Mission Sisters Hospital in New Delhi. We had only gratitude for their work.

Nonetheless, over time I became increasingly distressed at the divisions caused by religion. Missionaries refrained from a collaborative effort in their work overseas. Here in the United States, Christians often had angry and intolerant exchanges among themselves and, even more disturbing, confrontations with Muslims. On retiring from the Foreign Service, I sought ways to contribute in some small way to the attenuation of these problems. Ecumenism seemed an extension of what all diplomats do: promote coexistence, dialogue, and mutual understanding. Diplomacy is the art of building bridges across barriers of race, religion, culture, political and economic systems, and competing national interests. Coexistence is not a naive, feel-good ambition but the reality that the alternative, war, is unacceptable in a world of nuclear weapons.

Building those bridges that make coexistence possible is one of the fundamental roles of educational institutions. On the educational front, I was not only deeply involved at American University but also engaged with two other North American educational institutions, St. Michaels University School in Victoria, British Columbia, and La Roche College in Pittsburgh. I had attended St. Michaels in the 1940s, and they invited me to become an advisory governor. I was the 2007 commencement speaker at La Roche College, now a university, which asked Susan and me to join their board. During the period of my involvement, both institutions went through a strategic planning process in an effort to confront the reality of declining financial resources, a shrinking applicant pool, and the need to increase diversity. Figuring out the skills and knowledge needed in the twenty-first century was a challenge for these two vastly different institutions, as it had been for the Foreign Service. Both have tried to determine what students will need in the decades ahead, always emphasizing that an educational institution should give students the moral compass to navigate the rapidly changing societies in Canada and the United States.

My time teaching at American University was a fitting coda to a long professional life. It confirmed in many ways the motto of my own secondary school: *Finis origine pendet* (The end depends on the beginning). I was raised in the belief that tolerance of diversity was essential. What Andover drilled into me was that what one did was not for oneself, *Non sibi*. In the words of the St. Michael's School's motto, *Nihil magnum nisi bonum* (Nothing is great unless it is good).

It would be easy to dismiss these words as empty and outdated Latin tags with little relationship to the life that students led after they left the classroom. But in diplomacy, an ability to understand the other, to recognize the complexity of events, and to perceive the nuances that lie at the heart of international relations depends on an ability to get beyond oneself, to put aside one's own parochial interests, and to seek the common good. That is what education is all about. That is what diplomacy requires. American University provided me with the opportunity to bring my academic background, intellectual interests, and professional career into focus and to transmit some of the lessons learned over a long career to a new generation.

Epilogue

Christian, Gentleman, Cricketer

Almost nine decades ago my paternal grandfather expressed a hope that I would turn out to be a Christian, a gentleman, and a cricketer. Others may judge the first two qualities, but I can bear witness to the fact that I never became a true cricketer. I played a little cricket as a small boy in Victoria and a little more in my gap year at Sherborne, and I formed a part of pick-up teams at Princeton and St. Antony's College, Oxford. My final appearance on a cricket pitch came in Lima. In a one-day match, I joined the British ambassador's team at the Lima Cricket Club, one of the last remaining vestiges of Britain's large and important commercial presence in Peru. As a batsman, my scores never reached double figures, and my bowling was at best erratic; but in Lima, to everyone's amazement, in two brief overs, I bowled so badly that an overly ambitious batsman swung and missed and was out when the ball rolled tamely into his wicket.

I entered the Foreign Service at the end of the Eisenhower administration. The gentleman's three-day multiple essay examination had just been done away with. Vestiges of Victorian expectations remained. In my oral examination I was asked whether I smoked and what I drank before dinner. Officers still left calling cards, wives paid formal visits to more senior wives, and white tie entertaining lingered on. In some posts male ambassadors still wore a morning coat and top hat when presenting their credentials to the ruling head of state. In short, it was a world in which the European view of what it meant to be a gentleman was also what it meant to be a diplomat. An Oscar Wilde aphorism on diplomacy was apt: "To make a good salad is to be a brilliant diplomat: the problem is entirely the same in both cases—to know how much oil to mix in with one's vinegar." That culinary skill was one that gentlemen presumably knew. It could not be learned; it could not easily be taught. I sometimes got the quantities wrong.

I was raised with solid white middle-class sensibilities and with many of the prejudices of a bygone age. There was little diversity in my early life. My parents did have several gay and Jewish friends with whom they socialized regularly, but there was no racial diversity in the world in which I grew up. My parents lived in a world of gentlemen and ladies, in which decorum was a highly prized virtue. They brought me up in the same tradition, in which proper table manners were almost as important as correct speech and in which dance cards determined with whom one could or should dance. Most of the trappings of that genteel society have passed away, as, indeed, has the very concept of a gentleman. Nonetheless, I was deeply marked by my upbringing, although I did not entirely succeed in living up to the ideals that that upbringing tried to impose.

With respect to religion, I was raised a Roman Catholic, as my mother had promised when she married my Anglican father. I remain one still. Whether I have been a Christian is a more complicated question. Only others can judge. However, throughout my life I have moved easily between the worlds of Rome and Canterbury, reflecting my parents' faith and broad tolerance and my own experience. In my post–Foreign Service years I have been active in ecumenical and interfaith work, having served on the boards of the Interfaith Council of Metropolitan Washington and the Washington Theological Consortium, where I twice served as chairman. I have long believed that building bridges across faith communities is one of the most urgent tasks of our increasingly diverse and polarized society. Those bridges, however, are only useful if people are willing to cross them. I have not always found that to be the case.

In a short book of sermons that I wrote while at American University and gave at St. Alban's Episcopal Church in Washington, I characterized myself as a "Roaming Catholic." Although fascinated by liturgy and the externals of religion, I have not been much interested in dogma. I have been more interested in how one lives a Christian life. I have made this effort, with many failures along the way. I have tried to observe the commandments and not be overwhelmed by the temptations increasingly put before me as I rose in the diplomatic service of my country. Dean Quainton, were he to take an inventory of his grandson's life, would, I hope, give me a passing mark. Distinction in the three qualities he considered important would remain problematic. Readers can award their own grade.

Index

Costa Rica, 196
Council of the Americas, 167
counternarcotics programs in
    Peru, 234, 240–41, 243–44
counterterrorism, 144–45, 156–59.
    See also Office for Combating
    Terrorism; terrorism
Cox, Una Chapman, 275
Craig, Gordon, 46
cricket (sport), 23, 40, 289
Crist, George, 226
Cronkite, Walter, 226
Cuadra, Joaquín, 187
Cuba: Alliance for Progress and,
    213; Catholicism in, 173; econ-
    omy of, 207, 208; and Sandini-
    sta relations, 166–67, 196–99,
    210, 211, 216, 217; and Soviet
    relations, 204
Cutler, Walter, 165

Dacca unrest (1971), 106
Dacko, David, 127
Dam, Kenneth, 204, 215
dancing, 53–54, 62, 110, 139, 222,
    267. *See also* debutante balls
Dar es Salaam, Tanzania, 266
Dario, Reuben, 169
Davis, Nathaniel, 48
Dawn (publication), 90
DCM (deputy chief of mission)
    work, 117–25
DEA (Drug Enforcement Adminis-
    tration), 240–41
Deakin, William, 58, 59
debating, 30–31, 46, 53
debutante balls, 5, 83

de Courcel, Geoffroy, 113
de Gaulle, Charles, 139
de la Puente, Oscar, 247
Delhi Symphony Orchestra, 104
Delta Force, 146–47, 153
democracy: author's early opinion
    of, 40–41, 85–86; in India, 98–
    102; in Kuwait, 225; in Nepal,
    120, 123; in Nicaragua, 186, 189,
    190–91, 194, 195, 198, 208, 212;
    in Pakistan, 93; in Peru, 238,
    239–40, 243–44, 246–47, 257
Democratic Front for the Libera-
    tion of Palestine, 156
Denton, Jeremiah, 186
d'Escoto, Miguel, 168, 172–73, 177,
    185, 206, 211–12
de Soto, Hernando, 241, 285
Diamond Distributors, 129
Diaz Alejandro, Carlos, 206
Diplomatic Security (DS), 260–67.
    See also U.S. State Department
The Diplomats, 1919–1939 (Craig),
    46
discrimination against government
    employees, 261–62, 267–68
Ditmer, Clark, 261
dog racing, 79
Domenici, Pete, 206, 212
Dominican Republic, 213. *See also*
    Bogotá hostage incident (1980)
Drug Enforcement Administration
    (DEA), 240–41
drugs, 122, 234, 240, 247. *See also*
    counternarcotics programs in
    Peru
Dubois, Hubert, 115

India: author's language studies for, 85, 87; author's service work in New Delhi, 98–105; and Nepal relations, 123
Indo-Pak War, 93–95, 96, 105–9
Inman, Bobby, 165
Inman Commission, 266
Innes, Michael (J. I. M. Stewart), 52
Interfaith Council of Metropolitan Washington, 285–86, 290
interfaith work, 285–87, 290
International Court of Justice, 193
Iran hostage incident (1979–80), 153–54
Iran-Iraq War, 220, 227
Ireland, 42
Irish Republican Army (IRA), 156
Irwin, John, 113, 114, 116
Isham, Heyward, 144
Islam, 89, 136–37, 143
Islamabad, Pakistan, 90–91, 92–93, 94, 99, 105
Israel, 156, 158, 202
Israeli special operation forces, 146, 150
Italian Communism, 58, 59. *See also* Communism
Italian language studies, 58, 162
Italy, 38–39, 55, 156

Jacobson, Roberta, 269–70
Japan, 78
Japanese Red Army, 156
Jews, persecution of, 201–2
Jinnah, Fatima, 93
Jinnah, Mohammed Ali, 93

John Paul II (pope), 172, 176–79
Johnson, U. Alexis, 101
Johnstone, Craig, 164
Joulwan, George, 245–46

Karachi, Pakistan, 89–91
Karachi Boat Club, 89
Kashmir, 96, 100, 103
Keasbey Scholarship, 50
Kemp, Jack, 206
Kennan, George, 55–56, 58
Kennedy, John F., 90, fig. 5
Khan, Saeed, 87, 88
Khrushchev, Nikita, 66
kidnappings, 144, 151, 153, 154–55. *See also* terrorism
Kipling, Rudyard, 20, 85, 91
Kirkland, Lane, 206
Kirkpatrick, Jeane, 198
Kissinger, Henry, 106–7, 204, 205, 206, 213
Kissinger Commission, 200, 204–15
Korean delegation in Moscow, 68
Krys, Sheldon, 261
Kuwait, 215, 219–28

Laghi, Pio, 150
Laise, Carol, 118, 126
La Prensa (publication), 185, 203, 208, 209, 216
La Roche University (formerly College), 287
Latin studies, 19, 29, 30, 34
Lebanon, 153
Leiken, Bob, 167
Lenin, Vladimir, 67

Napoleon Bonaparte, 138, 140, 142
Nation (publication), 4
National Association of Students, 65
National Bipartisan Commission on Central America (Kissinger Commission), 204–15
National Cathedral School, 110
National Catholic Reporter (publication), 176
National Policy Association (NPA), 276–79
National Security Council (NSC), 107
Navy Seal Team Six (U.S.), 157
Naz, Hamid, 87
Nazism, 39
N'dayen, Joachim, 142
Negroponte, John, 191, 283
Nepal, 118–26
New Delhi, India, 98–105
New Republic, 4
newspaper job, 10
New York Times, 68, 201
New Zealand, 157
Nicaragua: author's appointment and preparation for, 144, 162–69; Catholicism and the revolution in, 167–68, 171–80; claims of Jewish persecution in, 201–2; Kissinger Commission on, 204–15; secret war in, 169, 190–95; U.S. policy and tactics in, 169–71, 175, 180–89, 197–215. *See also* Sandinistas
9/11 attacks, 283

Nixon administration, 106, 108, 128
nonviolence, 85–86
Norgren, William, 63
North, Oliver, 206, 211
North Africa, 114, 115
Northern Ireland, 156
North Korea, 68
Nouwen, Henri, 176

Oakley, Robert, 116
Oates, Arthur Faulkner, 3–4, 15, 16, 17
Oates, Florence, 16–17, 22, 23, 24
Oates, Josephine, 15, 16–17
Oates, Marjorie. *See* Quainton, Marjorie Oates
Obando y Bravo, Miguel, 171–72, 205, 209
Odom, William "Bill," 151, 187–88
Office for Combating Terrorism, 143, 144–46, 152–57. *See also* terrorism; U.S. State Department
Office of the Inspector General (OIG), 229–33. *See also* U.S. State Department
O'Hanlon, Bob, 266–67
oil industry, 220–21
oil platforms, 157, 191, 193
oil tanker protection, 220, 228
OPEC (Organization of the Petroleum Exporting Countries), 220–21
orchestra, 104, 110, 226
Organisation of American States (OAS), 196–97

87, 90, 99, 103; CAR service, 126, 129–43; childhood year in Mexico, 9, 11–12, 163; courtship and marriage to Susan, 54–55, 60, 63; as deputy inspector general at OIG, 228–33; as director general of the Foreign Services, 267–72; dissent against Indo-Pakistan crisis, 106–9; distinguished honors for, 143, 195, 216; at DS, 260–67; early Seattle life of, 3–13; ecumenical and interfaith work by, 285–87, 290; entrance in the Foreign Services, 64, 75–76, 289; family in Victoria of, 14–18, 22–25; FBI surveillance of, 69–70; first jobs of, 8–9, 10; health of, 5, 22, 36; Hindi language studies of, 85, 87; honeymoon of, 61–62; Italian language studies of, 58, 162; Kuwait service, 215, 219–28, fig. 10; loss of Margaret and, 97–98, 105; meeting the Duke of Edinburgh, 56; Nepal service, 118–26; New Delhi service, 98–105; Nicaragua service, 162–63, 169–72, 175, 181–95, 199–208, 218, fig. 9; NPA work by, 276–79; at Oxford University, 42–43, 50–63; Pakistan service, 87–98; Paris service, 111–17; Peru service, 234–59, fig. 11; at Phillips Academy Andover, 26–31, 287; at Princeton University, 44–49; retirement from the Foreign

Service of, 271–72, 275; Russian language studies of, 45, 47–48, 56; security measures in Peru for, 251–54; at Sherborne School, 32–33, 34–37, 39–43; Soviet Union trips by, 64–71, 263, figs. 2–4; Spanish language studies of, 144, 163–64; at St. Michael's School, 7, 15, 18–22, 23, 32–33; Urdu language studies of, 87–88, 164; Washington DC service and life of, 105–10

Quainton, Cecil Eden (father of author), 3, 9, 11, 12, 15

Quainton, Cecil Samuel, 3, 15, 291

Quainton, Dalla, 22, 23, 25

Quainton, Eden (son of author), 87, 88–89, 94, 103, 116–17

Quainton, Elizabeth, 99, 103, 105, 116–17

Quainton, Eric, 22–24

Quainton, Gladys, 22, 24–25

Quainton, Katherine. *See* Britton, Katherine Quainton

Quainton, Margaret, 90, 94, 97–98

Quainton, Marjorie Oates, 3, 9, 16–17

Quainton, Rodney, 8

Quainton, Stephanie, 22, 23, 25

Quainton, Susan: Australia life of, 78–79, 83–84; courtship and marriage to author, 54–55, 60, 63; employment of, 89, 110, 122; evacuation of, 94–95; honeymoon of, 61–62; Kuwait life of, 226; language studies by, 88, 219;

Quainton, Susan (*cont.*)
loss of Margaret and, 97–98, 105; meeting the Duke of Edinburgh, 56; New Delhi life of, 98–99, 103–5; in Nicaragua, fig. 8; in orchestras, 104, 110, 226; at Oxford University, 55, 62–63; Pakistan life of, 88, 89–90, 91, 94–95, 96–98; Paris life of, 111–12, 116–17; Peru life of, 235, 253; pregnancy and childbirths of, 77, 78–79, 87, 90, 99, 103; volunteer work of, 96; Washington DC life of, 109–10

Quayle, Dan, 240, 256

Queens' College, Cambridge, 3, 15, 23, 32

Qureshi, Moeen, 277

Rabb, Maxwell, 162

racism: in academic environments, 284; in Australia, 84; against bureau staff, 261; discrimination cases of, 268, 272; in Seattle community, 7

railroad, 5, 14, 16, 27, 83

Rajasthan, 103

Ramos, Julio, 210

Randall, Jonathan, 133

Rangel, Charles, 255

Rasgotra, Krishna, 123

rationing, 6, 8, 21, 36

RATS (Rawalpindi Amateur Theatrical Society), 97

Rawalpindi (Pindi), Pakistan, 91–98

Rawalpindi Club, 92

Reagan administration: ambassadors and, 163; counterterrorism policies of, 160, 161; Nicaraguan policy and secret war of, 169, 175–76, 182, 190–95; on OPEC, 220–21

Red Brigades, 156

refugees, 106, 107, 108, 120, 166

Reich, Otto, 166

Relais Bisson, Paris, 61

religion. *See names of specific faiths and denominations*

retirement, 271–72, 275

Rhodes Scholarship, 28, 46, 50, 59, 62

Ringling Bros. and Barnum & Bailey Circus, 11

Roche, Hannah Josephine, 4

Roche, Violet, 27

Rockefeller Commission, 213

rodeo, 225–26

Rogers, William, 101

Rome, Italy, 38, 55

Rouillon, Fernand, 113–14, 115

rugby, 33, 36, 40

Russia. *See* Soviet Union

Russian language studies, 45, 47–48, 56, 71

Sabah, Jaber al-Ahmad al-, 222, fig. 10

Sabah, Salem al-, 220

sahibs and memsahibs, 88, 89

Sandinistas, 164–65; author and, 166–67, 182–83, 216–17; Catholicism and, 168, 171–80; CIA and, 169, 187–89, 190–95; Claridge

on, 168; and Cuba relations,
166–67, 196–99, 210, 211, 216,
217; hymn of, 180; Kissinger
Commission and, 205–15; and
Soviet relations, 204, 216–17;
U.S. offer of peace to, 195–96.
See also Nicaragua

Sandino International Airport, 177,
192, 195

San Roman, Máximo, 249

Sarles, Margaret, 281

SAS (British Special Air Service),
146

Saudi Arabia, 221, 224, 225,
264–65

savings bond program, 7

Sayre, Robert, 161

Schneider, David, 105

school punishment, 19, 35–37

Scottish dancing, 53–54, 62, 110,
267

Scottish Society (Oxford), 53–54,
57

SEATO (South East Asia Treaty
Organization), 87

Seattle Art Museum, 27

Seattle First National Bank, 10

Seattle Rainiers, 6, 7

Seattle Savings and Trust, 10

Seattle WA, 3–13

secret war (U.S.-Nicaragua), 169,
190–95

security: author's DS work on,
260–67; in CAR, 131; in Nepal,
119–20; Office for Combating
Terrorism and, 153–55, 159; in
Peru, 251–52; queer govern-

ment employees and, 261–62;
at U.S. embassies, 219, 266. *See
also* terrorism

Seeger, Peggy, 68

Semana Cómica (publication), 182,
200, 216, fig. 9

servants, 88, 89

Sherborne School, Dorset, 32–33,
34–37, 39–43

Shining Path (Sendero Luminoso),
234, 235, 236, 240, 248, 256–58

Shirburnian (publication), 41

Shmeelk, Richard, 277

Short, Laurie, 82

Shultz, George, 215

Sikkim, 100

Silber, John, 206, 207–8

Sisco, Joseph, 101, 106, 109, 111

Sisters of Charity of the Blessed
Virgin Mary, 6

Smith, Grant, 133

Smith, Peter, 28, 29

Smolny Institute for Young Noble
Ladies, 67

Socialist Party (U.S.), 4

Solarz, Stephen, 186

Somoza, Anastasio, 181, 186, 187,
206, 209

Soviet Union: author's trip to,
64–71; counterterrorism and,
158; and India relations, 107;
and Sandinista relations, 204,
216–17; U.S. personnel security
in, 263–64. *See also* Russian language studies

Spain, 57

Spanish Civil War, 4

Spanish language studies, 144,
163–64
Special Program in the Humanities
(Princeton), 45, 50
Specter, Arlen, 226
Spielman, Harry, 92, 93
sports, 20, 23, 30, 33, 40, 226, 232
squash (sport), 40, 226, 232
Stalin, Joseph, 67
St. Anthony's Parochial School,
6, 7
Starr, Richard, 151
Steigman, Andrew, 116
Steinberg, Donald, 135
Sterling, Claire, 158
St. Michael's School, Victoria, 7,
15, 18–22, 23, 32–33
St. Michaels University School,
Victoria, 25, 287
Stoessel, Walter, 167
Stone, Galen, 100, 104
Stone, Richard, 198
Sudan, 153
surveillance, 69–70
Swing, Bill, 130
Sydney, Australia, 77, 78–79
Syria, 57, 112, 113, 158, 285

Taft, Orray, 78
Talbott, Strobe, 270
teaching work, 89, 110, 271, 280–
85, 287–88
Tehran hostage incident (1979–
80), 153–54
Teotihuacán, Mexico, 12
terrorism, 156; arrest and detain-
ment incidents, 133; assas-

sinations and attempted
assassinations, 129, 144, 252,
254; hijackings, 152, 159; hostage
incidents, 146–51, 152–54, 157;
kidnappings, 144, 151, 153, 154–
55; in Kuwait, 219, 227; in Middle East, 119, 265; in Nicaragua,
144–61; in Peru, 234, 235–36,
242–43, 248, 252–53, 256–58.
See also counterterrorism;
Office for Combating Terrorism; weapons assistance
The Terror Network (Sterling), 158
Thapa, Bhekh Bahadur, 120
theatrical productions: aboard
sea vessel, 89; during author's
early life, 6–7, 10, 30, 46–48; in
India, 104, 267; in Kuwait, 227;
in Nepal, 126; in Pakistan, 97; in
Peru, 252–53
Third Secret of Fátima, 152
Thomas discrimination case, 268,
272
Thompson, Llewelyn, 69
Tinoco, Victor, 185
Tito, Josip Broz, 39, 41, 59
Treki, Ali, 159
trekking, 124–25
Trevor-Roper, Hugh, 52
Tripoli embassy incident (1978),
159
Trudeau, Pierre, 24
Trypanis, Constantine, 63
Tucker, Shelby, 69
Túpac Amaru Revolutionary
Movement (MRTA), 258
Turkey (country), 57, 62, 264

Ullman, Richard, 28–29, 56, 60–61, 62
Una Chapman Cox Foundation, 275–76
United Nations, 101, 109, 145
United States Conference of Catholic Bishops, 167–68, 171
Urdu language studies, 87–88, 164
USAF plane attack (1992), 244–45
USAID (U.S. Agency for International Development), 92, 118–21, 135, 137–38, 241, 244
U.S. Foreign Services entrance exams, 64, 75–76, 268, 271, 289
USIA (U.S. Information Agency), 122, 226
USIS (U.S. Information Service), 69, 131, 244
U.S. Southern Command (SOUTHCOM), 245–46, 249
U.S. State Department: author's first assignment of, 79–83, 84–86; author's last assignment of, 267–72; DS (Diplomatic Security), 260–67; gift acceptance policy of, 82, 257; India desk in Washington DC, 105–10; Office for Combating Terrorism, 143, 144–46, 152–57; Office of the Inspector General, 229–33

Vance, Cyrus, 144
Van Hollen, Christopher, 106
Vargas Alzamora, Augusto, 237
Vargas Llosa, Mario, 234–35, 237–39

Vatican: author's visit to, 38; on revolutionary Nicaragua, 168, 174, 177, 178; terrorist incidents and, 149, 150, 152. *See also* Catholicism
Velarde, Arnaldo, 249
Velasco Alvarado, Juan, 249
Venezuela, 217
Venice, Italy, 38, 39, 61
Victoria BC, 3, 7, 14–25. *See also* Canada; St. Michael's School, Victoria
Vienna, Austria, 229–30
Vienna Youth Festival, 70
Vietnam War, 109
Villanueva, Pedro, 249
Voroshilov, Kliment, 66
voting laws, 81

Walker, William, 214
Walsh, George, 92
Warner, John, 226
war rationing, 6, 8, 21, 36
Warren, Lionel de, 115
Washington, George, 130
Washington Theological Consortium, 285–86, 290
Watson, Arthur, 113
weapons assistance: in Central America, 168, 191, 196, 197, 207; in Europe, 156; in Southeast Asia, 86. *See also* terrorism
Wegener, Ulrich, 147
West Africa, 114
Whig-Cliosophic Society (Whig-Clio), 46, 47

Related ADST Book Series Titles

Prudence Bushnell, *Terrorism, Betrayal, and Resilience: My Story of the 1998 US Embassy Bombings*

Herman J. Cohen, *The Mind of the African Strongman: Conversations with Dictators, Statesmen, and Father Figures*

Charles T. Cross, *Born a Foreigner: A Memoir of the American Presence in Asia*

John Gunther Dean, *Danger Zones: A Diplomat's Fight for America's Interests*

Harriet Elam-Thomas, *Diversifying Diplomacy: My Journey from Roxbury to Dakar*

Brandon Grove, *Behind Embassy Walls: The Life and Times of an American Diplomat*

Allen C. Hansen, *Nine Lives: A Foreign Service Odyssey*

Nathaniel W. Howell, *Strangers When We Met: A Century of American Community in Kuwait*

Richard L. Jackson, *The Incidental Oriental Secretary and Other Tales of Foreign Service*

Dennis Jett, *American Ambassadors: The Past, Present, and Future of America's Diplomats*

Charles Stuart Kennedy, *The American Consul*

Dennis Kux, *The United States and Pakistan, 1947–2000: Disenchanted Allies*

Robert H. Miller, *Vietnam and Beyond: A Diplomat's Cold War Education*

William Morgan & C. Stuart Kennedy, *American Diplomats: The Foreign Service at Work*

David D. Newsom, *Witness to a Changing World*

Richard B. Parker, *Memoirs of a Foreign Service Arabist*

Raymond F. Smith, *The Craft of Political Analysis for Diplomats*

James W. Spain, *In Those Days: A Diplomat Remembers*

Monteagle Stearns, *Gifted Greek: The Enigma of Andreas Papandreou*

Jean Wilkowski, *Abroad for Her Country: Tales of a Pioneer Woman Ambassador in the U.S. Foreign Service*

For a complete list of series titles, visit adst.org/publications.